The Sporting Year

THE SPORTING YEAR

A Selection of the Best
Sports Writing of 1976–77

Edited by
John Rodda and Clifford Makins

COLLINS
St. James's Place, London
1977

William Collins Sons & Co Ltd
London · Glasgow · Sydney · Auckland
Toronto · Johannesburg

First published 1977

ISBN 00 0 216737-9
Set in Baskerville
Made and Printed in Great Britain by
William Collins Sons & Co Ltd Glasgow

Contents

18th September 1976–11th September 1977

Acknowledgments

We are grateful for permission to reprint articles from the following papers: the *Daily Express*, *Daily Mirror*, *Daily Telegraph*, *Evening News*, *Evening Standard*, *Financial Times*, *Guardian*, *News of the World*, *Observer*, *Sun*, *Sunday Express*, *Sunday Telegraph*, *Sunday Times* and *The Times*.

Illustrations

Introduction

England has been the crucible of most international games – athletics, soccer, boxing, rowing, Rugby football, and, within its imperialist strictures, of cricket too – and the reporting and writing about such events has deep historical significance. Coaches and players may sometimes shake their heads in disbelief at what they read, but there is a marvellously rich reflection of the British and internatonal sporting scene daily throughout the year in the sports writing of the main Fleet Street papers. What *The Sporting Year* sets out to test is whether that work, otherwise dispatched to the library files, has an independent life of its own. We believe that it has – and that this anthology reproduces many outstanding pieces of sports writing only devalued by the need to get out the next day's paper.

For all that, the making of anthologies is a mug's game. If they are confined to the dead the living protest vehemently about what has been left out. There is usually even more complaint when the choice includes the living. Those writers who are not included feel cross, as do their devoted readers. It is a hopeless task.

Our brief has been to select the 'best' pieces written on sport that have appeared in our national newspapers from September 1976 to September 1977 – it being better to go by what is roughly a 'sporting year' than a strictly calendar one. And by the 'best' we mean the work of Fleet Street's sports writers, reporting at home and abroad throughout the season, sometimes with time to spare, but mostly meeting savage deadlines, phoning copy in the dark from the booth at the end of the lane, or from the sweat, din and confusion of a press box. Of course there are reflective pieces too, and we have tried to keep a balance between these two kinds of journalism. What has surprised us is that so many pieces written under pressure have lasted so well; Tony Lewis's piece in the England/Wales Rugby match, for instance, was actually dictated to his paper *ad lib* over the phone within minutes of the end of the match.

For this year's collection we have considered over eight hundred pieces from the 'pops' and the 'qualities' – inadequate, even hateful terms, but they are widely used and understood and have served our purpose. Perhaps inevitably, the majority of the pieces selected come from the 'quality' end, although sometimes the 'pop' press was able to recapture the excitement of certain sporting events better than any of their more prestigious rivals. David Benson's reports on James Hunt's motor racing world championship victory are a case in point.

One matter we would like to mention is ghost writing. Though by no means confined to the sports pages it plays a big part in the way sport is treated in the 'pops.' It is an increasingly virulent strain, and operates when prominent sportsmen who cannot write 'talk' to journalists who can. Some excellent work is done in this field but, in the main, the effect is lowering and depressing. This is a category which we have excluded.

We are only too aware of a number of failures in this first year. We set out, for instance, to include pieces from outside Fleet Street, from the *South Wales Echo*, the *Sheffield Telegraph*, the *Liverpool Post* and a host of other provincial newspapers, but the good sports writing from the main metropolitan newspapers was so considerable that for this year at least we were forced to narrow our sights. Sadly also, we were unable to include any of the gifted sports writers from the *Daily Mail*, which paper felt it did not wish to be represented in this anthology. We only hope that they may join us next year. Again, while we have tried to cover the main events of the year, we have not included reports where there seemed none of sufficiently high standard. Thus supporters of Barry Sheene, Henley Royal Regatta and England's South American football tour, to name only a few subjects that were given press coverage, will sadly find no mention of these events in these pages.

What kind of sporting year was it? Undoubtedly the main theme for our first twelve months has been cricket – from Greig's triumph in India and the Centenary Test in Melbourne to the emergence of Kerry Packer as sports tycoon of the year and the thrashing of the Australians in the Test series in England. And, of course, there was Geoffrey Boycott judging the right moment to back into the limelight.

After that there was Liverpool, Kevin Keegan, Don Revie and the Arabs, and finally Greenwood – and the plain truth that England's footballing talents are on a par with Australia's cricketing skills. There was the Lions tour of New Zealand, Tom Watson's astonishing performance at Turnberry, Virginia Wade, at last, winning Wimbledon, the faintly boring business of Nastase, Connors and Borg. The animals to steal the thunder were Red Rum and The Minstrel. There was nothing really outstanding from the world of athletics or boxing: it might be a pleasant change if those who persistently state their intention of retiring once and for all – George Best, Muhammad Ali, Joe Bugner, even Pele – would do just that. But the public is long-suffering and the tendency grows to regard sport as just another branch of showbiz. Perhaps that is fair enough: it is the age of exploration and sponsorship, the amateur spirit has wilted and all sport is now penetrated by finance. What is perhaps more worrying, and is reflected by pieces in this anthology, is that few sports remain free from hysteria, sheer bad manners, senseless chanting and hooliganism.

The taste has gone a little sour, but even in this context we believe that the writers in this anthology, though differing in age, background and approach (only two women are included; our prejudice or that of the sports room?) manifest much wit, liveliness, invention and sheer enjoyment in the shadows of the deadline and breadline. Perhaps we miss essayists such as Bernard Darwin, C. E. Montague or a Neville Cardus. But the overall quality of sports writing, we believe, has improved enormously over, say, the last fifteen years, and the sports pages – or rather their editors – have refused to be isolated, like a necessary evil, at the tail end of the paper. There is progressive integration with 'news' and 'literature,' both of which in the past were frequently regarded as inherently superior to 'sport'. There is room for improvement, and in our view no doubt at all that the public can easily assimilate much higher standards both of reporting and of interpretation.

CLIFFORD MAKINS

September, 1977 JOHN RODDA

SEPTEMBER

Motor racing on the slide

JOHN BLUNSDEN
The Times

18 September 1976 *The roar of the engines, the smell from the pits, the chequered flag and champagne for the winner are the romantic's view of motor racing—and one fostered by most of the media. But here John Blunsden stops and takes a look at the complex organisations which control motor sport—and questions their competence.*

An open letter to the people who run one of the world's most colourful and controversial sports:
I cannot be more explicit because I am no longer certain who really does run motor racing, only that they are making an appalling mess of it. So this is addressed to you all – the *Federation Internationale Automobile* (FIA) as the supreme authority; the FIA's *Commission Sportive Internationale* (CSI) as the rulemakers; the various national automobile clubs, who either organize themselves or sub-contract the individual races; the Formula One Constructors Association (FICA), who seem to be manipulating the whole thing to suit their own ends and under whose protective umbrella the once vociferous Grand Prix Drivers Association has chosen to become shielded, and anyone else who has a finger in the pie.

Last weekend we had the tenth and final race in the European section of this year's 16-race World Championship and during those 10 weekends I estimate that some 750,000 came to watch your sport (or should I be honest and call it a business?). Be assured that many of them went home feeling that they had been shortchanged. They paid a lot of money to get in, a lot more to get a good view, and a lot more still for a close-up look around the paddock. And what did they find? That the timetable in their expensive race programme was useless because it had been changed without warning to suit the latest whim of the FICA, that in many places their only view of the circuit was through a maze of wire-mesh fencing, and that the drivers, when they were not cocooned in their cars, were cocooned in their motor-homes, hidden from the very people who had come to hero-worship them and seek their autographs.

But motor racing enthusiasts are a resilient lot, and at the end of the day they cheered long and loud as the leading driver crossed the finishing line, was garlanded and champagned and sent off on his lap of honour. Only when they returned home to join those whose only contact with the race was through the mass media did they find that their cheering had all been in vain. That the winner had not been the winner after all, or – even more confusing – that maybe he had been and maybe he hadn't. Never mind, the authorities would sort it all out, in a few days, or perhaps a few weeks, or months.

Those of us whose task it is to report on Grand Prix racing share the bewilderment of our readers. From our privileged view of what goes on around us we are dismayed and baffled that people who have so much to gain, as well as to give, through the sport should be seen to be systematically tearing it apart from the inside.

No doubt a major cause of your strife is that motor racing has become not so much a healthy contest between one sportsman and another but an activity motivated by avarice. A victory or a high placing in individual races – and, therefore, in the championship – can be richly rewarding, no matter whether the 'success' is gained on the race track or afterwards, through the exploitation of the deficiencies of a cumbersome, ambiguous, often contradictory and misunderstood rule book.

It happened in Spain, again in France, then in this country, and a week ago in Italy . . . four excellent races marred by the intricacies of the small print, and, curiously, James Hunt became (at least temporarily) a victim of them all. In Spain it was the width of his car (disqualified from first place, later reinstated). In France it was the height of the rear wing (until it was found that the officials were using their measuring equipment incorrectly, whereupon his win was confirmed). In the same race John Watson was removed from third place (later reinstated) because one rear wing tip was a fraction too high.

At Brands Hatch the trouble was of a different sort: Ferrari's protest against Hunt's inclusion in the re-run Grand Prix (which he won) after his car had been crippled in the melee which had halted the original race, and subsequently put right again. As the original accident had been caused by a Ferrari driver (Regazzoni), Ferrari's refusal to accept the subsequent verdict by the RAC upholding Hunt's inclusion in the re-run race, is, I suggest, the least sportsmanlike act of this dismally controversial year. Ferrari's appeal will be heard by the FIA next week.

But surely the most recent Grand Prix, in Italy, illustrates most clearly of all the extent to which control of the sport has been lost. By all means analyse fuel if you wish to do so, but leave sufficient time for the job to be done properly (I am assured that accurately to measure the octane rating of several fuel samples by the Research Method takes days, rather than the few hours after which the figures were announced). Hunt and Mass were banished to the back of the grid on the grounds that they were using 101.6 octone fuel whereas officials claimed the limit was 101 (100 plus the permitted one per cent tolerance). But the rule book states that the highest-grade fuel sold commercially in four European countries, including the UK, is permissible. Texaco, who supply the McLaren team, sell 101 octane fuel in the UK. McLaren boss Teddy Mayer is appealing, not for the race to be withdrawn from the championship as had been mooted, but to clear his team's name and reputation – a modest enough demand bearing in mind Hunt slid out of the race in his desperate effort to claw his way through the field.

But that day, at least, the drivers had the last word. When it sprinkled with rain before half-distance, a hesitant official paused on the startline with two black flags with which to halt the race. Almost pushed on to the track by FICA spokesman, Bernard Ecclestone (so the constructors *do* run racing, after all) he held the flags aloft. Three drivers stopped next time round and two more slowed down. The rest carried on racing – harder than ever – for the full distance. At that moment Grand Prix racing was seen to be out of control.

When drivers (and team managers) do not even know the signal for stopping a Grand Prix it is time to tear up your rule book and start again. Only this time make it simple, make it short, and make it quickly, before the public turn their backs on you and let you get on with it on your own. It could happen.

Hide and seek

HUGH McILVANNEY
The Observer

26 September 1976 *Orienteering, a sport with strong roots in Scandanavia, has a following in Britain. What better way to advertise it than stage the World Championships? Hundreds of officials and supporters went north to Aviemore to organise the event, and with them a dozen British journalists; some were induced to go out in the forest and try their hand. After all, it attracts children of eight and grandmas of 58... Hugh McIlvanney got back to report how he fared.*

Orienteering, a sport that gives the impression of having been thought up by David Livingstone after an evening with Lasse Viren, is now far more ready than it was even a week ago to spread its sane and natural pleasure through the woods and wild places of Britain. By their ambitious staging of the sixth World Championships in the enchanting forests of the Eastern Highlands of Scotland, the British Orienteering Federation have achieved an evangelical impact that would do credit to a Billy Graham crusade.

It is the identity rather than the numbers of those converted than can be regarded as significant, because this is an activity that must be practised in remote and densely wooded stretches of countryside where any spectator who means to follow the action had better come with more electronic equipment than a Foxbat jet.

The fact does not prevent the Scandinavians, who are the established masters of the sport and have managed a predictable domination of the men's and women's competitions at these championships, from having crowds of up to 20,000 clustered around the finishing points of their major events. But Lisa Veijalainen, a disturbingly attractive Finnish girl whose blonde hair streams down to her shapely buttocks when it is not tied out of the way of molesting bramble and rhododendron bushes, was in no danger of being involved in a mob scene as she panted towards the Earl of Moray's Darnaway Castle on Friday to take the women's world title.

That there was no hint of sexual prejudice in that muted reception was soon confirmed when Egil Johansen, a 22-year-old Norwegian whose class had already been proved by double victories in both the junior and senior championships of his own country, completed the men's course at a speed that left him nearly two minutes ahead of the Swede who was his nearest rival. Most of the few hundred onlookers who were on hand to see Johansen finish were people personally involved in orienteering and, although the principles of sending the runners out into the forest at three-minute intervals inevitably blurs the outline of the contest while it is in progress, they were sufficiently knowledgeable to realise that taking just 91 minutes and 22 seconds to check through 24 cunningly, almost sadistically, concealed control points set along a route that involved not less than 12 miles of running and about 1,800 feet of climbing, represented a marvellous performance.

Apart from being a notable athletic feat it was a classic demonstration of the ability to use a compass and a detailed topographical map, and a highly-cultivated instinct for attuning the senses to an unfamiliar wilderness. Yet Johansen's accomplishment will bring him little celebrity and no financial gain. He says that even in Norway, a nation where there are about 50,000 registered orienteers out of a population of four million (compared with perhaps 10,000 active participants in Britain from a population that is about a dozen times as large) his previous successes have not brought him as much as an invitation to a dinner. The situation suits him fine.

A television repair technician from Kristiansand, he is a good example of the kind of friendly, intelligent young people to be found at the forefront of orienteering. It is one of the strengths that it can provide exercise and enjoyment from childhood virtually into old age but, naturally, its most formidable practitioners are under 35. Most of them share Johansen's leanness and sculpted look of fitness but, like him, the majority are free of that alienating air of self-absorption, that aura of egomania that so often marks the track and field athletes who become obsessed with the pursuit of Olympic medals. There is no suggestion of the spurious when Egil Johansen, asked to single out the most compelling attraction of orienteering, says simply: 'It is the fellowship of the other orienteers.'

Maybe as orienteering becomes more global, as competition intensifies and spreads to embrace more than the 19 nations and 130 contestants who assembled in Scotland, it will lose some of its innocence, but it seems better protected against corruption of its ideals than almost any other sport. It will never have to worry about accommodating masses of spectators, about adjusting to the values of television or even the problems of largescale Press coverage (those reporters allowed into the dappled beauty of the Darnaway and Logie estates over this weekend have had to lurk behind trees like poachers, emulating the unobtrusiveness of the control point marshals who must crouch for hours in camouflage suits and total silence to avoid betraying the positions) and commercialism should not become a serious menace.

The real guarantee of a developing future for orienteering in Britain as elsewhere, however, has nothing to do with politics. It resides in the intrinsic and utterly natural appeal of the sport, in that evangelical impact mentioned earlier, in those qualities that converted even a bunch of jaded Fleet Street reporters to the idea of trying to lose their paunches and bar-room pallors in the woods. Some of the gamer spirits, armed with map and compass, were let loose in the forest belonging to the Thane of Cawdor last Thursday. The maps had been prepared over the last two-and-a-half years by a small team of surveyors under Robin Harvey, who trained as an architect but has decided to devote himself to this fascinating cartographic work. All those involved in the map-making operation worked with a degree of secrecy that makes the CIA look about as clandestine as an advertising agency, because an orienteering course is useless if competitors have the slightest inkling of its whereabouts.

A farmhouse hideout was provided by the Earl of Moray and all but one or two of the estate workers were left in the dark about the doings of the strange characters who were glimpsed occasionally flitting through the trees or bending down to note topographical features in a way that presented an inviting target to an uninformed gamekeeper.

Robin Harvey's maps are magnificent creations, artistic and so brilliantly accurate that he was accorded something close to a standing ovation at the presentation ceremony. But they were not good enough to keep the journalists from getting lost. We were to be observed describing bewildered circles on the ferny floor of Cawdor Wood or stumbling out from a thicket, staring down at the compass with that look of rapt concern that Glasgow drunks turn upon their fish suppers.

Those hours as a guest of the Thane reinforced a long-held suspicion. Macbeth was framed. And it wasn't his lady who did in the King either. My theory is that when she got to Duncan he was already a goner, knackered, heaving his last after a day spent wandering in Cawdor Wood.

Goodbye to the greatest

FRANK McGHEE
The Daily Mirror

30 September 1976 *The decline but not quite the fall of The Greatest. Frank McGhee signals from New York, after Ali's battle with Ken Norton, that the end is nigh for the man who first as Cassius Clay and then as Muhammad Ali used his skills in the ring and his verbosity out of it to become the best-known man in the world.*

Muhammad Ali still has one title, the world heavyweight

championship, but he has lost another. He is no longer 'The Greatest'. He forfeited all rights to that bombastic claim when over fifteen desperately close rounds at the Yankee Stadium, he miserably failed to dominate an opponent he had guaranteed to crush – his challenger, Ken Norton.

Most American observers, apart from the blind, biased Ali idolators who don't know the difference between a left hook and a meat hook, thought Norton had won. Norton, convinced that he had, was led from the ring crying like a child, his massive frame shuddering with sobs of grief and outrage.

When the final bell went he had snarled at Ali: 'I beat you, I beat you' – and was full of leaping joy. Still stunned an hour later in a dressing room more crowded than that of any loser I've ever known, he said quietly: 'I know I outfought him completely. I was sure I won at least ten rounds and in the middle rounds I was playing with him.'

If you want to start another fight in New York right now you only have to disagree with him and say out loud you thought Ali deserved to keep his crown.

The two judges thought so. Both scored it eight rounds to the champion, seven to the challenger – though judges are notoriously reluctant to take away a world heavyweight champion's title on points. It hasn't happened since Jim Braddock beat Max Baer in 1935. A capable referee, Arthur Mercante, thought so, too. He made it eight to Ali, six to Norton one even.

Whisper it, I also thought Ali quite rightly kept his crown – but only just, I had them with six rounds each and three even and scored in a draw.

Perhaps I'm less impressed than American critics by mere aggression, which Norton admittedly produced aplenty. The age-old tried and trusted system of counting punches correctly delivered on the target area will still do for me. And, for me, Ali threw enough of those, particularly in the last third of the fight when he was trailing.

In retrospect, however, that is less important than the feeling of being let down by Ali. Too many of his antics and actions in Yankee Stadium were cheap, degrading, unworthy, unnecessary.

All Norton really had was strength, fitness, determination

and a booming, looping, swinging right-hand punch. Those assets were enough to make it obvious that the years Ali spent in the ring and the punches even he has had to take have chipped away at his enormous talent until too little of it is left. The immortal has become ordinary.

Sure, we all owe it to him to acknowledge what he has been – but 'has been' is a derisory, derogatory expression in sport and on this evidence it is what Ali has become.

He didn't even sound much like himself afterwards in the bedlam of his own dressing room.

'They wouldn't have given it to a man like me if they thought it was close,' he mumbled as he lay flat on a table, looking somehow deflated. 'I thought I won. I had him hurt more than he had me hurt.'

He talked about the switch in tactics when he stopped flatfooted slugging to come up on his toes, jab and move and dance in the later stages.

'I switched because the flatfooted fighting wasn't going like I thought it would. And anyway the judges always like it when I dance.'

He talked about retiring – but then he always does.

'It is time to get out, I don't need this game. It is getting too hard for a man my age, but the money is sweet. I got six million for this one. I'll get more when I fight George Foreman in six months' time.'

Frankly, I believe that on last night's form and performance Foreman would beat him.

Ali very quickly had to abandon any idea that he could or would knock out Norton – something he tried in the first three minutes when he stood leaning into his punches. But when he did that he was immediately vulnerable to right swings from Norton.

Each time it happened he feigned injury, wobbling at the knees, rolling his eyes in a vaudeville parody of a punch-drunk. Norton refused to be fooled. When Ali tried to turn the fight into a farce in the fifth, lounging and laughing against the ropes, wiggling his hips in a silly hula-hoop routine, his challenger took the chance to pile up more points.

By the seventh Ali was a man fighting for his life, able to put together only occasionally the outstanding flurries of punches that have always been his trade mark. Now it was Norton snarling the insults. Ali was having to save his breath. He had boasted before the fight that there was no way Norton could make him change his chosen course to stand there and slug it out, but he admitted afterwards that when his corner told him before the ninth that the fight was drifting away from him he had to do something different.

He had to get on to his toes, start back-pedalling and jabbing – and stealing points.

It served its purpose. I thought Ali landed enough of those stinging, flicking jabs to inch his way level again – but now Norton was winning the psychological battle. In the eleventh he was actually taunting Ali, laying back on the ropes, doing to the champ what Ali has done to so many others: mocking him. Ali didn't like it, tried to make him pay for it and two proud and brutal men did each other no good at all.

Until then it had not been dirty, though it became so briefly at the end of a furious and even twelfth round when Ali's left thumb sank deep into Norton's right eyeball – to provoke further snarling exchanges.

On my scorecard Ali was still trailing then, but he was gradually drawing level. Although Norton continued to hit the harder and seemed the stronger throughout the final rounds, Ali was landing more often – just often enough to keep his title.

OCTOBER

The 'big grudge fight'

ROB HUGHES
The Sunday Times

10 October 1976 *The quality of professional boxing in Britain and throughout most parts of the world has been getting thin, yet because of television the sport now has a larger audience than ever before. Promoters have to delve deep among their adjectives to make their product sell. The Sunday Times keeps a fairly lone vigil in this area, and for Rob Hughes the Richard Dunn–Joe Bugner British Commonwealth and European title fight was never an attractive match.*

British heavyweight boxing reaches its natural conclusion at the Empire Pool, Wembley, on Tuesday. Don't let me mislead you; I hope that doesn't read flatteringly. What I mean is that this is *it* – the end of the road, the final depths to which the heavies can sink. And since I can't feint as adroitly as the men in the boxing publicity business, I won't pretend to be at all sorry.

They are calling it the Big Grudge Fight, hoping public gullibility will swallow a match between the only British heavies whose names mean anything, but who are patently a reluctant athlete and an honest plodder. They want us all to know that Joe Bugner is dropping his reticent guard and coming out of retirement with 'hatred for the first time in my life' to take away Richard Dunn's British Commonwealth and European titles.

Only trouble is, when they get the boys in front of camera, they are no Muhammad Alis. Earnest Joe admits he doesn't hate anybody; likeable Richard couldn't convince even my trusting mother-in-law that he looks or sounds like a man in whom a major passion is aroused. But those of us who are conscientious objectors to the fight game can't take it all in fun. Boxing impinges on our sporting ethics. Whenever I feel enticed towards a boxing hall, usually through the athleticism and theatrics of Ali, I remember Bugner v Phil Smith, and I re-read Norman Mailer's chilling account of a real grudge fight, *The Killing of Benny Paret*.

Phil Smith? You don't remember Phil Smith? He was probably Bugner's least-publicised victim. The beating of Smith was the last I witnessed ringside. It provoked me to study and report, as thoroughly as a journalist can, the medical aspects of brain damage in sports. Smith, a black American, was imported to oppose (I use the term hesitantly) Bugner at the Royal Albert Hall almost seven years ago to the day. He was the fall guy needed to restore the golden image of the 19-year-old Bugner who, following the death of Ulric Regis after their fight earlier in 1969, had some unimpressive victories and then lost on points to Dick Hall, another American.

Smith looked the part – 6ft. 2in. and 15st. 28lb. But he couldn't fight, or at least that night he couldn't. Easy? It was obscene. I see, even now, the confusion and fear in that black man's eyes as he stood before Bugner like a rabbit paralysed before a stoat. When Bugner saw it too he pounded in with clubbing punches you normally see sunk into a punchbag. The Negro's mind was about as agile, his evasive technique as astute, as that punchbag. But his body was less resilient. His only response was to be hit and fall, to rise too fast, get hit and fall again, to whimper and finally to cry on his feet as, after one round and 80 seconds, the referee stopped it, and a baying crowd hailed Bugner's punching power.

In boxing terms, perhaps, nothing was amiss that night; nor will it be if Bugner can similarly outclass and spank Dunn. Yet even Mailer, a ringside devotee, emotively describes the way Emile Griffith, 'like a cat ready to rip the life out of a huge boxed rat,' barbarically took the life of Paret in 1962 after Paret had taunted him with homosexual insinuations.

So, if Dunn v Bugner *were* a true grudge match, thank heavens that the British ring is a more civilised arena, and that neither man has the ammunition, mental or physical, to do a Griffith. Beneath the fanfares of mock hate the amount of real needle is mercifully shallow, based on Bugner's unkind (and unwise, following his own passive encounters with Ali) televised comments that Dunn had no right to climb into a world-championship ring.

Dunn, of course, went five aggressive, hurtful rounds with Ali, and the ex-paratrooper who hit the deck 67 times with a chute on his back woke up to a lifetime's ransom of £100,000 for being dumped on canvas five times by the world champion. 'Dropping like a bloody great bag o' tatties,' says the Yorkshireman, unfortunately referring to parachuting rather than the six times he's been knocked out in the ring (or the 19 kos he has administered, mostly around small-time northern halls).

The faces of the two men tell you much about what to expect on Tuesday: Dunn's is weathered and scarred indelibly, a fighter who gives and takes; Bugner's is the clean mask of a man principally intent on avoiding punishment.

Who really cares, so long as boxing itself loses? And it will, because education and the Welfare State have diminished its lure and TV satiates those who still crave violence, with makebelieve or the real thing, the close-up gore of war almost daily in news bulletins. Thus, with fighters of great greed but no great need, there is neither public demand nor tolerance for the spectacle of the ring in which levels of skill and willingness have become second rate.

Hooliganism: still awaiting the remedy

Compiled from contributions by JOHN BALL, NORMAN HARRIS, CHRIS LIGHTBOWN, JOHN LOVESEY and BRIAN WILSON
The Sunday Times

17 October 1976 *Violence at and around football matches has been a social problem for several seasons. With anxiety and passion*

five Sunday Times writers combine to unravel the mess—and point out a few root causes.

If the eruption of the fans of the Rangers Football Club at Aston Villa last week was simply the latest incident in a long postwar history of teenage hooliganism it would not take account of the special factors affecting this club. The type of violence perpetrated by the Rangers' support differs from normal football hooliganism in its sheer malice and arrogant viciousness, and this would appear to be attributable to the religious dimension so long established within football in Glasgow. However, if the fans of a club like Glasgow's Rangers represent the ugly apex of football hooliganism in Britain they are only one part of the whole.

Rangers are only different in degree when their general manager Willie Waddell calls some of his own supporters 'animals'. All football clubs in Britain will tell you that their so-called hooligan element is extremely small. Leicester City, for example, say they have approximately 2,500 juveniles of 15 and under in an average crowd of 21,000 and of those the hooligan element numbers about 200.

But the hooligan problem is not a boil that can be easily lanced. It is abundantly clear, for instance, that the quasi-religious posturings of Rangers are extremely profitable. Moreover, the trouble thrives everywhere in an area of support that is crucial to professional football's survival and, to some extent, certain commercial hangers-on.

If the 50 or so coaches which went down the M6 last Saturday from Glasgow to Birmingham had been required by law (as last year by the Northern Area Traffic Commissioner) to arrive at a football ground within one hour of kick-off then arguably Aston Villa and the people of Birmingham might have been saved such an onslaught. As it is, the drivers of those coaches had to arrive early because the law requires an 8½-hour break on long journeys and only two drivers would have overcome that, thus cutting into the operators' profits.

There are others, also, who do well out of such young football supporters though not consciously contributing to the problem. British Rail run a total of about 700 football specials in a season and even the wrecking of the odd train does little to dent a worthwhile gross. As it is, British Rail has had to cut down on bar facilities despite the subsequent cut in profits because drink is recognised as a potent element fuelling the flames of hooliganism today, of the broad number if not the hardened leaders and the very youngest. Other commercial interests have had no such compunction. Clubs have bars on their grounds but argue that closing these will provide no solution as a result of the case with which a youngster can 'tank up' before a game in pubs, or by buying canned beer and bottled spirits as freely as milk in supermarkets.

It is the police who find that strong drink, more often than not, emerges as a major factor in creating football hooliganism. In Scotland police patrols now tour supermarkets and off-licences before matches looking to arrest 12- to 16-year-olds and to prosecute any who sell them alcohol. And although English clubs protest it is impractical to search fans before they go into the ground Glasgow police do.

Overall our society stands condemned for allowing so much money to be allocated in advertising to persuading young people that drinking is not only desirable but, by implication, is part of successful adulthood and even involvement in sport. The sensitivity of the advertisers to this charge was made clear to the *Sunday Times* last week when Scottish and Newcastle Breweries took refuge in their copyright to prevent us reproducing one of their posters showing footballer Roy McFarland with a pint of Tartan bitter.

Apart from drink most police organisations say that trouble flows largely in the wake of a highly successful team as opposed to a team that strikes a bad patch or is stuck in the doldrums. And this exacerbates the major problem: there is still no effective counter-force to the propaganda which is based largely in the profit and is directed at today's youngsters.

Almost a year ago exactly we said in these pages that the voices expressing concern over hooliganism 'grow shriller by the year as they call for severer penalties, instead of searching for what is wrong . . . It is almost six years since the report of the working party on Crowd Behaviour at Football Matches was published by the Government. . . .

In 12 months, will the elements of our society have changed in such a way that our youth can find an identity that will stop football hooliganism?'

Not only is the answer to that question still 'no', but the situation is worse. There is unemployment among young people and the economic crisis has created even more calls for cuts in those services that might ease the problem if wisely used.

Surely the time has come for the buck to stop being passed. Even if the clubs that are 'responsible' for youngsters only three hours in a fortnight – a minimal time compared with employers, school teachers and parents – the fact is that the problems are manifest at, or around, their football games, and this is the place where they must operate their social responsibilities to the community. Not by starting the sort of youth club which Aston Villa did in the recent past, only to discover that they attracted 'only a hundred or so decent boys but of course not the toughs because it wasn't their scene.' Not, like Rangers talking about putting up fences to contain the fans (other football men point out that the pitch is a vital exit in the case of emergencies). Not by perpetuating the social gulf and incomprehension between the camel hair in the directors' box and the denim on the terraces. And not by herding them in and out like so many cattle through the turn-stiles. But, as we said a year ago, by involving them more in their clubs – with a two-way benefit.

We are talking about the club being able to identify its worst elements and ridding itself of them. We are talking again about the club as a community centre because the greatest restraint on most youngsters is to have a place in a community, a community that knows and judges them. The Minister of Sport Denis Howell briefly took up the issue of community involvement as raised by the Harrington Report in 1968 and the Lang Report the following year, but has always talked in terms of moats and ditches whenever hooliganism goes over the top.

Such talk offers no hope of solving the broad issues. Neither does Mr Waddell's statement that Rangers will 'divorce itself completely from sectarian and religious bias in every aspect of the field of play and on the terraces' until that is seen actually to happen. The danger and the truth is that where there is no trouble nothing happens. The storm blows over. In what terrible way does hooliganism have to spill over amongst us before all the solutions in all the reports are implemented?

The pocket genius

DAVID GRAY
The Guardian

21 October 1976 *David Gray moved from writing about tennis to being one of its most important administrators, the general secretary of the International Lawn Tennis Federation. The loss to journalism was great, and this piece, a portrait of Ken Rosewall woven round a book review, is a reminder of that loss.*

Twenty Years At The Top. It is the right title for a book about Ken Rosewall. The marvellous thing about him is that his talents have lasted so long. He played at Wimbledon first in 1952 when Frank Sedgman, Dick Savitt, Jaroslav Drobny, Eric Sturgess, and Vic Seixas were ruling the championships. In 1974 he reached the final there for the fourth time. He had outlasted his contemporaries and the generation which followed them.

Lew Hoad was betrayed by his back; Rod Laver's left arm lost its strength; Tony Roche's series of injuries forced him into secondary stuff like Team Tennis; and Roy Emerson, lean, keen, and trained to the last ounce throughout the 1950s and 60s, gave up serious competition to become the darling of the summer tennis camps. But Rosewall stayed on, a survivor from the age of Hopman, when all the Australian kids looked stringy and short-haired, in the world of Connors and Borg where the courts are paved with dollar bills.

Perhaps he is the last of the old-style professionals. Easy, fluent shots; grace and speed of movement; intensity of concentration. Nature gave him a great deal, even if it did not endow him with Hoad's ability to summon up thunder, lightning and absolute majesty of shot. Ken is a genius who is only 5ft. 7in. and weighs only 140lb. A ghost with a rapier in his backhand.

His are the quiet virtues of tennis. On his good days it is a pleasure to watch him slip into his best attacking rhythm. His smashes, passes and volleys are object lessons in the art of placement, but the serve is a weakness and its vulnerability (particularly the tendency to double-fault) has always been most marked on days when he is under pressure. The child was father of the perfectionist.

The most interesting parts of Peter Rowley's new biography (Cassell, £4.50p, pp 239), which is the fruit of a great many fascinating conversations with the player himself, deal with Rosewall's tennis education. Samuel Smiles would have admired it as a study in self-help. Rosewall père was a grocer in a modest Sydney suburb.

Ken, an only child, was presented with a shortened racket when he was three. At five, Bob Rosewall stopped the little boy hitting double-handers and made him use his right hand. He bought a dozen tennis books and started to turn him into a champion. 'From books I taught Ken Fred Perry's forehand and Don Budge's backhand. The volley, overhead and lob he developed naturally. We would get up at four and five in the morning. We would spend weeks hitting only one stroke at a time. I would drop a handkerchief on the ground and he would hit to it.'

The child practised volleying against a white wall with a painted advertisement, and on another side of their house his father dug away a slope so that the earth was flat enough for him to practise his ground strokes. His mother, who broke a hip playing tennis, made sure that his white clothes were immaculate.

When he was nine he entered his first tournament and lost to the winner. At eleven he won the Metropolitan Hard Court Championship, defeating a boy two years his senior and over six feet tall in the final. 'In my heart I thought I had a champion, but I never told him that,' said Bob Rosewall.

He enjoyed the distractions of rugby and cricket. Bob Rosewall told him: 'Ken, if you quit rugby and cricket and concentrate exclusively on tennis, I think you have what it takes to be a champion. Or you can be good in all sports, but champion in none of them. Think it over for a week and let me know.'

Three days later Ken told him: 'Dad, I want to be a champion.' The sessions of two or three hours of practice in the early mornings continued. 'The reason I got to the top is due to many sacrifices by my parents and later by my family. When I was a youngster of 11, 12 or 14 I used to go to bed at 8 pm and get up to play tennis with my father at 5 am before he went to work and I to school.'

Jack Kramer watched him beat Hoad 6–0, 6–0 when they were 12-year-olds. Ted Schroeder asked him what he thought about them. 'We had better get the hell out of the way before these kids get much older because they'll be beating our ears off,' said Kramer. Seventeen years later he remembered that match: 'It was just like it generally is. Lew makes all the miraculous shots and Kenny wins all the matches.'

He suffered from eczema. Slazengers gave him a job. Carnation Milk sponsored him and Hopman chose him and Hoad for the Australian Davis Cup tour of Europe and the United States in 1972. Bob Rosewall told him: 'If Mr Hopman tells you to change this stroke or that stroke, listen, but afterwards you only do what you feel is right.' There are touches of asperity whenever Ken mentions Hopman in the book. The pupil doesn't remember that particular teacher with absolute charity.

He fell in love. He met Wilma McIver, from Brisbane, when he was 14, began writing to her (one hundred letters in three months) and sending her chocolates. When he was on tour he carried eight photographs of her, and Lew and the other boys used to tease him by hiding the one that he kept on his bedside table. When he was 21 they were married.

He won the first of his two French and four Australian titles in 1953, and the following year he was runner-up to Drobny at Wimbledon. Most people remember that final because of the overwhelming support that Drobny, the sentimental favourite, received. The centre court reckoned that Rosewall, the elegant teenager, belonged to the future, but it was Drobny's turn because the Australian would soon be making a habit of winning the title.

Ken, taking his usual commonsense view, merely thinks that his strategy was mistaken: 'I was badly advised. Harry Hopman was the team coach. I'm not saying that he advised me badly but you have read that he went out and found Lew Hoad and me and developed me. He did try to help my serve, but he had no effect on my backhand or forehand.

' "Dumb" is the way I'd describe my game against Drobny. I should have come to the net on my serve and return of serve. I'd serve to his backhand and instead of following it to the net he'd hit a soft, deep return and come in to the net himself, knowing I wouldn't come in.'

Rowley quotes plenty of analyses like that. Ken's views on his own and other people's tennis are those of a dedicated professional. It is always a joy to watch a match with him. His insights are always practical. He can get a ball through the eye of a needle and he tells you why other people can't.

He lost in the 1956 Wimbledon final to Hoad, but then spoilt Lew's grand slam by defeating him in the final at Forest Hills. When that match was over he amazed even those who knew him by going to a side court and practising serving with Don Budge. Soon afterwards he turned professional.

On the pro tour he overtook Hoad, gradually overcame Gonzales ('On my first tour with Gonzales I felt as though I was being thrown to the lions,') and then began his marvellous rivalry with Rod Laver, with so many great matches hidden away in the small one-night-stand towns of the American professional circuit.

Looking back, it is impossible to imagine why we allowed so much brilliant lawn tennis – the sort of stuff which should have been shown to crowds in the world's great stadiums – to go to waste. If the game had been open to the professionals in 1960 (as it was so nearly) Rosewall's name wouldn't be on the list of talented players who never quite won the men's singles at Wimbledon. As it was, we had to wait for open tennis until 1968 and his late harvest was remarkable. Aged 33, he beat Laver at Bournemouth in the game's first open final, and went on to win Paris in that month of June when the rioting students could almost have thrown their stones into Roland Garros.

He regained the Australian in 1971 and retained it the next year. He won South Africa, ruled Forest Hills in 1970 and WCT at Dallas in 1971 and 1972. Newcombe beat him in one more Wimbledon final in 1970 and Connors, punishing that medium-paced serve, knocked him out in 1974, a year when the centre court was awash with emotion, and repeated his overwhelming victory in the final at Forest Hills.

The veterans are waiting for him now. He will be 42 next month and doesn't think that he can go on playing against younger players. 'You have to be realistic. My career is waning because it is physically and mentally impossible for me to play as much as I know I should.'

It has been a remarkable career. If Wimbledon, the biggest prize eluded him, he ends as the most respected competitor in the game, a player for those who relish its beauties and its disciplines, the perfect professional.

Rowley's book illustrates that well. The champion's character was moulded in those 5 am practice sessions with Dad: 'Youthful tennis training has to be good and stays with you for the rest of your life – the same as if you learn good manners,' Ken remarked once. Every would-be Rosewall ought to have that engraved on his tennis racket.

Last lap

DAVID BENSON

The Daily Express

22 October 1976 *All eyes turned to Tokyo for the last Grand Prix of the World Driver's Championship. Could James Hunt pull it off? If he did then all but the Daily Mail in Fleet Street would be losers, for the Mail had signed up Hunt exclusively. But that was tomorrow's problem; David Benson looked forward to the race in the Express and traced the drama of Hunt's twelve-month battle with Nicki Lauda. For the Express it was a wordy piece, but it was an excellent way of setting up the climax.*

Grand Prix motor racing's most dramatic season reaches its climax on Sunday on an 'unknown' circuit in the shadow of Japan's mighty Mount Fuji, a 90-minute drive from Tokyo.

After 15 races only two men are still in contention for the World Driver's crown – Britain's James Hunt with 65 points, and reigning champion Niki Lauda, of Austria, with 68 points and the odds favouring Hunt at the moment.

The confrontation between these two men has excited public imagination as never before. In the first half of the season it seemed that Lauda and his Ferrari were unbeatable and he kicked off with victories in Brazil then South Africa (with Hunt a mere 1½ secs. behind).

Clay Regazzoni, in the second Ferrari, won at Long Beach, California, while Hunt was sidelined after a crash.

Hunt roared back in Spain to win in his Marlboro McLaren, with Niki second – only to be disqualified because his car was alleged to be ⅝″ too wide and the race was awarded to Lauda, who had competed with broken ribs strapped up after an accident at his home near Salzburg.

In the next two races – Belgium and Monaco – Lauda won at a canter. Hunt failed to score at all and it seemed all over. Niki now had a total of 51 points in the championship and Hunt just six.

South Africa's Jody Scheckter won the Swedish Grand Prix. Lauda was third and Hunt fifth. *The score* – Lauda 55 points, Hunt 8.

The next round, in the South of France, was the turning-point. Lauda blew an engine and scored no points while Hunt collected nine for his victory.

The next day the FIA – world motor sport's governing body – reinstated Hunt as winner of the Spanish Grand Prix. That meant James had scored 18 points in 24 hours, while Lauda had lost three by being downgraded from 1st to 2nd for Spain. *The score* – Lauda 52, Hunt 26.

Still a long way to go . . . but in Britain a fortnight later Hunt won after a first lap pile-up involving his McLaren and Regazzoni's Ferrari.

The race was restarted from scratch, Lauda was second and Ferrari protested to the FIA about the validity of Hunt's success. *The score* – Lauda 58, Hunt 35.

Getting closer . . . but the two-man battle almost ended

in tragedy in Germany on the long and dangerous Nurburg-ring. Lauda badly burned his face and lungs in a second-lap crash and almost died in a German hospital.

The race was restarted and Hunt led from start to finish to pick up another 9 points. *The score* – Lauda 58, Hunt 44.

Niki was still hospitalised when the Austrian Grand Prix came round and Hunt was firm favourite. But Belfast's John Watson won his first-ever Grand Prix, while Hunt finished fourth for just three points.

It was a great opportunity missed, but two weeks later – on his 29th birthday – Hunt made no mistake and won the Dutch Grand Prix in fine style after a duel with Watson. Niki was still convalescing. *The score* – Lauda 58, Hunt 56.

Incredibly, Niki came back two weeks later for the Italian Grand Prix and finished fourth to earn three vital points. But it was a disgraceful weekend of off-the-track wrangling. On the Sunday of the race Hunt was relegated to the back of the grid after an allegation – quite unfounded – that his petrol had too high an octane rating. Hunt crashed trying to get into contention with the leaders. *The score* – Lauda 61, Hunt 56.

Between the Italian and the Canadian Grands Prix the FIA heard the Ferrari protest over the British race. They disqualified Hunt and placed Niki first, taking nine points from James and giving three extra points to Lauda. *The score* – Lauda 64, Hunt 47.

A grim and bitter Hunt hit back in Canada to win while Niki finished eighth and out of the points. *The score* – Lauda 64, Hunt 56.

A week later – at Watkins Glen, U.S. – Hunt drove the race of his life to win again. Lauda finished third and the seemingly impossible hope that Hunt could get back into contention had become a reality. *The score* – Lauda 68, Hunt 65.

Now, victory on Sunday will ensure that the championship comes to Britain.

Even if Lauda finishes second – leaving both men on 74 points – Hunt will be champion because he would have seven Grand Prix victories this season compared to Niki's five wins.

King James

DAVID BENSON
The Daily Express

25 October 1976 *The biggest sporting thriller of the year comes to an appropriate, British end. Lauda drops out and James Hunt takes third place. He miscalculates and thinks he hasn't won, but finally he is convinced that in a season where at one stage he was 45 points behind Lauda he has beaten him—by a single point. David Benson puts the story together vividly.*

James Hunt is world champion – after a season in which the gods first frowned on him, then held him in suspense up to the last lap of the last race, the Japanese Grand Prix.

Appropriately, the final drama was played out in the shadow of Mount Fuji, where the gods of Shinto reward courage and determination. No one has needed these more than Hunt who has overcome disasters personal, political and mechanical to beat the world.

He did not win. Victory went to American Mario Andretti, in a British John Player Lotus. And when third-placed Hunt stepped out of his car at the end of 73 laps he thought he had failed.

He pulled off his black helmet with the Wellington School colours emblazoned on its side and started to complain to his team boss, Teddy Meyer, that he had lost the title because of lack of pit information. Someone shook him and told him he was the champion.

They dragged him to the victory rostrum and gave him third prize – he only needed fourth to become champion once Niki Lauda had dropped out, because he had won more races.

But he charged back to his pits and missed the lap of honour. He would not say anything until he saw it in writing. And after the reverses of this season, who could blame him?

The day began in gloom and heavy rain, with mighty Fuji covered in cloud that eventually crept down its lava face and seeped across the circuit which was flooded for the morning practice. Each car left a rooster-tail of spray that hung in the air making visibility impossible to following drivers.

South African Jody Scheckter, whose six-wheeled Elf-Tyrrell was seen aquaplaning on all four front wheels, said: 'If they run a race here today there will be a disaster.'

Hunt and Lauda wanted the race run as a non-championship event, but finally they lined up on the grid . . . for the world championship decider.

Hunt made a brilliant start and edged ahead of Andretti. Reigning champion Lauda was 10th after one tentative lap. Halfway through the next he faltered, dropped back and trailed into the pits.

Hunt led for 61 of 73 laps, holding off all-comers. One challenge came early from Vittorio Brambilla. He shot from eighth to second in three laps then called into the pits to change his right front tyre.

Again he attacked and by the 16th lap he was once again on Hunt's tail. But James was already driving like the champion he was about to become. Halfway through the 21st lap Brambilla drew alongside.

Hunt seemed to allow him the line, but quickly chopped back on to the inside, leaving Brambilla stranded. The Italian spun and Hunt hurtled away.

But the track was drying rapidly and Hunt was trying to preserve his wet-weather tyres which, like everyone else's, were overheating.

On lap 2, Patrick Depailler of France, in the six-wheeled Elf-Tyrrell, swept into the lead. Then Andretti passed Hunt. Depailler pulled in to change a flat rear tyre and Hunt was back to second. But on lap 68 he sped down the pit lane, skidding to a stop, his tyres in shreds. The McLaren pit took 27 seconds to change all four wheels and Hunt roared back in fifth place.

With two laps to go he managed to pass Alan Jones in the Durex-Surtees and Clay Regazzoni in the second Ferrari on the same bend. Suddenly he was third, with four points in the bag, one ahead of Niki and the new champion of the world.

Hunt told me: 'I didn't realise I had won the championship. I had been waving at the pits, begging them to call me in for a tyre change. No signal came and then it got so dark I couldn't see the signals. Then I had to come in. I thought I had blown it.'

How They Finished:

WORLD DRIVERS' CHAMPIONSHIP

1 James Hunt (G.B.) 69
2 Niki Lauda (Austria) 68
3 Jody Scheckter (South Africa) 49
4 Patrick Depailler (France) 39
5 Clay Regazzoni (Switzerland) 31
6 Mario Andretti (U.S.) 22

Britain's other world champions:

Mike Hawthorn (1958), Graham Hill (1962 and 1968), Jim Clark (1963 and 1965), John Surtees (1964), Jackie Stewart (1969, 1971 1973).

JAPANESE GRAND PRIX

1, M. Andretti (U.S., J.P.S.). 1 hr. 43 min. 58.8 sec., 114.117 m.p.h.
2, P. Depailler (Fr., Elf-Tyrrell)
3, J. Hunt (G.B., Marlboro-McLaren).
4, A. Jones (Aus., Durex-Surtees).
5, C. Regazzoni (Switz., Ferrari).
6, G. Nilsson (Swe., J.P.S.).

WORLD CONSTRUCTORS CHAMPIONSHIP:

1, Ferrari, 83 pts; 2, McLaren, 74; 3, Tyrrell, 71; 4, Lotus, 29; 5eq., Ligier-Matra and Penske, 20.

NOVEMBER

The power of prayer

ALAN GIBSON
The Times

5 November 1976 *Alan Gibson lives, loves and writes about sport in the West country—which is a pity, for his style and enthusiasm deserve more varied pastures. As Gibson says, the effect of prayer on sporting success is an old question. It goes beyond the cricketing field, where a preponderance of the clergy down the years may be responsible: Ronnie Delaney dropping to his knees at the end of the Olympic 1500 metres final in the 1956 Games at Melbourne and many a boxer has bowed his head, or dropped to one knee in the moments before the first bell. But for the moment Gibson looks to God through cricket.*

Once P. F. Warner was taking a cricket team to Australia, and asked a bishop travelling by the same boat whether it was permissible to pray for victory. The bishop, as I remember (I have mislaid the reference), said that 'anything which conduces to the glory of England' was a proper subject for prayer, and Warner undertook that his petitions would be regular and devoted. He won the rubber, so the thesis was at least not disproved, though I do not recall, when it came to offering thanks and praise at the end of the tour, that he included any but temporal members of his team.

It is an old question, this praying for sporting success, and I suppose it contains much the same traps and illogicalities as praying for success in war (especially when the other side are doing the same), and praying about the weather (when two equally earnest worshippers may want quite different sorts of weather). But I am not going to be drawn into the theology of the matter.

Even if it is foolish, there is no doubt that it is a temptation to which many of us succumb, especially when we are young. Sir Neville Cardus has told us how at Old Trafford he would pray that, as it might be, Mold should bowl out Ranjitsinhji with the third ball of the next over, middle stump. He felt that by specifying both the middle of the over and the middle stump, he was giving the Almighty a reasonable margin of error.

In my youth, I was firmly discouraged from praying about sporting encounters, but I do remember cheating occasionally. There was a Cup Final between Newcastle United and Arsenal. It was in 1932, when I was eight, and I am not sure why I felt so passionately about that particular encounter. But I have the clearest recollection of how, after I had punctiliously completed my regular prayers, and mother had said goodnight and switched out the light, I would dive under the bedclothes and add a secret, urgent postcript on behalf of Newcastle.

This turned out to be one of the Lord's more spectacular triumphs, for not only did Newcastle win, but did so by a disputed goal, when – every infuriated Arsenal supporter maintained – the referee had momentarily been struck blind.

Many a cricketer, at all levels of the game, must have uttered some kind of prayer when he has seen a high catch coming towards him in the deep. Albert Knight, of Leicestershire and England, was, so far as I know, the only one in the first-class game who, the ball safely caught, would pay his public acknowledments to his Maker, bowing his head and even, according to some accounts, bending his knee. I thought of Knight on the occasion when David Sheppard, on a tour of Australia when nothing had been going right with his fielding, at last caught one. He did not bow the head, but ran round in a happy little circle of thanksgiving, throwing himself catches. He was interrupted by a bellow from his captain. It had been a no-ball, and the batsmen were still running.

Knight would also pause to pray when he began his innings, as automatically as taking guard. That explosive Lancashire fast bowler Walter Brearley threatened to report him to MCC. Sir Neville, again, recalls the incident in his preface to *Hit Hard and Enjoy It*, by T. C. Dodds, which was published last summer. The preface was probably the last thing Sir Neville wrote. It is not my purpose to review the book, except to say that it is well worth reading, amusing as well as thought-provoking.

But it so happens that I have known Carter Dodds (he was known to cricketers as 'Dickie') for a long time; knew him, indeed, at the time he was beginning his first-class career, and remember very well talking with him in those days on the subject of prayer and its relationship to life, including cricket. I can therefore vouch – not that it needs vouching for – that the views he sets out in his book are not in any way coloured by subsequent success. I am sure that had he been a failure as a cricketer his faith would be unchanged.

The case of Knight and Dodds are not on all fours. Knight's, I understand, was a simple, evangelical faith. 'If ye shall ask any thing in my name, I will do it': so why not 100 runs? Dodds is a supporter of the Moral Re-Armament movement (to which he gave the proceeds of his benefit) and MIRA take a slightly more sophisticated view of prayer. I am not going to discuss its merits as a movement – I am not a supporter of it myself. For them, prayer, or 'guidance' as it is more commonly called, is a two-way communication with God. You have a 'quiet time', in which you put the problem to him, and you note, with pen and paper if possible, what thoughts he puts into your mind in reply. You are not *asking* for anything, except advice.

Now this, always assuming that you believe in a personal and loving God, is sensible enough. Thus Dodds did not pray that he might score 100. He asked God: 'How do you want me to play cricket?' And the answer came: 'Hit the ball hard and enjoy it.' It took some time, incidentally, as he honestly records, before he had the courage to carry out God's instructions. When he did he was transformed from one of the slowest opening batsmen in the country to one of the fastest, overnight, which made Frank Rist, the Essex coach, call him 'the miracle man.'

When he took his benefit match (the match was the most important thing in a cricketer's benefit in those days) he wondered whether to insure against the weather. His guidance was not to insure, because God had said: 'If I want you to have the money, you shall have it.' He accepted this, and the weather cleared at the last minute, and Compton scored a century before lunch, and the benefit was a huge success. He then asked what he should do with the money, and God answered if I may risk an august paraphrase: 'Give it away,' which he did.

This does not, I suppose, tell you a great deal about God, but it tells you all you need to know, and all you need to admire, about Dodds, who has the quality of the saints.

The trouble with this kind of prayer is that it can degenerate into superstition. Dodds had, according to his own account, already several clear indications from God that he should marry a girl called Ann, with whom he was not in love. This is his description of the decisive moment:

'We were playing Somerset at Valentines (!) Park in Ilford. It was a hot day, and two Somerset batsmen were set, and were despatching our bowling to all parts of the field. In the middle of the afternoon Bill Greensmith was bowling his leg-breaks, and just as his arm was coming over for one delivery the thought popped into my mind that if a wicket fell to that ball, then Ann was definitely the girl I was meant to marry.

'To my consternation I saw the ball was one of those that all leg-break bowlers deliver occasionally. The ball slipped out of his fingers and bounced halfway down the wicket. The batsman could have hit it to any part of the field. Instead he hit it straight at me and I caught him out!'

This is no good at all. It is entirely pagan, like examining the entrials or touching wood, or touching the peak of your cap before the bowler delivers. It reduced God to a hazard and all the other cricketers concerned to automata. If God wants to assure a happy marriage he has better ways of doing it than making the ball slip out of Greensmith's fingers. We can all understand what made the incident so vivid to Dodds at that time, but it spoils his argument, and does no justice to his faith.

To return to my starting point; is it any good praying that you might make 100 runs when next you go into bat, or about the steepler coming to long-off, or even that you may hit the ball hard and enjoy it – for some of us are not given the requisite talents? I quote to you a few lines from Leslie Weatherhead, as saintly a man as Dodds, which he made in the course of an address concerned with praying about the weather. He said, bluntly, that he did not think it was, but he added:

'I am sure a man can be as good a Christian who believes in praying about the weather, as a man who does not. And if bad weather makes you pray when good weather would leave you prayerless, it could be argued that it is a good thing to pray whatever you pray about. It is a good thing for a child to talk to his father about *anything* that worries him.'

One way or another, then, all those prayers of Warner and Knight and Dodds and you and me: they may not have been wasted after all.

Those little perforations

PETER DOBEREINER
The Observer

7 November 1976 *With all the hazards that go with the game of golf—the rough, bad weather, bunkers, wrong clubs, even the nineteenth hole—the smooth part round the cup itself always seemed a safe, unblemished area. Peter Dobereiner spikes that idea.*

The average golf shoe is fitted with 11 spikes. The average golfer has two feet and walks, on average, 50 paces on each green. So if an average of 200 golfers play the course then each green receives an average of 110,000 spikings on an average day, always accepting that my grasp of mathematics, which is well below average, has not failed entirely.

The concentration of these spikings is obviously highest in the area around the hole. Assuming that every golfer holes out and retrieves his ball from the hole, there cannot be fewer than 2200 spikings per square yard on that part of the putting surface where the ball is slowing down and most susceptible to deviation. By my reckoning there cannot be fewer than two spike marks per square inch around the hole by evening.

All this only goes to prove what everyone knows already:

that the area around the flag quickly gets worn and cut up, particularly when the ground is soft, and that golfers who play late in the day are at a considerable disadvantage.

It was for this reason that the PGA introduced a temporary local rule, with the approval of the Royal and Ancient Golf Club, permitting damage caused by shoe spikes to be repaired. This local rule is experimental and it is no secret that if it proves to have been a success the R. and A. will consider incorporating it into the rules of golf. It is no secret, either, that there is a strong lobby forming in America to resist the introduction of such a rule if and when the time comes.

The PGA is to meet the R. and A. in December to discuss the way the spike mark rule has worked out in practice and George O'Grady, one of the tournament administrators, certainly believes that it has made the game fairer and that it has also speeded up play.

That last point is slightly surprising, but he points out that instead of spending ages agonising over the problem of judging the effect of putting over spike marks the players now simply tap them down and get on with the job.

That is not to say he is in favour of incorporating the concession into the rules of golf. On the whole he believes that amateurs spend much less time surveying the putt and that allowing them to indulge in wholesale repairs of the line would make play slower.

The main weaknesses of the present local rule are that it gives no guidelines about what is a spike mark, nor does it attempt to define any limits as to how extensive the repairs may be. As such, the rule is difficult to police, and rules which cannot be enforced are bad rules. It is obvious, for instance, that it is unlawful for a player to hammer away along the line of his putt until he has created a groove for the ball. But between that extreme and the restraint of a player who confines himself to the odd tap with his putter head on a raised tuft of grass there is a wide range of possibilities for gardening.

In the French Open one of the contributory causes to the wrangle between Rafe Botts and Howard Clark was that the American thought Clark was overdoing the repair work. Then last month in the Piccadilly Severiano Ballesteros was aggrieved when the referee ruled that the damage he sought to repair was not a spike mark but a scuff caused by the heel of a shoe.

Having formed that opinion the referee had no option but to rule as he did but the incident was faintly ludicrous (and tragic for Ballesteros)* and it exposed one weakness of the rule. In an ordinary tournament Ballesteros – or anyone else – would have repaired that blemish without a second thought. It was only when there was a referee on the spot, and one who was prepared to act like an Indian scout tracking a war party, that the rule could be enforced.

Normally it is quite impossible to determine whether a tuft of three blades of grass has been raised by a shoe spike, a pecking bird, a running dog, a dropped putter, a carelessly lifted ball-marker or anything else. In practice everything gets a bonk from the putter. If this rule is to be retained – and it certainly makes for a fairer game – then I believe it should be amended to read: Damage to putting greens may be repaired. It must be all or nothing.

There is another possible line of approach to the problem of spike marks and that is to introduce legislation to limit the size and number of spikes on golf shoes. It is quite obvious that half the spikes on golf shoes are unnecessary except for the sake of symmetry when walking on hard surfaces. The spikes on the outside of the right shoe perform no golfing function in the swing. All they do is prevent you from turning over your ankle when you are walking about in the locker room. There must be scope for ingenuity by the manufacturers to design shoes which do far less damage to greens.

Meanwhile the professionals at least can look forward to another season of being able to tap down spike marks. If it does nothing else the experimental local rule ensures that we will have no repetition of the absurd sight of two years ago when Peter Townsend had to take his sand wedge for a two foot putt and chip the ball over an obstruction.

* Upset by what he regarded as an unfair and uninformed decision Ballesteros let his concentration falter and he lost the match. To his mind the referee's intervention was tantamount to an accusation of cheating and, as Ballesteros says, 'I do not cheat. I am a good enough player not to need to.'

A poisoned well

BRIAN GLANVILLE
The Sunday Times

21 November 1976 *Of all the soccer correspondents Brian Glanville has the deepest understanding of the game in Italy. In this assessment of England's performance in Rome—where they lost 2-0—he points to the problems which beset players, clubs and the national team manager alike and also to those Latin flaws which may finally help the England cause.*

'I want to play in England. I want to play for an English Club, for Liverpool or Manchester United.' Thus Francesco Graziani, Italy's centre-forward, said when I met him on a television programme a few hours after Wednesday's international match in Rome. Nor would he be discouraged when I told him that he would earn substantially less money than he does now with Torino. It was reassuring that after so mundane an exhibition by our international team an Italian player should still be so keen to come to England.

It is always foolish to place too much significance on any one result, and the lesson is particularly emphasised when one remembers that less than six months ago, after the surprise of New York*, Italian football seemed to be in pieces, the sweeper and man-to-man marking game quite out of date, while last Wednesday it was England who looked old-fashioned. The Italian defenders, indeed, frequently broke forward with great verve and pace as soon as they had won the ball, while England's were of relatively little help to their attack. The most alarming feature of the English defeat, however, was that this was probably the best, or the least bad, team that Revie could have put out under present circumstances.

This meant, inevitably, that Stan Bowles had to be integrated within 90 minutes into a team which knew him not.

* In July England, together with Brazil and Italy, played a number of semi-exhibition internationals in various centres throughout the USA. In New York England came back from 2-0 down to beat Italy 3-2.

He said to me after the game that he felt things were going well in the second half, adding that he was sure England would beat Italy at Wembley: 'I don't think they're a good team.' It meant also that there was no alternative to Gerry Francis as the co-ordinator of the midfield, that Revie perforce had to choose a couple of wing-halves to play alongside the splendid Trevor Brooking, England's one major success. It meant that he had to choose at left-back Mick Mills, a large-hearted player of modest attainments and with no left foot, who prefers to play in midfield and was predictably at a loss against the extraordinary Causio.

When a league throws up so few players of any quality there is not a great deal a manager can do. True, Revie did not much help matters by his obsessional fiddling about with tactics, but there is no evidence that it would have made much difference had he been more consistent. It was logical enough to put the limited but determined Cherry on Antognoni, and the selection of Brian Greenhoff was well justified.

The debate between man-to-man marking and zonal defence seemed to be resolved strongly in favour of man-to-man in Rome. Yet it is worth remembering that in New York Italy's man-to-man defence fell to pieces. After Wednesday's game the Italian team manager, Enzo Bearzot, remarked that it was the close and decisive Italian marking which made Channon and Keegan look ineffective, that a ball player can show what he can do with the ball only when he is given time to get it under control. Had Keegan been playing for Italy he would have shone.

Then there was the question of the second Italian goal, which, by the way, would never have come about at all had Keegan not attempted that aberrational flick, and put the Italians in possession. Dave Clement explained to me that he had moved out to the wing to counter Benetti. Behind him, defender or defenders unknown had failed to pick up Bettega, the scorer.

Bettega himself, a young man of refined good looks, told me that he had found this often happened in an English, zonal type of defence, that one player tended to leave an opponent to another. The truth is, however, that without Causio it is most doubtful that Italy would have won. Two moment of exotic brilliance brought two Italian goals, even if the first was made possible only by a lucky deflection, while the second required Bettega's fine header.

Causio, as the Italians themselves say, and as one saw clearly enough even within the context of this game, is a player who can alternate the brilliant with the bad. But at least he has the courage, as well as the supreme skill, to attempt the difficult, the supreme virtuosity. Bowles can do that, too, but by and large we breed this out of our players. Our football for years has been a poisoned well in which individualism, the one quality which can unlock today's well-organised defences, is discouraged and despised.

It would be futile and reactionary to condemn all kinds of coaching, as futile as it would be to condemn all kinds of psychiatric treatment, but just as there are many more inept psychiatrists than good ones, in the very nature of things, so there are many more harmful and restrictive coaches in England than there are helpful ones: not least at schools level.

One has written often enough of the dead tactical hand which descended on our football after England's World Cup victory in 1966, when wingless play and the suffocating concept of work-rate deadened virtuosity. Don Revie's Leeds were for a long time as guilty as any successful team of furthering such methods, as he has admitted. Now both he and we are paying the penalty. The ironic thing is that Wednesday's result could well have been different. Scores can be illusory. Without in any way exculpating England's performance, it remains true that, as Clement remarked, they kept the crowd quiet for 35 minutes till that lucky first goal, while at the moment that the second came they were beginning to get a grip on the match against an Italian side that seemed clearly to be tiring. A 1-1 draw would not have been beyond them, and who knows what would have happened after an equaliser? Who, for that matter, could possibly have predicted at half-time in New York the collapse of the Italians in the second period?

We can see now, alas, that the fine days of summer, the results obtained in America and Finland, were something of a delusion, that the truth of our dull, virile, honest championship could not be obscured for long.

Hope of qualifying for the next World Cup is not extinct. Italian football has not wholly found its way out of the maze. But our club managers must be more adventurous, our international teams must continue to give talent a fling . . . continuously. Gradually, enlightenment may seep its way down into the schools, and the poison may seep out of the system.

The Ugly Face of Sport

PETER WILSON
The Daily Mirror

25 November 1976 *Peter Wilson began writing for the Daily Mirror in 1935 and was Fleet Street's most prolific and pungent writer through four decades. From retirement in Majorca he returns to Wimbledon and other events in summer and occasionally dips into the past to remind us that he is a gentleman who expects people involved in sport to be sportsmen. In this carefully angled stab at Ilie Nastase he argues that the financial rewards now available to top sportsmen are undermining the structure and administration of sport.*

Sportsman: one engaged in sport, fair-minded person, good loser (*Everyman's English Dictionary*).

Just how many of today's sporting stars who – in teams or individually – hog the headlines, live up to the above definition?

If you go to a football match it's even money that if the players aren't trying to maim each other in the sacred name of sport – and the hope of greater financial rewards – the spectators will be slashing, stabbing or trying to garrotte one another, before setting out on an orgy of destruction.

The malaise seems to be spreading wider and wider in ever-increasing circles which taint the whole pool of sport.

But if I had to spotlight one international figure in sport, who typifies what it should all not be about, my pen would be pointed at Ilie Nastase, the Rumanian lawn tennis maverick.

In a United States tournament the referee, Charles Hare, an Englishman of the older school, rightly disqualified the Rumanian, because, in the official's Americanised words, 'he showed me his ass.'

Recently, in Hong Kong, in the process of being beaten 1—6, 6—4, 7—6, 6—0 by the 42-year-old Ken Rosewall – just as great a stylist and a far greater sportsman than Nastase has ever been – the Rumanian was asked to serve again because his opponent was not ready.

He thereupon slammed the ball out of the Victoria Park centre court and a report quoted the imperturbable Rosewall as commenting:

'I was glad to win, but not when he (Nastase) behaves like a child, a baby – I don't enjoy that at all.

'I suppose he got upset because I wasn't ready. But it's only courtesy for one player to wait for another. He doesn't have any courtesy.'

At Wembley last week Nastase, disagreeing with a linesman's decision – for the how many thousandth time? – spat in the direction of the official and later banged a ball towards him.

To be fair to the man I christened 'Muhammad Ilie', that's about as far as he will go in the expression of physical violence. He did, it is true, threaten last year to go over the barrier by the side of Wimbledon's centre court to 'sort out' some photographer who had offended him. But, as far as anyone could see, flicking a towel in the direction of the cameraman was the limit of Nastase's bellicosity.

However, when it comes to the short, ugly words, in a variety of languages, and the crude, lewd gestures – which constitute a universal language – Nastase is in a class of his own – thank goodness.

With prize money, endorsements and all the other benefits which now form the trappings of any sports star, it must be a bad year for Nastase if he doesn't rake in something approaching £250,000. Even if he were the greatest player in the world – which he has never proved himself to be – the foul mouth and foul manners of the Rumanian are attributes which makes the gold he garners really tarnished. When he is fined the amounts are usually derisory – and he takes his own sweet time in paying them. When he is suspended he manages to find some tournament which does not seem to come under the jurisdiction of any of the authorities.

And this is the canker of sport today. From Muhammad Ali to the most fumble-footed Soccer star, the financial rewards have become so overblown that these primping prima donnas think that they inhabit a world of their own.

It's a world where the standards of decency and straightforward, respectable behaviour exhibited by ordinary folk are discarded as unnecessary to the swelling self-glorification of the so-called super-stars.

We do not want youngsters modelling themselves, in all sports, on stars who do not so much flout as utterly ignore the conventions of civilised society.

We do not want crowds, in any sport, who think that, if it's permissible for the star to spit and swear and defy authority, it must follow that the spectator can do likewise with 'bovver boot' and blade. Nastase, of course, is not the only sinner. But, to me, he is probably the most notorious. I wish he would take the money he has made, through insult and defiance – and go.

DECEMBER

Salute to The Bishop

FRANK BUTLER
The News of the World

5 December 1976 *Boxing is marvellous for the characters it creates, and for the manner the boxing writers reflect them. Later in the book Dudley Doust writes about Henry Cooper; here Frank Butler, the longest serving boxing correspondent in the 'Street, talks to Cooper's ex-manager—one of the oldest professionals.*

Back in 1894 Gladstone resigned as Prime Minister and Gentleman Jim Corbett was the heavyweight champion. An event that didn't catch the eye of historians was the birth of Jim Wicks, son of a docker from Bermondsey, the toughest punch-up community in London.

Tomorrow, Jim Wicks – ex-docker, ex-bookie, ex-publican and ex-fight manager – is 82. And some of those 'good boys' he once managed like 'Enery Cooper and brother George, Joe Lucy, Alex Buxton and Vic Andretti are joining 700 guests to give Jim a birthday 'do' at London's Cunard International Hotel.

Few fight managers are held in high esteem by all their ex-fighters. Few have been as independent as Wicksie. Always his own man, he told Jack Solomons and Harry Levene when they sought to get Henry Cooper's services:

'I don't care who 'Enery fights for. He'll box for the geezer who pays most.'

Wicks, of the pink, bald and shiny head, is known as 'The Bishop,' but is no saint and knows he's not in danger of ever being canonised.

'My father was a docker earning 30 bob a week,' he explains. 'Us kids in Bermondsey were a bunch of thieves and hooligans. We had to be to survive.

'What saved most of us from becoming real villains was a couple of real good guys – one a Protestant Dr Stanfield and the other a Catholic, Mr Potter.

'They started up boys clubs giving us soccer and boxing. The best way to stop violence on the streets is for the kids to let off steam at each other. We were in the gym every day and every night. It became a way of life.'

A born gambler, Wicks as a young man became a street bookie, dodging the cops. He explains:

'I did well and went legit and became one of four proud bookmakers allowed in Tattersall's at Ascot before the Tote and before bookies were allowed their tools' (boards, umbrellas and prices).

Henry Cooper is good to Jim. They've been in partnership 25 years. Even though Henry retired five years ago he still has his old manager running his business commitments and insists that he takes his percentage. Henry meets Jim once a week for lunch and Wicks is always saying: 'That 'Enery. He's a real angel!'

Though he remembers the old days as though they were only yesterday, like many old-timers as the years roll faster than the Thames past Bermondsey he can't recall all the names.

'Remember that great middleweight Charlie Wotsisname?' he asks, and gets irritable first with himself and then with the listener for not remembering. 'Blimey. You ought to know. He used to box old Bill Waddycallim in the jimmynasium at the Thomas A'Beckett.'

Jim Wicks is the last of the great characters disappearing from the fight game. The best tribute to him is that all his ex-fighters living in Britain will be at the Cunard tomorrow to honour him.

Henry Cooper sums it up best: 'I would never have been the same fighter without Jim. He fought all my financial battles and never once picked my pocket.

'I knew he was in there fighting for every penny for me, and he'd still take his coat off and have a go for me at 82.'

Happy birthday, Shamus, old boy. All those angels, those good boys of yours, will be raising their glasses to you tomorrow.

A dazzling debut

CLIVE TAYLOR
The Sun

20 December 1976 *Christmas, yet the best sporting news is about cricket. Clive Taylor tells the story of how Peter Lever broke down India's batsmen. Early in the new year Taylor became ill during the Centenary Test in Melbourne, returned home and died. His loss to cricket and cricket writing was a grievous one, as this piece shows.*

John Lever, his fair hair flapping round his shoulders like a Viking, yesterday brought down India, the lords of the East, in the First Test.

For the first time in 12 years they suffered the humiliation of being made to follow on before their own countrymen, who have grown sleek and content watching their success. That was the doing of Lever, who in his Test debut took 7 for 46, the best performance by anyone in his first bowl for England.

For all but three overs of the innings, as India were put out for 122, Lever occupied one end, always superb, swinging the ball into the pads with his left-arm deliveries and sometimes angling it across towards slips. The confusion he created on a pitch doped into unconsciousness was complete, yet his record says that while he has won his way into Test trials he has never before impressed enough for promotion. Indeed, even this time Cope challenged for his place.

With four wickets already landed, the Essex man went 80 minutes yesterday morning before he took another. Then Knott caught Patel off bat and pad down the legside and half India were out for 96. Three runs later Sunil Gavaskar, the most talented of all their batsmen, went for the hook despite three men posted for the shot and stood transfixed watching his own downfall. For 25 yards round the boundary edge Willis's giant strides ate up the ground as the ball hung in the air, then as he made the catch he stumbled, fell and hung on.

The other ten of the England team raced 80 yards over the outfield to congratulate him.

Immediately afterwards Willis, now a sort of gully in the tight ring of attacking fielders, flung himself to his right and slid his fingers under a sliced drive that Sharma had hit brutally hard. That wicket belonged to Underwood – the first time any bowler other than Lever had intervened.

When they started again Lever lifted out Kirmani's off-stump with an in-swinger so sharp that the batsman finished up facing mid-on. Then Old finished off Bedi, Chandra and the Indian innings in two balls.

Ten minutes later Lever, the edge gone by now, was starting his new opening spell of five overs. Yet the memory of his earlier success will keep him warm for the rest of his life as a professional cricketer. 'I began to worry when I hadn't got a wicket in the first hour,' he said.

'I kept telling myself that four wasn't enough and all the time Fletcher [his County captain] kept running up and telling me to keep my head and keep my line. He really kept me going until we got the break.

'Bowling in this country is all about stamina – just being able to keep running up and firing it in. Yet the ball swung so much this morning that I was able to aim it at first slip.'

With India 259 behind Lever had given England the chance to win this First Test just as they did under Tony Lewis four years ago. The prospect improved when after 25 minutes of their second innings Willis knocked over the stumps of Gaekwad, a good-looking player with too many sloppy shots to do the job of opener.

But India came back in a way they found difficult in the old days. Gavaskar, cool, tenacious and with a beautiful technique against the slow bowlers, has inspired them to 82-1. India are prepared to fight for their honour.

At times the frustration showed among the England bowlers and the appeals became more frantic. But Greig, so far at least, has stood by his maxim that this series will not be one in which the umpires are intimidated. Twice he waved Lever and Old back to their marks as they stood in the middle of the pitch ready to air their indignation as appeals were turned down. Apparently he wants peace as well as success.

JANUARY

The President's Putter

ROGER PAUL
The Financial Times

8 January 1977 *The President's Putter, which has survived the ice and wind of Romney Marshes, reflects a quality of sporting life from another age. Roger Paul's sketch set the event and the people who play in it apart from any other without taking the more obvious line of cynical disapproval.*

The President's Putter is a 4-day golf tournament played at Rye in Sussex in the first week of January, which makes it if not eccentric then at least a little whimsical. It is a midwinter exercise in combating cold and consuming Kummel; with cammaraderie the inevitable and welcome result. It is, as one member puts it, a compulsive re-union of the members of the Oxford and Cambridge Golfing Society, and yet over the years it has been more than that.

There was a time when the Putter field contained most of the best amateurs of the day. Among its winners have been Laddie Lucas, Leonard Crawley, Cyril Tolley and Roger Wethered. Nowadays the entry is less formidable. This year only three internationals, David Marsh, Michael Attenborough and Donald Steel entered, and only Attenborough survived the first round. But the Putter is a guide to a man's fortitude both in playing in extreme conditions, in accepting the bounces through and on the green and in surviving the social combat course that is set in places like The Mermaid, the Ship and the Hope Anchor. The latter's management, for instance, undergoing their first Putter this year, learned one valuable lesson. You can never have enough Kummel in stock: just when you think you're all right a bridge game goes on until four in the morning and everything's shot to hell.

The entry, if not formidable, is fascinating. There is the annual glimpse of the Boys Own Paper game of E. R. Dexter, Lord Ted, former England cricket skipper and once a Walker Cup possible.

There is, or has been for the last 36 years, Gerald Micklem displaying an enduring swing. This year he bowed out, before, as he put it, people began to be surprised at him getting through a round. He remains comfortably at the top of the table of most matches played, with 111, and doubtless to his immense satisfaction at the top of the table of matches won, with 76.

Then there is Freddie Brown, another former England cricket captain, who, in sharp contrast to Dexter and Micklem, has yet to survive a round. On Thursday night he took consolation at losing a four-hole lead and the match with joyous reflections of the England performance in India.

He told us, too, how, in the infamous 1932 bodyline series in Australia, he found himself made 12th man for the 5th time in five Tests. The series was won so he slipped the masseur a couple of quid in return for a mythical bad back and stole off to play golf.

The Putter began in 1920, and has been played at Rye every year since apart from the grisly winter of 1963 when the whole country was snowed under. The whole country, that is, with the exception of Littlestone just down the road which played host to the Putter and saw it through.

The competition was not, of course, played during the second world war, a fact duly and drily noted at the first AGM after it, on 16 January 1946. Lord Justice Morton put a resolution which received unanimous support that, so far as the Society was concerned, 'The years 1939–45 be reckoned non-existent.' Not all the members were able to attend, of course, and Mr G. D. Roberts, KC, sent a telegram from Nuremburg apologising because of 'a prior engagement with my old pal Goering,' and there were other manifestations that all was not yet normal. The retiring captain, G. L. Mellin, was presented 'in theory, as it has been temporarily mislaid on the railway,' with a canteen of cutlery.

The weather is the constant topic and a factor in every

match. Some people function better than others under three sweaters and some waterproofs; but strangely the Putter has run its course in its allotted time on all but five occasions. In 1953, 1955 and 1971 it finished one day late and in 1964 and 1967 the final was played in March, after the University match.

Indeed in 1964 they had to play the 5th round, the semi-final and final over 12, 12 and 18 holes respectively on the same day, leaving Donald Steel a slightly breathless winner. Steel has won the Putter twice, the second time in 1970, and, as a fellow golf writer, is the man who salvages our self-respect for us by actually being able to play the game.

Each winner is required to attach a ball to the Putter, itself a venerable old instrument once used by Hughie Kirkaldy when he won the Championship at St Andrews in 1891. It was bought by the Society's first President, John Low, who then used it to reach the final of the Amateur Championship, again at St. Andrews, and there hang on to Harold Hilton's coat-tails until the very last hole. The attached golf balls are a piece of potted golf history, ranging from battered old Silver Kings of Spaldings, through to sleek Dunlop 65s and, lately, two Titleists.

Rye, of course, is the perfect venue for an event of this type. The area survives winters better than most and the course is a hardy creature of a calibre sufficient to host the English Ladies Championship in 1970.

Then there is Rye Town itself, perched on a hill and seemingly shrivelled with age and yet entirely vigorous: full of fine shops and enough pubs selling good food and real beer to make the wintry evenings a delight.

As I write the sun is beating down strongly out of the clear blue sky, glinting on the sea now a mile away from what used to be a flourishing port. But all that means, in Putter terms, is a strong possibility of fog and frost tonight. Not that anyone is worried. It's all happened before; in any case Lord Ted's won again and the word has got around that the Hope Anchor has re-stocked with Kummel. All's well with the President's Putter at Rye.

Golly gosh, Clare!

FRANK KEATING
The Guardian

12 January 1977 *Clare Francis took part in what was regarded as the toughest in the series of Single-handed Transatlantic Races. In that unkind sea, her sinking craft wracked by gales, she spent almost a month alone, but moments in her journey were recorded for BBC television by the use on board of an automatic television camera. Frank Keating met Clare at the Boat Show several months later and, like many others, wondered how this dot of a girl won through.*

For my money, the second most staggering thing at the Boat Show this week has been the sight of queues waiting for an autograph – from Clare Francis. The most staggering thing was seeing the size of her boat *Robertson's Golly,* in relation to the 5ft. 2in. of Miss Francis herself.

How on earth, I would still like to know, did this pert knockout of a 7½-stone weakline, with wrists like twigs and a frame like Twiggy's, manage her Ohlson 38 – which along-side her has a mast like Salisbury's spire – through the most dangerous Single-handed Transatlantic Race yet?

In spite of the fact that the 1976 race had the worst weather, that it boasted a record number of competitors, that sailors died during it for the first time, and that one third of the boats had to drop out, Miss Francis succeeded in beating the French-held women's record by completing the course in 29 days and was the first British competitor in a conventional boat to finish. The smallest person ever known to have sailed the Atlantic alone, she survived two violent gales, a fearful storm, continuous fog for two weeks and almost permanent waves of over 35 feet.

Miss Francis, born in suburban Surbiton, began sailing at the age of five. After the Royal Ballet School she studied economics at London University. On getting her degree she set out on a career in marketing – and one of her jobs before she took to more dangerous hobbies full time was in the marketing department of Robertson's Jam. Hence her sponsor for the Atlantic race. She had sailed the Atlantic before by herself – for a bet.

Miss Francis has written a book on last year's race (*Come Hell or High Water*, Pelham, £4.25) and if the queues waiting for autographed copies at Earls Court this week are anything to go by she has a best-seller on her hands. Certainly, if my memory is right, she was out-signing last year's marathon by the Rt Hon. shoulder-shaking captain of the *Cleoud*. The tale, as the groanworthy title suggests, is racily told by a bright and courageous young lady. It is hugely readable in a lightweight sort of way. It has so many girlish exclamation marks that you think at the end that the boat should be renamed *Golly Gosh*.

Those who saw her memorable BBC film of the voyage (it brought even our eminent boxing correspondent to tears) will certainly want to buy it. Single-handed filming, in fact, was an awful chore to her at the time. 'One day it finally became too much for me. Turning on all the equipment I started making my usual type of report about the weather . . . then I suddenly found myself grunting. I followed this with a growl and a pronounced squint of my eyes. Then I gnashed my teeth. The lens stared back at me, completely unimpressed . . . and thrusting my chin forward I gave a series of monkey-like grunts, my best impersonation of an orangutan with plenty of armpit scratching and knuckle-trailing. Grabbing a banana from the galley I ate it with my back to the camera, throwing sly and threatening looks over my shoulder . . . and just to leave the BBC in no doubt, I finished with a fine impersonation of a gorilla rushing at a camera, with lots of chest-beating and loud shrieks.

'It made me feel marvellous. The thought of the BBC viewing the reel made me giggle with delight. The more I imagined the scene the more I grinned with anticipation. I could see the studio, the technicians, everyone watching, all thinking I had finally eaten too many bananas. Then a less pleasant thought occurred to me. Supposing they used it in the finished film? No, no, of course they wouldn't! Or would they? If they did everyone would think I was mad. So with that I threw the reel over the side.' What a pity . . . no, sorry, golly gosh, what a rotten swizz!

Merrie England

JOHN HOPKINS
The Sunday Times

England 26 Scotland 6

16 January 1977 *The poverty of England's rugby football, as John Hopkins points out, has reached the level of a music hall joke. Here he enthuses—and reflects the enthusiasm at Twickenham—as Scotland reel before a new power in the game. One swallow does not make a winter, but for the moment rejoicing was deserved.*

England found a captain, found a team, found their tactics and could well be on the way to finding true happiness after this compelling victory over the hapless Scots. Twenty points was England's biggest margin ever in the Calcutta Cup and the country's highest score in the championship for 10 years. They won by four tries to none, which was not a try too many, and had Hignell not failed with five penalties and two conversions out of 11 attempts then the margin would have approached the indecent. Four tries, by the way, is exactly twice the number England scored last season.

But that is not all, for midway through the second half one became aware that out of the throats of many of the 68,000 spectators was coming a patriotic fervour more normally associated with Cardiff Arms Park. 'Eng-land, England' it came down from the stands, descending like a heavy mist to cover and confuse further the by now bedraggled Scotsmen. Ask not for whom they roar, England, they roar for you.

And how one could identify with those enormous waves of support. England's rugby had recently sunk to the level of a music hall joke – yet after one of their worst seasons ever here were England playing as if every Scotsman in London was taunting and teasing them. There were men with the heart that John Burgess wanted so much when he was the team coach; and, showing that they had it, they won the support of every Englishman in the ground.

It was a team effort, but it was a victory that was based entirely on England's forwards. The bald statistics revealed that the lines-out were nearly shared; England won 19, Scotland, largely due to the beanpole Donald Macdonald at the back, won 17. The big difference, though, was at the mauls, where England won four for every Scottish success and at the rucks, which England won at a rate of two to one.

Such figures barely reveal how often, even at rucks set up by Scotland, it was an Englishman who fed the ball back. But it was in all aspects of the game and not just the rucks that the Englishmen were so impressive. They went into the fray with such vigour!

With all this possession England were able to play the limited tactical style that they always said they would. They didn't make mistakes – it would hardly have mattered if they had – and with the eight men in front of him marching triumphantly forward like courtiers announcing the arrival of the king Young in particular and Cooper and Kent outside him were able to play precisely the way they wanted to.

All the known limitations of Young were gone, and he had time to pass. The shortness of it hardly mattered as Scotland's back row were more often than not going backwards. With this extra time and space Cooper was able to kick, which in the main he did accurately, to run, which he hardly did, and to utilise his backs, which he did more often, and most successfully in set moves.

Corless will feature in no despatches from this game, but only because in his position he was often missed out by Cooper, the better to get to the ball to the waiting, thrusting Kent, who could make such a mess in Scotland's midfield. McGeechan and Cranston tackled well but it was a charge by the fair-haired Rosslyn Park player that set up the ruck from which England scored the first try. And then when England were wanting to twist the dirk that was already stuck into Scotland's heart it was Kent they chose to do it.

The flag of St George was standing out in the wind but it was growing dark as after a scrum Young popped a delicate kick to within a yard of the Scottish line. As in his try, when he had plunged over after a five yard scrum and after a hint of a wheel by England had disrupted Scotland's back row, Young had all the time in the world.

England charged around the front of the line-out but met a solid wall of Scotsmen. From the maul the ball came back beautifully, Cooper was able to run across in front of the Scottish posts, and Kent, charging diagonally, plunged through a thicket of Scottish shirts to score. Hignell's attempted conversion hit the post and rebounded but the score moved to 20–6. By now it was approaching a slaughter.

Scotland's sole hopes lay in running the ball; their talented backs looking the better equipped for that sort of game, on paper at any rate. But where was the ball they needed? With Englishmen, that's where, and with it went any hope that Scotland had of winning.

They had taken an early lead with a penalty goal by Irvine only to lose it three minutes later when Slemen took a high overhead pass from Cooper on the blind side of a ruck and went over in the corner. There was an unreal quality about this try, the way it was set up and then brought off. Who knows how many centres throughout Britain were practising just such a move in training sessions last week – racing into their opposition to set up the ruck, their forwards piling in after them and then, with the ball quickly heeled, moving it fast to the blindside? It's an old move, and an honest one.

A penalty goal by Hignell was answered with a similar score by Irvine. Just before half-time came Young's try and then after the re-start another penalty goal by Hignell.

Now there was no doubt about the better side. It didn't matter that Tomes ungraciously stamped on Horton, or for that matter that Cowling was being pressurised by Sandy Carmichael in the set scrums. It was 16–6 and the cheek of the Englishmen was never better represented than by Hignell, who tried a dropped goal from miles out on the touchline.

Then came Kent's try and in the last minute of the game Roger Uttley picked up the ball from a scrum five yards out and Hignell was successful with this conversion. Uttley was helped off the field at this time with what was later diagnosed as a bloody nose. He missed the jumping for joy by his team mates and the atmosphere of elation in the ground, but it didn't matter. He had done his part and he will be back again.

ENGLAND: A. J. Hignall (Cambridge U), **P. J. Squires** (Harrogate), **B. J. Corless** (Moseley), **C. P. Kent** (Rosslyn Pk), **M. A. C. Slemen** (Liverpool), **M. J. Cooper** (Moseley), **M. Young** (Gosforth), No 8, **R. M. Uttley** (Gosforth, capt) Second Row, **M. Rafter** (Bristol), **N. E. Horton** (Moseley), **W. B. Beaumont** (Fylde), **P. J. Dixon** (Gosforth), Front Row, **F. E. Cotton** (Sale), **P. J. Wheeler** (Leicester), **R. J. Cowling** (Leicester)

Tries: Slemen, Young, Kent, Uttley;
Conversions: Hignell (2);
Penalty Goals: Hignell (2)

SCOTLAND: A. R. Irvine (Heriot's FP), **W. C. Steele** (London Scottish), **I. R. McGeechan** (Headingley, capt), **A. G. Cranston** (Hawick), **L. G. Dick** (Swansea), **R. Wilson** (London Scottish), **A. J. M. Lawson** (London Scottish), No 8, **D. S. M. MacDonald** (Oxford U), Second Row, **A. K. Brewster** (Stewart's-Melville FP), **A. F. McHarg** (London Scottish), **A. J. Tomes** (Hawick), **W. Lauder** (Neath), Front Row, **A. B. Carmichael** (West of Scotland), **D. F. Madson** (Gosforth), **J. Aitken** (Gala)
Penalty Goals: Irvine (2)

REFEREE: M. Joseph (Wales)

Taking an early bath

NEIL WILSON
The Observer

16 January 1977 *Whatever the era, sporting endeavour and determination can be seen and understood; only the stop-watch can show the improvement that one generation makes upon another. In swimming it is not even a generation apart. Here Neil Wilson writes about the talent of Cheryl Brazendale and the way she overcomes the frustrations of a swimming life in Britain.*

In its endless pursuit of the impossible the sport of swimming never establishes solid milestones. Today's record is tomorrow's qualifying standard. One Olympic record was improved three times in 35 minutes in Montreal. Nothing grows old in swimming.

Last August, at the age of 13, Cheryl Brazendale became the first British girl to swim 100 metres inside one minute; forty-two hundredths of a second inside, to be precise. She was 14 years too late for it to make even a ripple on the world pool. An Australian, Dawn Fraser, swam the distance in less than 60 seconds in 1962, and so commonplace was it in Montreal that six girls who did it failed to reach the semi-finals.

But what makes Miss Brazendale anything special is the background to her achievement. For her there is no organised, computerised, State-supported training of East Germany nor the sun-kissed scholarships of the campus pools of Miami. Cheryl drags herself out of bed at 5.30 in the morning to catch a tram along Blackpool's sea front to train in a hotel pool no larger than the garden variety in the stockbroker belt.

A few hundred yards away along the Golden Mile, Blackpool's famous Derby Baths, one of Britain's few international-size pools, stands empty, the water drained from it from October to March because the local corporation cannot afford the upkeep when the summer visitors have gone.

So Cheryl dives into the hotel pool knowing that in her 90-minute pre-school session she will have to turn 250 times. 'It's great for her turns, but hardly conducive to speed,' says her coach, Frank Naylor, who set up the hotel club four years ago when his own daughter was locked out of the Derby Baths in winter.

Today he is still protesting at the local indifference. 'Here we have the fastest girl sprinter in Britain in a town with one of the country's best pools, and she can't use it. In East Germany they'd open a pool just for someone like her.'

Cheryl is accustomed to overcoming life's hurdles. She has never known her father, rarely sees her mother, and the grandfather she lived with died last week. Her aggression in the water, thinks her coach, is the result. 'She hates to be beaten by anything or anybody. She won't settle for second, even in training.'

Cheryl, a slim, green-eyed child already tall for her age, shyly denies the aggression. But does she like to win? 'Oh yes, of course. That's what swimming is all about, isn't it?' Last August, in her first national senior championship, she won the 100 metres freestyle, was second in the 200 (the first time she had ever swum the distance), fourth in the 400 and second behind a Canadian in the 800, a range of events that would do justice to Kornelia Ender.

In East Germany, with such potential, she would be moved to better facilities, as Ender was. But Naylor's only compromise in the face of their disadvantages is to take her once a fortnight to a full-size pool in Wigan. Even his own coaching knowledge is second-hand, gleaned from books and other coaches since he began spare-time coaching four years ago. His own sporting experience was confined to the rugby field playing fly-half for Waterloo in the 'fifties.

But he has established firm views on swimming. Discipline is top of his list of priorities. Dedication is another demand he makes. Cheryl is a model pupil.

'Most swimmers have parents pushing them; Cheryl has to drive herself. Swimming for her is a way of improving her chances in life. That's a powerful incentive.'

Trips abroad are also an incentive for most, but next weekend Cheryl will celebrate her fourteenth birthday in Geneva, swimming for England's junior team, and she is unimpressed by the prospect. 'It's okay, I suppose. A day off school anyway.' Naylor is even less enthusiastic. 'Fancy trips don't help much. They'd do her more good spending the money on opening Derby Baths.'

Greig's crowning glory

HENRY BLOFELD

The Guardian

20 January 1977 *Cricketing tours often go down into history with one incident sprouting like a cactus. England's of India will be remembered for the long-awaited victory and also for the 'Lever affair'. The England bowler used a gauze strip across his forehead to stop perspiration running into his eyes (strange that no one has come up with a simple all-sport solution for this problem). But he was accused of using the oil substance in the gauze to polish the ball and bring back the shine, a most helpful aid to fast bowlers. The accusation came from India's captain, Bishan Bedi, and while it was rejected by England's players and management there was no apology.*

England finished off the Indian batting in Madras with the quiet, almost methodical efficiency that has been so characteristic of their cricket in this series. India were bowled out after 90 minutes for 83 in their second innings, and England won the Third Test match by 200 runs. They have also won their first series in India since Douglas Jardine's side were successful in 1933-4, for they have now taken an unbeatable 3–0 lead.

It was appropriate that, though Underwood and Willis destroyed the innings, Lever should have taken the last two wickets to fall. He was unjustly treated in the match, and he may never receive an apology. Yet he behaved marvellously during the last three days, and it will have given him and the rest of the England side great satisfaction that he should have made victory at Chepauk a fact.

It seems extraordinary that the wheel should have turned a half-circle so quickly. At the end of August England had lost a series 3–0 to the West Indies and, without fast bowlers or batsmen who could play fast bowlers, the future was bleak. Now, four and a half months later, England have won the first three Test matches of the series in India – and all by resounding margins. In April, too, these same Indians scored more than 400 in the fourth innings to beat the West Indies in Port of Spain.

At the end of the match yesterday Greig and his players were in a state of euphoria; after all the problems they have had in the last two years one could only feel that they deserved every moment of it. It was only in August that it was being seriously suggested that another captain should be found; since he arrived in India at the end of November it has been impossible to fault Greig as a player, as a captain or as a diplomat.

He himself is insistent that it has been a team effort, and he does not like singling out individual players for praise. There is no one, though, who deserves greater credit than Greig himself. His example has been magnificent, his inspiration has been felt by all the players, and his behaviour, both on the field and off, has been exemplary.

Greig was probably even more upset and angry at the recent accusations than Lever, yet he acted with a calmness and authority I did not think he had. He has shown how much he has matured and also that he has digested the obvious lessons of the youthful impetuosity that, even last summer, he showed in England, when he made his now infamous and at the time, unthinking 'grovel' statement about the West Indians.

Though this tour has reflected credit on everyone involved – not least on the selectors, who chose the original party and are often forgotten afterwards – it could be dangerous to think that England's problems have been solved in two months in India. They have not, though a significant start has been made. In each Test match the Indian spinners have almost taken control. In Delhi, on the first morning, England were 65 for four: in Calcutta they lost four wickets for 90; and, in Madras, they were 31 for three on the first morning.

The early batting has not been good and each time the middle order have had a tremendous struggle to put things right. That they have done it has been a reflection of Greig's influence on his players. He is a great competitor and no keener cricketer has ever taken the field.

The bowlers have all been splendid in India where, admittedly, they do not play fast bowling well. But Australians have been reared on Thomson and Lillee and, though Willis and Old may seem pretty quick in India, this may not be so when they bowl again at Doug Waiters and Greg Chappell. Fielding, on the other hand, should not change and, in India, with Randall, Lever and Barlow in the side, the English performance has been positively Australian.

This has never been better illustrated than yesterday morning when four catches were held in the slips, three of them good and one – by Brearley – brilliant. In the third over, Patel, who had looked as if he was trying to restrain his natural inclination to play strokes, tried to steer a ball from Willis to third man and was caught by Old at third slip to his right with deceptive ease. Willis yesterday bowled as fast as he probably ever has, and after the match Knott said that, even in Perth, he had never had the ball thump into his gloves in the same way.

This was off the last ball of Willis's over, and the first ball of the next over, bowled by Underwood, turned and lifted sharply to Viswanath. He came forward and the ball flew off the edge over Knott's shoulder to Brearley's left at first slip. Somehow, as he fell, Brearley managed to get his left hand under the ball and hold on. If, or when, Fletcher comes back into the England side, he surely cannot replace Brearley, who held five catches in the match and who should, in my opinion, have been awarded the prize for the outstanding fielder in the match in place of Randall, at first slip.

Viswanath's dismissal made the score 54 for five and saw the end of any faint hopes that India may have had of saving the match. Three runs later Kirmani played back to another short one from Willis which he could not avoid, and Brearley caught him up by his chest at first slip. Two overs later Madan Lal, who had been stepping away to leg every time Willis bowled, hooked at a short one and Knott held the catch above his head.

Another fine crowd – there was almost a full house – watched all this in good humour, and people twice ran on to the field and put garlands around Greig's neck, which he accepted with great amusement. One fan was chased back and caught by one of the ground-staff, who, much to the crowd's displeasure, gave him a hard time. Greig, who never misses a trick, tried to intervene on the spectator's behalf.

Lever now replaced Willis and he soon had Mankad caught at third slip as he drove at a ball that slanted across him. He finally uprooted Chandra's off stump with a yorker. The crowd did not seem remotely hostile to Lever yesterday and when one of his throws from the boundary came into Knott's gloves over the stumps he received a big round of applause.

Though, perhaps, the 'Lever Affair' was not handled too cleverly, one hopes that it will now fade into the background. One or two questions by local journalists at the Press conference in Ken Barrington's room afterwards suggested that this might not be so. Whatever they write or say, none of them can dispute the fact that the better side won the series. It has been a marvellous performance by England and side-issues cannot take away from that.

(*for scoreboard see following page.*)

ENGLAND: First Innings 262
(J. M. Brearley 59, A. M. Greig 54, B. S. Bedi 4–72)

INDIA: First Innings 164
(J. K. Lever 5–59)

ENGLAND: Second Innings 185
(D. L. Amiss 46, B. S. Chandrasekhar 5–50)

India: Second Innings Overnight 45–3

D. B. Vengsarkar retd. hurt	1
G. R. Viswanath c Brearley b Underwood	6
B. P. Patel c Old b Willis ...	4
A. V. Mankad c Old b Lever	4
S. M. H. Kirmani c Brearley b Willis	1
S. Madan Lal c Knott b Willis	6
B. S. Bedi not out	11
B. S. Chandrasekhar b Lever	6
Extras (b 5, lb 1, nb 2) ...	8
Total	**83**

Fall of wickets: 40, 45, 45, 54, 54 57, 66, 71.

Bowling: Willis 13–4–18–3, Old 5–1–11–0, Underwood 14–7–28–4, Lever 6.5–0–18–2.

England won by 200 runs

England won the first Test in New Delhi by an innings and 25 runs and the second Test in Calcutta by ten wickets.

FEBRUARY

90,000 people can't be wrong

MICHAEL HART
The Evening Standard

10 February 1977 *Michael Hart is Fleet Street's youngest chief association football correspondent. He followed the Arsenal and England player Bernard Joy, and shows in what was one of his first judgements of the international team that the Standard have made a sound long-term investment.*

Don Revie has nine months and nine matches to repair England's withered football reputation and avert the crisis of confidence that threatens to engulf his players.

With November's crucial World Cup qualifying tie against Italy looming on the horizon, England were again reminded of their lack of world class players in the disappointing 2–0 defeat by Holland.

The man who summed it up best for me was Queen's Park Rangers striker Stan Bowles. Clutching his boots in a plastic bag, hair still wet from the shower, he said mournfully: 'It was like putting Richard Dunn in against Muhammad Ali.'

England have now lost four of their last nine games – against Scotland, Brazil, Italy and Holland – a sequence that must surely be the most depressing in our international history.

Those who feel most depressed, of course, are the players. 'I don't know what we have to do,' said Bowles. 'I'm bitterly disappointed, and so are the rest of the players. I think we've got to work at our skills – basic control of the ball. The Dutch have it, we haven't.'

Bowles is right: that is the long-term answer. But the

Football League – acclaimed by us as the greatest competition in the world – represents a system that stifles the development of technique and intelligence in our footballers.

As we do not have time to change this system before next year's World Cup, what is the answer?

Well, first I would like to see Revie revert to an orthodox centre-forward adept in the air. When Manchester United's Stuart Pearson came on as substitute for Paul Madeley I felt that it immediately gave the England attack a greater potential.

The powerful centre-forward who attacks the ball in the air is one of the traditional strengths of our game, but this avenue to goal was denied success, and Bowles, all demanding passes along the ground, were greatly restricted by the tight man-to-man marking of the Dutch defence.

I would also like to see Revie develop some cohesion and consistency in his selections. In two years he has not produced a settled side. He made six changes to the team for the 2–0 defeat by Italy in Rome. He made five changes to the team for last night's game with Holland. He has used the incredible total of 49 players in two years.

It is now time he settled on a side, based on England's sole surviving qualities of strength, courage and endurance.

It is also time he settled on his tactics. I think he should persevere with another of our traditional strengths – the midfield destroyer. Johan Cruyff, wearing the number nine shirt but playing his customary deep role, had the freedom of the pitch in the first half – and a hand in both the goals scored by Jan Peters.

Revie, having witnessed the majesty of Cruyff and the damage he had done, detailed Paul Madeley to tight-mark this Dutch master after the interval. But by then it was too late.

The first Dutch goal was a thing of beauty, and emphasised the great chasm in class separating the teams. Cruyff, arrogant, assured, out on the left, lingered on the ball for about 20 seconds, tempting opponents into false positions while looking for the most destructive pass.

He found it – to his Barcelona club-mate Johan Neeskens, who had drifted unmarked into a central area about 25 yards from goal. Neeskens gently lofted his pass, first time,

1. *above* Kevin Keegan jumps over Berti Vogts of Borussia Moenchengladbach in the European Cup. Liverpool won the game and Keegan landed in Hamburg

2. *over* Red Rum (Tommy Stack up) wins his third Grand National. The crowd is jubilant – while a policewoman looks in another direction

minster Bank

eting

3. Clare Francis, single-handed Transatlantic sailor

4. The eyes of James Hunt, world motor racing champion 1976, seen through the eyes of Chris Smith, Sports Photographer of the Year

between two England defenders. Peters, a player of unlimited promise, was there, taking the ball smoothly and turning it past Clemence.

It was a goal of thought and supreme artistry, the culmination of a move that sliced through the industrial wasteland of England's defence. It was not the sort of goal you will see very often in the Football League.

By the time Peters had scored his second goal the derision of a 90,000 crowd was ringing in the ears of the England players. A football nation, once impregnable at Wembley, were being humiliated.

This was, in fact, Holland's first victory over England and only the sixth time a foreign side had won at Wembley.

It was a mistake not to have marked Cruyff tight. Sir Alf Ramsey made a similar error in the Nations Cup against Germany in April 1972, when the gifted Gunter Netzer, allowed to roam free, engineered the 3–1 defeat of England. Revie himself has experienced the freedom of Wembley as a player. In the 1956 FA Cup Final, playing for Manchester City as a withdrawn centre-forward in the Hungarian style, he murdered Birmingham City, who lost 3–1.

You could argue that the withdrawal of Brian Greenhoff with an elbow injury after 30 minutes upset the balance of England's midfield, but that is only scratching the surface. The truth is, quite simply, we are not good enough.

Jan Zwartkruis, the Dutch manager, said: 'The English style is kick and rush, give and go. It is nice for spectators. I like English football.' I'm not surprised! He added: 'The Dutch game is different. It is a fantasy game. We use our imagination, we create, we take risks.'

Holland, beaten by West Germany in the 1974 World Cup final, will go into their important qualifying tie against Belgium next month greatly encouraged by this result. 'I was very satisfied,' said Cruyff. 'We have not played as well as this since 1974.'

England will go into their qualifying tie against Luxembourg at Wembley next month with trepidation. It is a match in which England must score heavily and last night's match gave little evidence that this can be achieved.

'I think we have learned a lot from this defeat,' said Revie. 'If we're honest it has shown us just how much work we've still got to do. They have wonderful control and feel for the ball. They put just the right weight on their passes. They were world class, there's no doubt about that.

'My players are very despondent, that's natural. They were given a lesson in control and passing, and not giving the ball away. Big hearts and endeavour are not enough against world class teams like Holland.

'At the end of the day you've got to go right back and look at our skills. The Dutch were absolutely brilliant, but these are the sort of teams we will have to meet in Argentina.

'Luxembourg is the next problem. I'll stick with the same squad, more or less, for that match.'

England's successes were few. Trevor Brooking, Ray Clemence, Francis and Bowles could be said to have made a positive contribution, but the centre back partnership of Mike Doyle and Dave Watson could not cope with the sophistication of Holland's attack. 'It was men against boys,' said Doyle.

When England left the field the crowd chanted: 'What a load of rubbish.' Ninety thousand people can't be wrong.

Sitting among the crowd, diligently taking notes, was Enzo Bearzot, the Italian manager. He will return to Rome with a smile on his face.

All is not lost for England – but time is running out.

Tommy's girl

MAUREEN CLEAVE

The Evening Standard

11 February 1977 *Maureen Cleave talks to Europe's only woman boxing promoter, not so much about boxing as the man whom Beryl Cameron Gibbons loved. The devotion and the memories are weaved round a sketch of a boxing gymnasium in London's Old Kent Road—and the high life it can bring.*

The Thomas à Becket in the Old Kent Road is a Courage pub that has been the centre of London boxing for 30 years.

It is run by a woman called Beryl Cameron Gibbons.

How Beryl came by the pub and by her grand name I will later explain, for there are other remarkable things about her. There is the fact that she is the only female boxing promoter in Europe, and then there are her looks. Her perfect nose, her golden skin, her neat lobeless ears, her beautiful hands all suggest centuries of breeding of the rarest kind. These features, however, Beryl leaves to make their own quiet statement, while choosing rather to accentuate her bodily charms.

They are considerable. 'Life is what you make it, you know,' says Beryl, 'and the older I get the more I enjoy it.' Not a muscle of that shapely form hints that she is 42 in April; she could be playmate of that or any other month. She knows her power, and is confident, decisive and cheerful as a result.

She lives with her 24-year-old son in a large flat above the pub. At 3 pm the floor of her sitting room begins to shake because the punch-bag in the gymnasium is suspended from the ceiling directly below. Boxers love the Thomas à Becket. When Ahumada came over to fight Conteh they tried to fix him up a practice ring at the Café Royal, but he couldn't concentrate.

'Not with all them chandeliers,' said Beryl. 'They had to bring him down to the Becket.' She has never met a boxer she didn't like. She married one called John Cameron when she was 16.

The sitting room is a snug, smallish room – though at one point Beryl obviously had other ideas for it. It seems she intended it to look like the kitchen of a medieval castle. The cavernous fireplace, charred as though from roasting oxen, now houses her record collection. Oil paintings of Beryl herself are stacked against the wall. There is a harmonium she bought because it looked nice, and on it a china shire horse in full harness.

Carved in a corner of the chimney-piece is a heart pierced with an arrow, 'T loves B.' 'T' is for Tommy Gibbons. the much-loved ex-amateur boxer who used to run the Thomas à Becket before his untimely death seven years ago, and with whom Beryl lived the seven years before that.

'It was the biggest funeral since Ivor Novello's, they said.

Six hundred wreaths – they had to put them on a lorry. Even the nurses in the hospital asked to come, though I had him home to die.' Miraculously, Beryl produced a copy of his funeral oration, carefully protected by tissue paper, from what appeared to be a sack of cuttings in the hall. 'He spoiled me, Tommy did. An out-and-out gentleman.'

She laughed the warm rich laugh that is entirely in keeping with the rest of her, and said nobody could call her an out-and-out lady.

Tommy died at 7 o'clock in the evening and the brewers came round the next morning. They let her have the pub on nine months' trial and she's had it ever since. Then she put on a nice suit and went to see the Boxing Board of Control. She paid her deposit and they let her become a promoter.

The pub is scheduled to come down but she thinks it's too famous. Even the football and rugger fans from up North come here. 'Good as *gold,*' she said firmly. 'I like pub life. This is my home. If it was me personally myself and I won the pools I'd still stay here. I love Bermondsey.'

If she isn't in the pub people come up the back stairs to visit her. There's Fred who comes morning and evening in his carpet slippers; he does her shopping.

'You've missed him,' she said. 'Wednesdays he goes to meet his daughter in my other pub in Peckham (the Walmer Castle). I often take him to the local fights with me.' From under a fresh pineapple she produced a photograph of Fred, all dressed up to go to a fight. 'Oh, you get some characters round here all right.'

She was born in Acton. Like her mother before her she was London Schools Diving Champion. The teachers liked her because she told the truth. 'Where were you yesterday?' they would say; and Beryl would say: 'At the pictures.' She never pretends or tells lies, and only took Tommy's name because he asked her to in his will.

She was happy then as she is happy now. 'I believe life's too short and sweet,' she said. 'If anything makes you unhappy do something about it. I don't believe in feeling bitter.' She and her sister were both very pretty. Their mother still enters their old photographs in beauty competitions; indeed her sister found herself in the heats of

Miss Great Britain when well into her forties.

'We have to keep an eye on Mum like that,' Beryl said. 'She was going to call me Pearl but my godmother insisted on me being called Beryl.'

When her marriage failed she found herself doing upholstery for Harrods and living in Queensway. She is forever grateful to Tommy for rescuing her from the hectic social whirl of Notting Hill.

She rises at ten and spends the morning on the telephone. Being a promoter means that you put up money for fights. Being a match-maker (a *very* rare thing for a woman to be) means you pick the fighters. She had to organise the meetings of her club, The Premier Ring Sporting Club, that meets every six weeks in the Royal Garden Hotel for Beryl's favourite entertainment – a nice dinner and dance. There are three boxing bouts and a cabaret arranged by herself, usually a comedian. 'People want a laugh out of life,' she said.

She must be good at these various jobs because they are all tough. 'I can let out a bit of verbal when necessary,' Beryl said, 'I'm well known for it. In this business they don't do me no favours and they don't do me no harm.'

Her private passion is clothes. She has two rooms of them, racks running the entire length, and they sit in a sea of shoes.

She had just bought £300 worth of things in cash at Bill Gibb's shop in Bond Street the day before, choosing them on her way to a meeting while the taxi waited outside. To Beryl there are two sorts of blouses: see-through and *completely* see through. She held up one for me to see and indeed it was quite possible to see through it the numbers of the buses coming up the Old Kent Road. The dresses are fantastic: ostrich plumes, sequins, silk, satin, topless, backless, sideless . . .

'I get so confused on the night,' said Beryl, scooping up a cream chiffon dress with rhinestones from the floor, 'that I have to go out and buy another dress. I had a good night out in that one—' she spoke fondly of a green beaded affair – 'the beads came off and people started slipping about all over the place. I got rid of my minks and now I'm mad on my foxes.'

She was pleased to discover some photographs among the shoes. 'Here's one of us laughing,' she said, 'and here I am with Betty – that's Keith Townsend's mother. Here I am sitting on Lady Somebody-or-other's knee.' She goes to Tramps and Annabel's and Morton's and Maunkberry's. She drinks white wine and Bucks Fizz. 'That's champagne and fresh orange juice – though I don't mind a light ale if it comes to it.'

(For business engagements she wears a nice Jaeger suit.)

It's hard not to envy Beryl because she seems to do exactly as she likes. If the sun shines she jumps on a train to Brighton and lies all day on the beach. A lot of her friends would like to see her married.

'They think I'm still pining for Tommy,' she said, 'but it's a thing you learn to live with. I used to go to the cemetery every fortnight but it didn't help me. Now I go at Christmas time and Easter and the day he died and his birthday. I'm so pleased I got married young; when you're young you don't know how to enjoy yourself. If I'd married late I'd have been tied down now with children. I'm very selfish in the way I want to live.'

Sometimes she meets the boxers in training road-running when she comes home from a night out at six in the morning. The week before she'd come in at eight. Her son, a foreman fitter at Heinz, had had to ring up the pub from work to see if she was home.

Beryl fished a photograph of this handsome young man from under a bronze saucepan for making Turkish coffee.

'Oh, yes,' she said, 'he often has to do that. You see, when I'm out I'm *out*.'

Bull's eye view

RICHARD BAERLEIN

The Observer

13 February 1977 *Bookmakers and Governments regularly make money from gambling. Whether too much, too little or whether gambling*

is bad for the punter is a matter for the Royal Commission, now well into its enquiries. Phil Bull, a racing man of many parts, has defined views on the subject, and even more precise ones on British racing; the Commission got it all—some 40,000 words of evidence.

Phil Bull believes that racing belongs to the people. He makes this quite clear in a 40,000-word personal submission to the Royal Commission on Gambling. It is a massive document dealing with most departments of the racing industry and backed up by strong logical and lucid arguments with facts and figures where necessary.

In itself the document is worthy of a paperback because it should be read not only by everyone in racing but by everyone who ever has a bet.

The submission will not only influence the Royal Commission. It will help the Chancellor of the Exchequer, educate Cabinet Ministers and MPs of all parties, and interest even those outside racing. Some of the main points are:

1. The stupidity and humbug of betting legislation.
2. The total abolition of control of racing by the Jockey Club.
3. The hypocrisy of betting office regulations and hours.
4. Formidable criticisms on the submissions to the Royal Commission by the Churches Council on gambling and by the Horse Race Totalisator Board.

I particularly hope that his evidence will not be lost on the Chancellor of the Exchequer, who has been singled out for special advice in an effort to combat some of the nonsense submitted by other bodies.

'Racing belongs to the people. Not to the Jockey Club, not to the owners, especially not to the breeders and not to Old Etonians,' Bull says with some passion.

The author discovered that 62.8 per cent of the Jockey Club members are Old Etonians. I can now understand why Francis de Cautley, headmaster of my private school, made such stress on the fact that he prepared boys for only two public school: Eton, and those going elsewhere.

'The reason the Bloodstock and Racing Industries Council and the Thoroughbred Breeders' Association hanker after a Tote monopoly is because they see in France a Tote betting set-up from which owners, breeders and trainers benefit through high prize money in a way that they do not in this country; and which regards owners, breeders and trainers as the rightful heirs to whatever racing has to bestow. That's how they would like it to be here.

'That racing is an entertainment for the public – not just those going racing, but for all people who are interested in it and betting on it – does not concern them: they are indifferent to that aspect of the matter,' says paragraph 214.

The Rev Gordon Moody and his Churches Council on Gambling come in for some of the sharpest criticisms in the opening paragraphs. 'Bishops see nothing particularly incongruous or outrageous in officiating with their blessings at the launching of Polaris submarines: but they have never been known to open casinos or racetracks; that wouldn't have the approval of the Churches Council on gambling. For their propensity to swallow unethical camels and strain at imaginary moral gnats the Christian churches are unsurpassed.

'What relevance has this for a Royal Commission on Gambling? More than enough. The attitude of churches towards gambling is humbug. But it is just such moralising humbug that has loused up all legislation on betting and gaming including that of the 1960s.'

Bull objects to the moralist's thumbprint on the statutory regulations relating to betting offices because in effect they say 'betting is bad for people; we cannot stop it, so we'll limit the facilities,' and then goes on to prove this point. 'The original intention to make it an offence to loiter in a betting office had to be abandoned as unenforceable, so every effort was made to ensure that no one would wish to loiter. No facilities may be provided in a betting shop which may be enjoyed: no music, no entertainment or refreshment of any kind and, in particular, no radio or television; strictly speaking the facility of a chair or the use of a table may not be enjoyed.

'A betting office is to be as bare and uninviting as possible, so as to ensure that a person will go into it only if he feels he has to, and will get out of it as soon as he can. This, doubtless, is the moral way to bet: quickly, furtively, uncomfortably, and, if possible, with a sense of guilt – the traditional Christian way of sex perhaps.

'That a man or woman may go into a bingo session or gamble in a casino in the evening but not back horses in a betting shop after 6.30 pm is anomalous to say the least. If betting in a betting shop is unobjectionable during the afternoon when most people are at work, why should it be objectionable for people to bet in their leisure time?'

Although a breeder himself for over 30 years, Bull is particularly critical of the Thoroughbred Breeders Association. He strongly objected to the idea of breeders' prizes and was largely responsible for them being turned down at the last meeting of the Racing Industry's Liaison Council.

Of them he says: 'Breeders frequently sell for substantial sums yearlings which subsequently prove incapable of winning a race of any description. Do they offer any recompense to the unfortunate purchasers of those yearlings, who paid for them so much more than they proved to be worth? They do not. It has never been known. Very well. Breeders cannot have it both ways. They breed horses for sale and they get for them the market price at the time of the sale. That is all they are entitled to.

'Doubtless British breeders are envious of the substantial bonuses paid to breeders in France. I am unmoved by their envy. Racing in France is run by and wholly in the interests of the big French owner-breeders, whose sole concern is not with the provision of entertainment for people but with lining their own pockets at the expense of punters who are so ill-informed and naïve as to bet on terms that can only be described as rapacious. Breeders would be pleased if punters could be plundered like that in England. Hence their hankering after a Tote monopoly. I regard this unprincipal pursuit of self-interest as deplorable.'

Bull's plan for a British Racing Board to take over complete control of the sport-industry is exactly on the lines I advocated in a series of articles in the London *Evening Standard* 25 years ago this winter. But Bull goes much further. 'No provision has been made for Jockey Club representation on the British Racing Board. It is appropriate, and contrary to the principles implicit in the constitution of such a national board, that any private club, whatever its traditions, history or background, should have as a club any right to participation in the control of racing. That its members may have an expertise born of experience is irrelevant. The place for the utilisation of that is elsewhere.

'It has been suggested that a new Racing Board might be set up in such a way as to leave the Jockey Club with authority over the rules of racing and disciplinary matters. This is completely unacceptable. It would create an intolerable situation, far worse than that which now obtains between the Levy Board and the Jockey Club, in which policies decided upon by the Racing Board could be frustrated by rules made by the Jockey Club.

'The British Racing Board must have complete authority. Anybody to which it might delegate responsibility, for rules or anything else, must be required to give effect to the Racing Board's directives.'

This means the total abolition of the power of the Jockey Club. When I made my plea 25 years ago I was hoping the Jockey Club would get organised before Government intervention eventually took place. I had one complimentary letter – from racing correspondent James Hilton Park, for whom I was standing in during his holiday. I don't expect Bull will receive too many bouquets either, but the Minister of Sport, Denis Howell, is determined to set up a Racing Board one way or another.

Then Bull goes on to deal with the efforts of the Jockey Club to get up to date. 'The Jockey Club, having been many times adjured by the Minister of Sport that it must set about broadening its base and constitutioning itself more democratically if it hoped to survive, and having ignored that advice, saw the advent of BRIC as a threat to the continuance of its authority as the governing body of racing.

'To meet that threat and cut the ground from under the feet of BRIC, the Jockey Club brought into being the racing industry's liaison committee (RILC), virtually a carbon copy of BRIC, on which all the various bodies, interests and associations involved in racing were given representation. It was, of course, an advisory body without executive powers. The Jockey Club would listen to it and it was invited to make recommendations which the Jockey Club would consider.

'What the creation of RILC does establish is how far the Jockey Club is prepared to go to meet the criticisms of those who regard it as an anachronism in the modern world. It will democratise its advice, but not itself; and it intends to hang on to the reins as long as it can, no doubt in the hope that the next general election will see the end of Mr Howell.'

Bull's treatise goes far deeper than the Jockey Club's own examination of the racing scene conducted under the chairman ship of Sir Henry Benson. Benson also advocated a British racing board; but that part of his report was quietly swept under the carpet.

An Indian winter

JOHN WOODCOCK
The Times

18 February 1977 *Tony Greig (even before the Packer affair) had his critics because of his attitude and tactics; John Woodcock was among them, but in this analysis of the tour he affirmed that the man's qualities and judgment had played a crucial part in the tour's success.*

Life is good for the England touring team at the moment. Last night they were able to celebrate their victory in the series against India on board *Queen Elizabeth II*, now in Bombay on her cruise round the world. Their next engagement is not until Saturday, when they fly to Sri Lanka for eight days' cricket before going on to Perth and finally to Melbourne for the centenary Test match against Australia.

It is no mean achievement to beat India in India. The only other England side to have done so was Douglas Jardine's, 43 years ago, and I doubt if even he made the impact here that Tony Greig has done in the last three months. Like some blond colossus, Greig has dominated the scene, both on the field and off.

'Where's Mr Greig?' has been the question that everyone has asked, followed, disarmingly, by 'What's your good name?' Without Greig this would be half the England side it is. With him it has done what it came to do in terms of results, without suggesting that it has the players to go on to great things.

One of the reasons why England began to get the worst of things in the last two Test matches was that Greig's own bowling was so erratic. He is also excitable when the game starts to run away from him on the field. He has had a compelling tour, though, not least in his relations with the great Indian public, and he has helped England, at least partly, to believe in themselves again.

The main disappointment has been how slowly the batsmen have developed. The fault for this is only partly their own. A young MCC batsman on his first tour, with his confidence to build up, can expect to find it easier these days to make a hundred against South Australia at Adelaide or against Barbados at Bridgetown than against East Zone on a dust track at Gauhati.

As for playing the Indian spinners in a Test match, on pitches now produced for them, there is nothing remotely simple about that. Randall's scores of 22 and 15 in the last Test were worth a couple of 50s elsewhere.

Because of their statistically poor Test returns it is difficult to be sure how good Randall will become and how much it is reasonable to expect from Brearley in the next two or three years, and whether, when the game is no longer exclusively to do with spin, Barlow and Woolmer will come into their own. We may know more about this in Melbourne. We shall certainly find out all about it next summer when the Australians are in England.

As preparation for a Test match against Australia, a tour to India is as much use as driving a vintage car from London to Brighton the day before hurtling round Silverstone in the British Grand Prix – except for the teamwork it creates. The teamwork of Greig's side has been conspicuously good, for which Ken Barrington, a well-liked and conscientious manager, may take considerable credit.

Technically, the most satisfactory aspect of England's play was the respect shown by their bowlers for length and line. Willis has come back with a bang on this tour, Old has been a valuable all-rounder and Lever has come on enough to raise hopes that his 26 Test wickets will be followed by quite a lot more.

With 56 Test wickets between them, these three took only six fewer wickets than Bedi, Chandrasekhar and Prasanna in 350 fewer overs. That was remarkable, and had a lot to do, of course, with the result. As did Amiss's 179 at Delhi, Tolchard's 67 at Calcutta, Knott's inimitable contributions, Underwood's fine bowling and the towering presence of Greig.

For batsmen whose last two years have been spent dodging bouncers not to have had to do so for three whole months has been a merciful relief. Which brings one to the future of Indian cricket and its almost total reliance on spin. Although there are dietary and physical reasons for this, as well as climatological ones (temperatures which induce lethargy), I believe India could breed fast bowlers, which is not to say they ever will.

There is certainly no way of their doing so while their game is played on slow, turning pitches. What they need most, and it would be possible to achieve, are faster pitches than they have and a return to truer batting conditions. If the series had been played on the plumbest pitches they could have prepared, India, because their bowlers have more guile than England's, would probably have won it.

If it were to be played all over again on the pitches as they were, I am not sure who would win. That is how closely matched the two sides were, at any rate in India. There is, in India, a critical lack of opportunities for the young, mainly for economic reasons. Indians are among the best natural cricketers in the world, yet they are able barely to scratch the surface of the great resources they possess.

Seventy-five per cent of the country's population of 600,000,000 live in the villages, where not one of them would play any organized cricket. Even in the vast majority of urban schools there is no cricket to speak of and, until more of the money taken from the Test matches is ploughed into the schools, so it will remain. Of the children of the country, no more than perhaps one in a 1,000 has the chance to play anything much more than cricket in the street.

Final averages for Test match series in India

India batting	Inns	NO	Runs	HS	Avge
S. Amarnath	4	0	180	63	45.00
S. M. Gavaskar	10	0	394	108	39.40

India Batting—(*contd.*)

B. P. Patel	10	0	286	83	28.60
K. Ghavri	6	2	99	35*	24.75
A. D. Gaekwad	8	0	165	39	20.62
G. R. Viswanath	10	1	175	79*	19.44
S. M. H. Kirmani	10	1	167	52	18.55
P. Sharma	4	0	62	29	15.50
Madan Lal	4	0	51	17	12.75
Yajuvendra Singh	4	0	50	21	12.50
B. S. Bedi	10	3	81	20*	11.57
M. Amarnath	4	0	36	24	9.00
E. A. S. Prasanna	8	1	55	13	7.85
B. S. Chandrasekhar	10	3	20	6	2.85

ALSO BATTED: D. B. Vengsarkar, 8, 1 (Rtd hurt): E. D. Solkar, 2, 3, A. V. Mankad, 0, 4; S. Venkataraghavan, 0, 4.

Bowling	Overs	Mdns	Runs	Wkts	Avge
E. A. S. Prasanna	232.4	79	389	18	21.61
B. S. Bedi	298	106	574	25	22.96
K. Ghavri	58	15	149	6	24.83
B. S. Chandrasekhar	194	40	537	19	28.26
Madan Lal	48	11	86	3	28.66
S. Venkataraghavan	34	6	94	2	47.00

ALSO BOWLED: M. Amarnath, 29–7–56–0; E. D. Solkar, 6–1–15–0; S. M. Gavaskar, 5–3–2–0; P. Sharma, 4–0–8–0; Yajuvendra Singh, 1–0–2–0; A. D. Gaekwad, 1–0–1–0.

England batting	Inns	NO	Runs	HS	Avge
D. L. Amiss	9	1	417	179	52.12
A. W. Greig	8	0	342	103	42.75
A. P. E. Knott	8	1	268	81*	38.28
J. M. Brearley	8	0	215	91	26.87
R. W. Tolchard	7	2	129	67	25.80
K. W. R. Fletcher	5	1	91	58*	22.75
J. K. Lever	8	1	122	53	17.42
C. M. Old	6	0	95	52	15.83
R. A. Woolmer	3	0	42	22	14.00
D. W. Randall	7	0	86	37	12.28
D. L. Underwood	7	1	71	23	11.83
G. D. Barlow	3	1	11	7*	5.50
R. G. D. Willis	7	2	19	7	3.80

ALSO BATTED: M. W. W. Selvey 5*

Bowling	Overs	Mdns	Runs	Wkts	Avge
J. K. Lever	149.4	29	380	26	14.61
R. G. D. Willis	135	25	335	20	16.75
D. L. Underwood	252.5	93	509	29	17.55
G. M. Old	88.5	20	201	10	20.10
A. W. Greig	131	28	336	10	33.60

ALSO BOWLED: M. W. W. Selvey, 15–1–80–0; R. A. Woolmer, 1–0–2–0.

*Not out.

MARCH

Conteh joins the rough, tough school

DONALD SAUNDERS
The Daily Telegraph

3 March 1977 *John Conteh, so often at odds with the boxing establishment, sought to cut out the middlemen of the business and keep in his bank account more of the six-figure fees which a world boxing champion is able to command. He virtually arranged his title defence in his home town, Liverpool, and showed as uncompromising an attitude in the ring against his opponent as he had done outside it towards those who normally arrange and promote world title fights in Britain.*

John Conteh returned to London from his native Liverpool yesterday still firmly clutching the world light-heavyweight title, while Len Hutchins, his wounded American challenger, was flying home to Kalamazoo, protesting loudly that he had been cheated.

Hutchins, battered to painful defeat after 65 seconds of the third round of an incident-filled, exciting but surprisingly one-sided bout, claimed he had been deliberately butted soon after the opening bell. Blatant infringement of the rules, he claimed, caused a deep, jagged, one-and-a-half inch cut near his left eye, blurring his vision and depriving him of the opportunity to mount the fierce challenge he had planned.

Conteh – who in any case, denies the charges – will not be at all perturbed by the uproar. Such controversy sells fights, especially in the United States and to television companies, now his most lucrative sources of income. The champion knows his savage destruction of Hutchins – and the howls of anguish it provoked – will heighten interest in his next defence, against Miguel Cuello, of Argentina, probably on 28 May, in Britain, Monte Carlo or Montreal.

Indeed, Conteh has emerged as a ruthless champion. He is now a fully paid-up member of the rough, tough society of two-fisted fighters the Americans have always admired – and, understandably, have for so long believed could not flourish in the stand-up, straight-left, Marquess of Queensberry atmosphere of the British ring.

That is why he is likely to continue to rule the light-heavyweight division, at least until he clashes with Victor Galindez, of Argentina, another merciless champion, who holds the World Boxing Association title.

Since watching Saturday's slaughter Galindez surely will have modified his opinion of Conteh as 'chicken'. The provocative Argentine must have noticed how much sharper, toughter and determined the champion was this time, than when he painstakingly outpointed Alvaro Lopez, last October, after a long absence from the ring.

Almost from the opening bell Conteh obeyed his corner's instructions not to allow Hutchins to settle. Quickly he took command with jolting left jabs, solid hooks and jarring rights.

Then, after missing with a long right, Conteh charged on through – and only deaf ringsiders failed to hear the sickening clash of heads.

Sid Nathan, the referee, promptly warned both men, because, as he confirmed when we travelled back to London yesterday, he was satisfied each was as much to blame as the other. I share Mr Nathan's view that this was not a deliberate butt by Conteh. But, though both men were careless, it seemed to me that the champion should take the major share of the responsibility – because he made no effort to check his vigorous follow-through.

Even so, I doubt whether Hutchins was as inconvenienced by the injury as his camp would have us believe. The wound, at the outer edge of the brow, should not have impaired his judgment.

'When they kept protesting during the interval I think they were looking for a disqualification,' said Mr Nathan. 'I told them the cut was not dangerous and that Hutchins could continue.'

From that moment, however, the American, who had scarcely oozed confidence earlier, seemed to have little stomach for the battle.

In his eargerness to finish the job Conteh was a little wild at the start of the second. But soon he was mercilessly driving home savage punches to the hapless challenger's head and body, with either hand.

So, though the end came suddenly and early, it was not really a surprise to the packed arena. Conteh, having shaken the American with a thumping right, missed with a following left, threw another right off-target then landed the hardest left hook he has employed for many a day, flush on his challenger's jaw.

Hutchins crashed to the canvas on his back, clearly in serious trouble. He rose uncertainly as the time-keeper tolled seven – I thought the count exceptionally fast – and was promptly rescued by the referee.

'He turned the wrong way as he got up and was obviously dazed,' said Mr Nathan. 'So there was no point in continuing the count to the mandatory eight.'

These boyos are not for burning

TONY LEWIS
The Sunday Telegraph

Wales 14 England 9

6 March 1977 *Any Welshman in England must have suffered a miserable week before going down to Cardiff Arms Park for the international match. So much talk and writing about the sorry state of Welsh rugby and how England would make it worse. . . Tony Lewis survived it, and here, tongue firmly in cheek, opens his match account with a delightful analogy which must have gone down well where the Welsh editions are sold.*

Open the parlour curtains, put away the cold ham and the bread and butter, the funeral for Welsh rugby is off. It had not been exactly a false alarm from the English undertakers, but there was always an unreal ring about the prediction which had made England the pre-match favourites yet Wales the most likely to win.

England were not easy to beat. They swallowed up their tackles midfield; Dixon and Rafter waged a frugal battle with Cobner and Burgess on the loose ball – a real connoisseur's piece; and Hignell was a model of safety. But it all amounted to effort within their known limitations.

To score points they needed Welsh handling mistakes – and there were none – or Hignell's penalty kicking – which was excellant but not quite productive enough.

Wales were miraculously unruffled by the experience of being the odd point down from much of the game. They were adventurous without taking chances and shrugged off many refereeing frustrations, too, by not only pursuing their normal counter-attacking methods but also by solid and sensible kicking by Edwards and Bennett.

So Wales go to Scotland in a fortnight's time with hopes of retaining the Triple Crown. England had got their fingers on the prize, but will not have thought themselves unlucky.

Their consolation is in the improvement they have made this season, and thoughts that they can get better still as soon as they improve the usage of the ball behind the scrum.

Possibly England's reputation before the game shaped an inaccurate assessment of the Welsh pack. How skilfully Martin reversed the previous form and nuisance value of Horton. How strongly Quinnell led from No. 8 and how splendidly the new young prop, Williams, held Cotton in the tight and played his part in loose play.

It was the English scrum which struggled from time to time and Wales, whose line-out weakness has been a talking point all the season, won that score 22–15.

The dullness of the day and the drizzle belied the brilliance of the sporting occasion – which had brought many English supporters bounding into the Principality. An immense rendering of the Welsh National Anthem ended the chatter – the Celt and the Anglo-Saxon were separated and the action was on.

England had some wind behind them. Bennett missed a penalty kick after a minute and Slemen and Hignell both made superb kicking recoveries which demonstrated the English confidence.

After five minutes Hignell had scored his first penalty goal. Cooper put a kick of rare delicacy over the Welsh backs and was obstructed in his chase by J. P. R. Williams. The kick went over from 22 metres and the Arms Park crowd roared Wales back.

After 11 minutes Hignell put over a second when Wheel threw a boot wildly at the ball which was safely in Young's hands. Cardiff went quieter.

England next took a heel against the put-in. What an affront. Dixon, on the flank, held down Windsor's hand-flap signal on the side of the scrummage. It was not a serious event because the ball was kicked away, but it was another prick in Welsh pride.

The signs of Welsh recovery were clear as the Welsh pack rose to the challenge. Meanwhile, England, with the ball they won, simply went through their familiar five-finger exercise of scissor and demi-scissor. Incredibly it confused no one but themselves.

Squires did get away on a charge or two, but mostly Cooper kicked, Young did little to draw the fire, and the Welsh defence organised its recovery as cleverly as ever. J. P. R. Williams, Davies and Bennett are long rehearsed in such matters.

English apprehension must have grown at the sight of Edwards, sleeves rolled up, looking sharp and kicking with immaculate judgment. Two of his kicks to the short side brought a scrum near the England line. Wales beautifully controlled their heel and Edwards ran through Slemen as if he were an open goal. It was Edward's 19th try for Wales, and this his 48th international.

Wales were uneasy with their kickers at this stage, Bennett and Fenwick had missed penalties and Martin the conversion. Yet by half-time they were in the lead. Fenwick had found his touch after Wheeler had been penalised for a foot-up offence. Most worrying for England, who were very much in contention, was the manner in which Martin won clean line-out ball while Horton frequently put Young under pressure.

Just after half-time Hignell put England into the lead again after a penalty kick had been awarded against Wales at a line-out. But thereafter, England simply plugged on, more and more committed to a tackling game.

This was the watershed as Wales unleashed the aggression of J. P. R. Williams, deft touches by Bennett and masterful control by Edwards. There was a break through the middle by Corless, but otherwise the only applause they encouraged came from decisions to take short penalties in their own territory.

Fenwick kicked his second penalty to restore Wales's lead and the final try was a model of flair and planning. Another Welsh line-out was won deep in English territory, but Edwards was under pressure.

With the inspiration we have come to take as his second nature, he flipped a reverse pass to Bennett. The ball was spun out to Burcher who carved a classical outside break. J. P. R. Williams thundered in, turned to look for Davies, who was outside him on the right, and dummied, not one, but three defenders over to the touchline as he cut in to touch down.

England's last win at Cardiff in 1963 looks now even more remote and if their defeat yesterday was not as crushing as their last Triple Crown effort in Jarrett's match in 1977, it certainly left Uttley, their brave captain, in no doubt that they were second best on the day.

WALES: J. P. R. Williams (Bridgend), **T. G. R. Davies** (Cardiff), **S. P. Fenwick** (Bridgend), **D. H. Burcher** (Newport), **J. J. Williams** (Llanelli), **P. Bennett** (Llanelli, capt), **G. O. Edwards** (Cardiff), **C. Williams** (Aberavon), **R. W. Windsor** (Pontypool), **G. Price** (Pontypool), **A. J. Martin** (Aberavon), **G. A. D. Wheel** (Swansea), **T. J. Cobner** (Pontypool), **R. C. Burgess** (Ebbw Vale), **D. M. Quinnell** (Llanelli)

ENGLAND: A. J. Hignell (Cambridge U), **P. J. Squires** (Harrogate), **B. J. Corless** (Moseley), **C. P. Kent** (Rosslyn Pk), **M. A. C. Slemen** (Liverpool), **M. J. Cooper** (Moseley), **M. Young** (Gosforth), **R. J. Cowling** (Leicester), **P. J. Wheeler** (Leicester), **F. E. Cotton** (Sale), **W. B. Beaumont** (Fylde), **N. E. Horton** (Moseley), **P. J. Dixon** (Gosforth), **M. Rafter** (Bristol), **R. M. Uttley** (Gosforth, capt)

REFEREE: D. I. H. Burnett (Ireland)

The great get-together

TREVOR BAILEY
The Financial Times

12 March 1977 *March is not normally the time to read about cricket, and the Centenary Test in Melbourne came as an unexpected bonus for followers of the game, while for cricket writers it was an unashamed excuse for anecdote and nostalgia. Trevor Bailey's piece captured the setting perfectly.*

Some two years ago Hans Ebling, the former Australian Test cricketer, had a dream. The first-ever Test match had taken place on 15 March, 1877, when the Australians beat James Lillywhite's all-professional side and made people in England realise that there were some good players in that vast colony. To celebate this historic occasion Hans envisaged not only a centenary Test between the two countries, but also an assembly of many of those still alive who had done battle for the Ashes in Australia.

Fortunately the Victorian Cricket Association took up his idea and has organised, quite brilliantly, the greatest cricket gathering the game has ever known.

For the English contingent it began appropriately enough with a champagne party at the Excelsior Hotel before flying to Melbourne. Just over 60 former Test players set forth on this unique pilgrimage. They were all instantly recognisable, which, as I had played first class cricket with all but two, was hardly surprising, though some were a shade thicker round the middle and thinner on top.

The oldest member in our party was Percy Fender, who had toured Australia back in 1920. Sadly there was nobody from the 1924 side, but all the succeeding tours were represented, including a good contingent from the 1932 controversial 'bodyline' tour which was captained by Douglas Jardine.

In Singapore we picked up Freddy Brown, as bluff and hearty as ever, the quieter Bob Wyatt, who is such an outstanding authority on the game itself and the laughing, ageless Les Ames. We found waiting for us in Australia Sir Len Hutton (typically combining a little business), Gubby Allen, Geoff Boycott, who has been making stacks of runs in club cricket out here and should really still be in the England team, and Willie Watson, who had come in from South Africa. In addition there was Harold Larwood, Peter Loader, Tony Lock, Barry Knight and Frank Tyson, who have all settled in Australia and done well.

Fred Trueman – whose remark to the Rev (now the Rt Rev) David Sheppard out here after he had dropped yet another catch: 'Put your hands together and pray like the rest of us,' has become a little classic – has not yet arrived. I shall know immediately he does, because I cannot fail to recognise that broad, loud Yorkshire voice saying 'Now then sunshine, how are things?'

Long air flights are usually exhausting and boring affairs, but on this occasion the time passed quickly, because quite apart from the quality of service of the Quantas staff and the drinks, both much appreciated by our party, there was so much to talk about. It also illustrated one way in which tours to Australia have changed.

Alec Bedser remarked to Eddie Paynter that it was very different from the last time Eddie had made the trip back in 1932. 'Aye,' said Eddie, 'it took five and a half weeks by boat.' On my three visits 'down-under' the MCC have also gone by ship and tours lasted for six months, even though we flew home. Travelling by sea did take a long time, but it enabled newcomers to get to know their colleagues really well and to forge a relationship which proved an asset in the battles that lay ahead. It also led to lasting friendships.

I sat with Charlie Barnett, one of England's most exciting opening bats, who looked far too young to have been on the 1936–37 tour, which, besides being one of the closest fought, had also done so much to heal the scars left by the 'bodyline' series. Charlie is a keen huntsman and said, 'Those big high black fences provide the challenge I used to have when facing really fast bowling.' Inevitably the late Wally Hammond, whom Charlie knew so well, came up in conversation. He reckoned he had never seen Wally with dirty trousers, because the speed of his reactions and his balance made diving to take a catch unnecessary.

Our first day in Australia was spent recovering from the rigours (some of them self-inflected) of the flight and then we were woken up with a bang as our hotel was invaded by over a hundred of our former foes. There was no escape. You met them everywhere you went, by the pool, in the bars, in the corridors, in the foyer, in every other room and in the lifts. I just managed to escape from the Cricketers Room in the Windsor Hotel, where the MCC always used to stay, and went into the restaurant with John Arlott to find Sir Donald Bradman at the next table, looking very spry and as always fascinating company. Besides having been the finest batsman the world has ever seen the Don is a brilliant after-dinner speaker, an outstanding administrator and shrewd businessman. I never played against him when he was in his prime, but, as he scored well over a century on the three occasions I bowled at him in 1948, this was just as well.

On Wednesday the Victorian Cricket Association held a cocktail party at the Melbourne ground for all the former English and Australian international cricketers and for the two teams who will be playing in the Centenary Test. It is safe to say that never before have so many Test players been gathered together in one room. It was an incredible experience as face after face from the past loomed up before you.

I confess I did not recognise all the Australians. Colin McCool, heavily camouflaged with a nautical beard, deceived me completely; on the other hand Keith Miller looked exactly the same. He immediately gave me a certainty for the races, which I fortunately forgot and saved myself some money. Ray Lindwall, Norman O'Neill and the Archer brothers were four who did not seem to have altered at all in appearance.

The Melbourne ground holds a host of memories for me, both good and bad. It was here that I collected a pair (out for ducks in successive innings). My only satisfaction was that my executioner was Lindwall, who swung the ball more than any other really fast bowler. It was here that Peter May's side, which looked so good on paper, and played so badly, hit rock bottom. Why this should have been is difficult to pinpoint, because Peter was an astute and popular captain, with a very tough streak beneath his considerable charm.

The good times on the Melbourne Oval had included fielding in the slips as Frank Tyson blasted his way through the opposition by sheer pace. How fast was Frank in Australia on that tour? Arthur Morris, who opened their batting, summed it up for me at the time when he said, 'Frank is faster than Brian Statham by just about the same amount as Brian is quicker than you.' As Godfrey Evans would stand about 10 yards further back from Brian than he did for me, it gives some indication of Frank's exceptional speed.

Godfrey is with us on this trip and though his face is now partially hidden by white mutton-chop whiskers he remains as lively and volatile as in his playing days. At the moment he is marketing some toy games he has invented with the same enthusiasm he displayed behind the stumps.

The Melbourne ground is well equipped and the biggest in Australia. It staged the Olympic Games in 1956, and the Australian rules football final is played there. It does, however, lack the beauty of Adelaide and the charm of Sydney. It also has some less than diplomatic gatemen.

We used to be given passes to show when we went into the ground and on one occasion during a State match several of us, having changed in our dressing room, went off to practice at a nearby school. We returned to the ground in our whites and wearing our not exactly inconspicuous blazers, to be refused admission because our passes were already in the dressing room. This was too much even for Denis Compton, one of the most tolerant of men. To our amusement, and the gateman's anger, Denis simply vaulted over the turnstile.

However, my fondest memory of Denis in Australia was at the Sydney races. He went to place his last bet, after having a bad afternoon, and a helpful bookmaker proceeded to tip him the winner at 10 to 1. Unable to decipher the ticket, Dennis went back after the race to ask if he had in fact won. The bookie paid him out £100 and then chased after him for well over half a mile because he had forgotten to return his stake money – just another example of how Compton acquired the tag 'Golden'.

All the cricketers taking part in this nostalgic reunion

have had two things in common, a love for the game and a passionate desire to win the Ashes, which have been in Austrailia's possession for rather too long, but otherwise they are so very different in character and outlook. I am sharing a room with Doug Wright, who was a great leg-spin bowler. When he retired from cricket he coached at Charterhouse for many years and now assists in running sport at Kent University. Doug is, and always has been, a quiet, kind, sensible individual, as might be expected from a former chorister.

If you want to know where a party is being held Bill Edrich is the right person to ask, always assuming that he is not already there. Last night I had dinner with Lindsay Hassett, whom I first met when he was leading the Australian services side immediately after the war. He is a very amusing gnome of a man with an impish sense of humour and a passion for fishing. Predictably there is a large golfing contingent, which includes Ted Dexter, Peter Richardson, the best impersonator in the party, Brian Close, who seldom stops talking, and jovial Tom Graveney, whose inn I shall be visiting the next time I am in the Cheltenham area.

My room-mate in Australia was often Reg Simpson, whom I once took to a New Year's Eve yacht club party in Sydney. As every table insisted on us having a drink with them it became a testing evening. I was grateful not to be performing on the following day, but Reg had to play. Nevertheless he scored a century, which I listened to on the radio in bed, and which showed not only skill but considerable stamina.

Colin McDonald, the former Australian opening bat, is an intelligent and interesting companion who, like most Australian ex-players, is worried by the noticeable increase of 'sledging' in senior cricket. This is a new term for me, which, roughly translated, means colourful abuse of opponents and officials and visible dissenting whenever decisions go the wrong way.

The great get-together with our toughest and closest cricketing enemies is thus proving a wonderful, if slightly exhausting experience, which, combined with the Test itself, has certainly caught the imagination of the public. Ray Lindwall reckons that by the time all the junketing is over

G

it will have taken far more out of him than any cricket match.

It is to be hoped that the English administrators have begun to think seriously about returning the compliment, as the centenary of the first Test to be played between the two countries at home is only three years away. Not altogether surprisingly, all the Australian players seem to think it is a very good idea, and have expressed a willingness to participate.

Yawn . . . wake up by Wednesday

COLIN MALAM
The Sunday Telegraph

Aston Villa 0 Everton 0

13 March 1977 *The Football Association are the controlling body of the game throughout England, embracing all levels and styles of club; the Football League control the 92 professional clubs who play in the four divisions of their league. If the two are not exactly rivals there is rivalry enough, and the popularity and charisma of the FA cup was the envy of the League. Ultimately they introduced their own Cup competition, but as Colin Malam reminds his readers the final at Wembley is a long time making an indelible mark on football's history.*

A memorable climax continues to elude the League Cup. Come to that, it requires a considerable effort of memory to recall the last time either of the two domestic Cup competitions produced a final that was anything like wholly satisfying.

Yesterday's excuse for a match, certainly, responded limply to a 100,000 Wembley full house, record receipts and a perfect Spring afternoon. After a reasonably promising start, it subsided relentlessly into utter mediocrity and predictable stalemate.

As a result of their failure to score, the two sides now move on to Hillsborough on Wednesday to try to decide the destination of the trophy and to settle the question of which of them will take one of the UEFA Cup places next season.

Away from the peculiarly intimidating atmosphere of Wembley perhaps they will rediscover, individually and collectively, the inspiration that deserted them totally on this occasion. If they do not this final could be one of the longest running shows since 'The Mousetrap' – and a good deal less entertaining.

Yesterday's pallid, tedious ninty minutes was particularly disappointing in view of the marked improvement in Everton's form recently and of the memory of Villa's stirring battles with Queens Park Rangers in the semi-final. On the day both teams seemed overwhelmed by the occasion.

In fact, so rarely was a goal even promised that one's most vivid memory was of the referee halting the game mysteriuosly in the second half to call both captains together following a foul on Gidman.

It seemed that Mr Kew was warning the teams to tone down the force of their tackling – a plea, boxing-style, for more action might have been more appropriate – but it transpired that he merely wanted to remove three stray bandsmen's spurs from the pitch.

The first half was certainly better than the second, which was practically non-existent; and if any one player came close to imposing his will on the match it was Andy Gray, Villa's lion of a centre-forward.

Twice in the first half the enterprising Scot overcame the twin problems of a solid blue barrier in front of him and unreliable lines of supply behind to drive powerful shots at the Everton goal – one of which Hamilton headed off the line.

Soon after the interval, too, Gray nearly enlivened the game by pouncing on a sloppy pass-back to Lyons, but Lawson came out quickly to block the shot and Deehan, who had wasted two reasonable chances earlier, could do nothing with the rebound.

McKenzie, audacity personified, had promised at the start to make his first full appearance at Wembley one to remember. After having a shot deflected for a corner and then cheekily chipping the ball on to the roof of the Villa net, however, the unpredictable Everton striker gradually disappeared from view.

Overall, Dobson and Goodlass were Everton's most influential figures. Dobson's experience and composure contributed significantly to the greater speed with which Everton settled to their task, while Goodlass kept nibbling away at the Villa defence throughout the first half.

It was Goodlass's clever overhead kick, for instance, that opened the way for a half-hit volley by King that Nicholl blocked. In addition, the darting Everton winger hit his side's one shot of any note in the match. The diminishing effect of Wembley apart, the only possible excuses for Everton's progressive loss of momentum and Villa's failure to play with any of the freedom and fluency one has come to associate with them were the absence of Rioch and Pejic, Everton's ineligible signings, and the damaging effect of previous injuries on Cropley, Villa's principal architect.

Nevertheless, there were still enough players of genuine talent on the field yesterday to have made the 17th League Cup final something more than one of the poorest matches ever to have been seen at this historic stadium. The only blessing is that there was no extra time.

A. VILLA: Burridge, Gidman, Robson, Phillips, Nicholl, Mortimer, Deehan, Little, Gray, Cropley, Carrodus
Sub: Cowans

EVERTON: Lawson, Jones, Daracott, Lyons, McNaught, King, Hamilton, Dobson, Latchford, McKenzie, Goodlass
Sub: Telfer

REFEREE: G. Kew (Middlesborough)

Replay, 16 March: A. Villa 1 Everton 1
Replay, 13 April: A. Villa 3 Everton 2 (after extra time)

Dad's army waltzes over colonials

JACK FINGLETON
The Sunday Times

13 March 1977 *When the Aussies put on a show they do not expect to be upstaged—certainly not by English cricketers. One suspects that the smarting behind Fingleton's humour was in fact much worse. But what a gem of a paragraph he writes on David Hookes—the observer blending in the facts to tell his readers all about the young batsmen in a compelling, entertaining style.*

The base ingratitude of it all! Here we Australians stage the greatest show ever seen on the cricket Earth, with reception after reception, witty speeches, and on all sides old enemies falling on one another like blood relations, and what happens on the field? Why, England return evil for good by rubbing our noses in the dirt before thousand upon thousand who came to acclaim the locals, but remained to praise the enemy.

I must say it is a bit thick, and hard to swallow, but those who called the last English team 'Dad's Army' are now seeking a new name for the revitalised guardsmen. That charming man, Ken Barrington, the England manager, told me only the other night that I would see a big difference in the team now that they had done so well in India.

Never has there been such a publicised cricket match. Only huge sponsorship by Qantas, our internal airline, TAA, Benson and Hedges and the Hilton Hotel has made this event of all lifetimes possible. The organisation has been fantastic, and only Melbourne would attempt such a game, bringing not only the English team from India but also inviting all who have played a Test in Austrailia for either country, and all who have umpired them.

Those few who have turned down the invitation will never forgive themselves. I sensed the spirit of Grace, Hobbs, Rhodes and all the rest permeating the ground as I arrived for the start of the match yesterday morning. Here the hospitality never wavers, and the beverages never stop flowing. The old-timers wear perpetual smiles.

I looked out of my bedroom window early, before eight o'clock, and already the cars and the queues were forming below. They have come from everywhere for this game, and there is not a vacant hotel room in the huge city. All ready for the Lillie kill. All, that is, with the notable exception of the England players.

Greig took a big risk by sending in the Australians. On a perfect pitch it was a cheeky, aggressive thing to do. But in no time Australia were in dire trouble. Davis tried to force, and was LBW to Lever, who sprayed them somewhat. McCosker tried to pull Willis, hit the ball, first on to his hand, then into his face, then on to his wicket. Then he went to hospital, where the news is not good. He has a fractured jaw, his teeth in splints and it will be six weeks at least before he smiles.

The Aussie batsmen had not a thing to smile about in the morning. Cosier went for a pull and skied it. Walters also tried to pull and muffed it, Greig running back and locking the ball in his hands as if it were a Crown Jewel. One wondered at Willis. He ran up faster, and with more gusto, than when he was here two years ago. No batsman thought much of him, but it was the pathetic attempts at hooking and pulling that upset us. The Yorkies say, 'Never cut before lunch.' Our motto should be, 'Never pull before lunch, or, if you do, at least get the feet positioned.' It was like it was at Sydney against Imran and Pakistan all over again. Evidently the Englishmen followed that series closely on their travels.

Then came Master David Hookes, 21, of Adelaide, at 23 for three. A terrible state of affairs for one so young in his first Test. He is the lad who hit four centuries in successive innings for South Australia, and forced himself into this game. The biggest crowd he had played in front of was 6000 in Adelaide. The tier-upon-tier of faces, 60,000 or so of them, could have daunted him, but didn't. He walked faster to the middle than anybody I have seen. I got the idea he must have been late for an appointment on the other side of the ground, but he soon set to and impressed us all. He is magnificent. Tall, strong and left-handed, he showed us some lovely shots on the off, though the leg side is supposed to be his strength. The old gaffers among us thought he left a gap between bat and pad, but this gem of an innings was enough to get him to England next summer. He could well have left alone the ball that dismissed him.

Chappell struggled and struggled, deep in torment. The over-rate was funereal, nine an hour. Chappell scored eight in 85 minutes. Marsh was better, but down in the 'outer' they sang *Waltzing Matilda* to inspire the batsmen. It would have needed Matilda to do a fast one-step to be any help. England's cricket was superb. The bowlers were on the spot, and the fielding absolutely glittered. Randall saved run after run. Woolmer was unerring, and there followed some almost 'miracle' catches by Greig, Knott and Brearley. Has Dad's Army been demobbed?

Chappell never looked like getting on top. Marsh alone promised, but never prospered. Underwood came on to worry Chappell more and more with Greig setting an ideal field, himself at impudent, imprudent silly point, breathing almost in Chappell's face, his long arms stretching out. Poor Chappell was frustrated. He had a desperation swing at Underwood eventually, and was out bowled after his worst innings for a long time, over three hours for 40 with five twos and 17 singles. I fear some of our young men, now wealthy business tycoons as well as players, have over-stretched themselves.

That was Underwood's 250th Test wicket, but it was the new Willis, hair almost down to his chest, who impressed me. I asked him the other night whether they didn't have any barbers in India. 'When I get it cut,' he said, ever so kindly, 'I'll see you get some.'

But what about this English fielding! Keen, fast, sure, with those freak catches. It's one-day cricket, I suppose, that's sharpened them all. They came on to the field like a Cup-final team emerging at Wembley, sprinting and leaping.

Greig's captaincy was faultless. He is now a great leader, full of guile and knowledge.

Off the field the old-timers are standing up well. Larwood is a great hit. Wherever he goes Percy Fender is being capably looked after by his grandson, and all are charm and smiles, the old grudges gone, as I thought they would be.

This is a fantastic show. It would need a Neville Cardus to do it justice. I like the story Ernie McCormick tells. He noticed an old chap looking at him as he was going up in the lift. 'Weren't you,' he asked, 'Ernie McCormick?' Ernie is still thinking of the answer.

With an hour to go yesterday there was pandemonium as Lillie prepared to bowl to Brearley to the crowd's chant of 'Lillee-ee, Lillee-ee.' Poor Mike. He played the first ball, got the second away for a single and then it was Woolmer's turn. Neither flinched. Two names on the wall, Hobbs and Sutcliffe, would have been proud of them. Straight bat, body in line. As it should be.

The smiles of the English spectators were as wide at the Cheddar Gorge. One would think the pound sterling had gone up 10 points. I don't think there will be much clamour for the return to the English fold of a certain Yorkshireman, whose courage I have never doubted, or his ability, but sometimes I wonder whether he faces two-eyed the prospect of failure against a certain fast bowler.

England will have lifted their hopes for next summer's series enormously if the batsmen can carry on where Willis, Lever, Old and Underwood, and the superlative fielding, left off. The pitch is a beauty, full of runs. Brearley is still there, but Woolmer isn't – he nibbled.

So many names of our friends come to mind at this time. My editor is a kindly soul, which is also poetic, and he may permit me to end with a quote: 'To be blest if it tells me, that midst the great cheer; a kind voice had murmured, "I wouldst he were here".'

AUSTRALIA: First Innings

I. C. Davis lbw b Lever	5
R. B. McCosker b Willis ...	4
G. J. Cosier c Fletcher b Lever	10
G. S. Chappell b Underwood	40
D. Hookes c Greig b Old ...	17
K. D. Walters c Greig b Willis	4
R. W. Marsh c Knott b Old	28
G. J. Gilmour c Greig b Old	4
K. J. O'Keeffe c Brearley b Underwood	0
D. K. Lillee, not out	10
M. H. N. Walker b Underwood	2
Extras (b4, lb2, nb8)	14
Total	**138**

Fall of wickets: 1–11, 2–13, 3–23, 4–45, 5–51, 6–102, 7–114, 8–117, 9–136.

Bowling: Lever 12–1–36–2; Willis 8–0–33–2; Old 12–4–39–3; Underwood 11.6–2–16–3.

ENGLAND: First Innings 29-1 (Brearley 12*, Underwood 5*)

A small band of gold

CLIFF TEMPLE
The Times

14 March 1977 *After the disappointments at the Montreal Olympic Games some gold-medal winning by Britain's athletes was a welcome change. The European Indoor Championships is small fry by comparison, but the performances in San Sebastian were welcome pointers into summer. For two of the winners, Jane Colebrook and Sebastian Coe, the victories were the first positive steps towards international recognition; for Mary Stewart it was a matter of maintaining a family tradition – her brothers, Peter and Ian, had won European indoor titles before her.*

On an afternoon of splendour which British athletics will enjoy reliving many times in future years, our small squad of athletes competing in the European indoor championships here today claimed three gold and two silver medals. The golden haul took just 25 minutes of track action, and left a queue of British winners waiting for the soft chair in the interview room. Katrina Jane Colebrook (women's 800 metres), Sebastian Coe (men's 800 metres) and Mary Stewart (women's 1500 metres) took it in turn to show the rest of Europe the way home, each in their own style.

Miss Colebrook, over whom perhaps the biggest question mark was hanging, because she qualified for the final only as one of the fastest losers in Saturday's heats, was content to sit in on the field and let them take her through 400 metres in a nippy 57.66 seconds. She made her move wide round the last bend to overtake her rivals in the classic style, winning in 2 minutes 1.1 seconds, and equalling the world indoor record. It has been an astonishing season for Miss Colebrook, a 20-year-old Lincolnshire secretary whose outdoor best is still only 2 : 7.5. 'I felt much better than in the heats,' she said, 'and when I was still with them and feeling comfortable at the bell I knew I had the chance to win.'

Coe, whose racing maturity has been a highlight of the championships as he won heat, semi-final and final in apparent relaxed comfort, was also only just outside the world's best in his event, winning in 1 : 46.5, a personal improvement of one second. He was delighted to have drawn lane one and made the best use of his luck, going hard from the gun to grab the lead at the 200 metres break. Then, as the rest of the field were knocking each other silly with wild pushes behind him, he sped, smooth as silk, towards victory. 'I'm going to try to make the best use of my strengths,' he told me just before the race and that is what it came down to: strength.

Miss Stewart made her effort with 400 metres left, after the Bulgarian, Tchavdarova, had obliged by setting a swift pace. 'It went pretty much as I expected,' Miss Stewart said. 'I had thought about going ahead earlier, but as she did it all for me what was the point?'

Miss Stewart's winning time of 4:9.4 was just over a second outside her own indoor world record, but the fact that she had become the third member of her family in six years to win a European indoor title will please her more than the time.

Britain's two silver medals came from a couple of previous indoor champions, Geoffrey Capes, in the shot put, and Verona Elder, in the women's 400 metres. Mrs Elder found that the East German, Marita Koch, who improved her own indoor world record to 51 seconds, had too much speed on the first lap, but held on to take second place in 52.7sec.

For Arthur Gold, the British Amateur Athletic Board secretary, the championships were a baptism of fire in his first major meeting since being elected president of the European Athletic Association. Basque separatist demonstrators marched into the arena after the morning's events began and they wanted him to lead them out of the arena to guarantee their safety in the face of the armed police who stood guard in large numbers outside the stadium. In the interests of the meeting he agreed.

The unexpected disturbance naturally affected performances in the morning events, and many athletes found themselves warming up for two hours or more, not knowing when, or even if, they would compete. 'That sort of thing wrecks your concentration completely,' Geoffrey Capes said, after his silver medal performance in the shot putt.

A little-known Icelandic shot putter, 27-year-old Hreinn Halldorssen, reached 67ft. 6¾in. with his opening effort. It was several feet further than Halldorssen had ever managed before, and, although normally within the range of Capes, it was sufficient to demote him to the silver medal. His best putt, 67ft. 1½in., came in the second round.

Randall makes a fight of it

RAY ROBINSON
The Daily Telegraph

18 March 1977 *The course which Lillee and Walker set in scattering the England batsmen for 95 in the first innings of the Centenary Test remained unchanged. But a score of 417 in their final innings by England brought them to within 45 of Australia's total, and Derek Randall's 174 gave stature and respectability to English batting once again.*

England were beaten, as expected, in the Centenary Test in Melbourne yesterday. What was not expected, however, was the slender margin of Australia's victory, and Tony Greig, the touring captain, was right to point out that the loss of this one match was outweighed by England's recovery of batting stature.

A thrilling last-day recovery, inspired by Derek Randall's 174 – the Nottinghamshire right-hander's first Test century – swept England to a total of 417, 11 runs beyond the highest winning fourth innings in any Test.

Alas for Randall, Greig and England, it was still 45 runs short of the asking total. So Australia triumphed, as they had in the first-ever Test between the countries, and by an identical margin.

Yet, for 7½ hours, England had threatened the impossible, clinging to the lifebuoy offered by Randall. England's latest Test hero is slightly built – 5 feet 8½ inches tall and 11 stone; yet his strokes skimmed over the Melbourne outfield as smoothly as the Queen's Rolls-Royce.

Randall, forever restlessly fiddling with his cap, maintained his aggressively watchful vigil for the equivalent of a day and a quarter, enabling England to average $3\frac{3}{4}$ runs an over. Most of his 21 fours were placed through the off field; his cover drives were unexcelled on either side.

He went through a difficult time after a Lillee bouncer had struck his cap, felling him. Amiss, his batting partner, walked anxiously towards him; but Randall moved a dozen yards to leg, then returned to shape up again.

However, he hung his bat out riskily at Lillee's outswinger and Chappell's outcutter several times, to Amiss's obvious concern. Soon, however, he had recovered his poise, and he and Amiss carried their third-wicket stand to 166 in $3\frac{1}{2}$ hours.

Amiss, except for brief uneasiness against the new ball, coped far better with Lillee than in the first innings. But he was surprised by an in-cutter from Chappell after reaching 64 off 185 balls in 233 minutes, and Marsh soon snapped up Fletcher, off Lillee.

Randall ploughed on, his serene progress interrupted by two untoward incidents. In Lillee's 23rd over one delivery reared past the Englishman's raised bat and right shoulder, hitting something en route.

Randall pointed to his shoulder; Lillee, appealing, pointed to the bat and spoke to Randall, who again fingered his shoulder.

Randall's end seemed to have come when, after making 161, he was given out by umpire Brooks to a catch by Marsh off Chappell. Randall, resigned to his fate, began to walk, when Marsh sportingly indicated that he had not caught the ball before it hit the ground.

Brooks conferred with Chappell, and Randall was recalled to continue his punishment of the long-suffering Australia attack. But he was soon to go. His fifth-wicket partnership with Greig had produced 56 when Randall, pushing forward to O'Keeffe's leg-break, fell to Casier's bat-pad catch.

Randall swished his bat disappointedly at the grass as the noise of the crowd's applause followed him off. His sterling innings earned him the 1600 dollars award as Man of the Match.

Two overs later O'Keeffe drew Greig into another short

leg catch by Cosier. It was 369 for six and the Australians sensed victory. O'Keeffe dismissed Lever LBW, and a smart catch by Chappell helped Lillee send back Old. Underwood soon followed.

Knott, meanwhile, had been vigorously run-hunting since his captain's departure; but after hitting five fours in 42 he tried to drag a straight ball off his stumps and became Lillee's fifth victim for 139. Lillee finished with a match analysis of 11 for 165. His jubilant team-mates carried him off; it was the least he deserved.

AUSTRALIA: First Innings 138

Second Innings 419–9 dec.
(R. W. Marsh 110 not, I. C. Davis 68, K. D. Walters 66, D. Hookes 56; Old 4–104)

ENGLAND: First Innings 95
(Lillee 6–26, Walker 4–54)

ENGLAND: Second Innings

R. A. Woolmer lbw b Walker	12
J. M. Brearley lbw b Lillee	43
D. W. Randall c Cosier b O'Keeffe	174
D. L. Amiss b Chappell	64
K. W. R. Fletcher c Marsh b Lillee	1
*A. W. Greig c Cosier b O'Keeffe	41
†A. P. E. Knott lbw b Lillee	42
C. M. Old c Chappell b Lillee	2
J. K. Lever lbw b O'Keeffe	4
D. L. Underwood b Lillee ...	7
R. G. D. Willis not out	5
Extras (b 8 lb 4 w 3 nb 7)	22
Total	**417**

Fall of wickets: 1–28, 2–113, 3–279, 4–290, 5–346, 6–369, 7–380, 8–385, 9–410.

Bowling: Lillee 34–4–7–139–5, Walker 22–4–83–1, Gilmour 4–0–29–0, Chappell 16–7–29–1, O'Keeffe 33–6–108–3, Walters 3–2–7–0.

Umpires: M. O'Connell & T. Brookes

*Captain †Wicketkeeper

Requiem for a champion

HUGH McILVANNEY
The Observer

20 March 1977 *Steeplechasing and hurdle racing are full of risks. Riders are injured, horses sometimes break down and have to be shot. But rarely does the end come for an outstanding jumper in the glare that goes with one of the greatest events, the Cheltenham Gold Cup,*

as it did for Lanzarote, winner of 19 races and over £60,000 in prize money. For Hugh McIlvanney, the death was 'an experience to make the raucous human turmoil at Cheltenham... seem for once like an intrusive sideshow'.

The tarpaulin they threw over the remains of Lanzarote on Thursday afternoon was a winding-sheet for our enjoyment of this year's Cheltenham Festival. Pleasure in the greatest of jumping race meetings died along with the best horse in the Gold Cup.

English attitudes to animals are often mawkish enough to turn the stomach but the emotional reaction to the freak accident that killed Lanzarote was robustly sincere, one that had to be shared by all who believe that great racehorses have a higher status than bingo cards. There was an unforced nobility about him that conveyed itself even to those of us who knew him only through his public appearances, something about his bearing and the carriage of his fine head, a blending of strength and good-natured placidity that tended to make respect and affection come in a single flood.

To see the brave light in his eye snuffed out so abruptly, champion turned to carcase in one slithering stride, was an experience to make the raucous human turmoil at Cheltenham, the betting and drinking and guessing and lying, all the marvellous nonsense that eddies through the place every March, seem for once like an intrusive side-show. There was an emptiness that couldn't be measured by the hand in your pocket.

Twenty-four hours later, as a thin and muted crowd of racegoers toyed unaggressively with the problems of a moderate card at Lingfield, John Francome, who had got up on Lanzarote before the Gold Cup with no more pessimism than Angelo Dundee feels when he slaps Ali on the shoulder at the first bell, still wore an expression of shocked remoteness. 'I feel bloody lousy,' he said at the door of the weighing room. 'I don't even want to go outside.'

It was 25 minutes after the second race, a novice steeplechase in which he had given a smooth and promising introduction to Clandestine from Richard Head's stable, and he had not found the inclination to change out of the blue and white hoops of the six-year-old's owner. He was preoccupied with things past. His young face is alertly, almost warily intelligent, but now the steady eyes under the long lashes were clouded with thoughts that were far away from the hard bench we sat on.

'We had jumped that ninth fence and going a stride or so away from it when Lanzarote's back legs went from under him,' he said quietly. 'He crumpled on his near hind and I knew straight away when I looked at it that it was broken just above the hock. It was twisted up, not grotesquely but bad enough to let me know how serious it was. At moments like that you don't have to be a veterinary expert to realise the worst has happened. I waited with him till the vet came. All I could do was to try to soothe him, hold his head down and keep him from trying to get up. Then the vet arrived and shot him, put him out of his misery.'

There was a heavy residue of misery among the humans who had worked intimately with Lanzarote. As he was carted from the scene of his death (near the fence that would have been the fourth from home on the second and last circuit in the Gold Cup) to a triangular space by the side of the course that is normally used for parking the ground staff's tractor, the sense of what had been lost reached achingly into everyone who had ever admired the horse. But it must have felt like a disembowelling knife to such as his owner, Lord Howard de Walden, to Fred Winter, the inspired trainer for whom the fatality was the latest in a series of disasters visited upon him by this race, and Harry Foster, the veteran stable lad who has cared for Lanzarote since the brown gelding went to Winter's yard at Lambourn.

'It's upset me more than enough but it's probably worse for the guv'nor,' said Francome. 'He was bound to think a lot of a horse that had done so much for him and he obviously felt all the closer because he rode Lanzarote quite often in work at home. But most of all I feel sorry for Harry Foster. Harry's getting on a bit now, he's nearly 60, and you can imagine what an important part of his life that horse had become.'

It is not difficult. A stable lad accepts that his job will have more to do with hard work on raw mornings than afternoons of triumph at the racecourse, and to be given charge of an animal like Lanzarote is a small miracle that warms and brightens the whole of his existence. It was a permanent cold that settled on Harry Foster as his nine-year-old hero and friend was put away on that wet hill at Cheltenham. Lanzarote had won 19 hurdle races, including the 1974 Champion Hurdle on that same course, and his three victories over fences had indicated that he could easily go on to dominate the tougher game and increase considerably his winning stakes total of £61,000. Foster had shared in a highly personal way in all those successes and the tears he shed on Thursday were not so much justified as inevitable.

There were other sad stories at Cheltenham, especially in a Gold Cup that saw the favourite, Bannow Rambler, and the formidable Fort Devon prematurely removed from the action and then, between its last two jumps, produced savage misfortune for another representative of quality, Summerville, who broke down dreadfully when the prize was at his mercy and will never race again. But much the saddest episode was the demise of Lanzarote. 'There's no point in talking or writing about it,' John Francome declared with sudden understandable bitterness at Lingfield. 'It's all irrelevant. The old horse is dead and that's it.'

The pain, however, will stay alive for him for a long time, no matter how many winners he adds to the two he rode on Friday. Nor will Fred Winter be easily consoled. After his previous ill-luck with Pendil and Bula (who was, for bad measure, severely injured on Tuesday of last week) and this most recent nightmare, Winter must feel that the fates have booby-trapped the Gold Cup course against him. 'If I were Fred I'd drive out of this place and never come back,' said a fellow trainer on Thursday night. Of course, Winter will be back. Timidity is no more a part of his nature than it was of Lanzarote's.

Relentless Green batters Stracey to defeat

DONALD SAUNDERS
The Daily Telegraph

21 March 1977 *The rewards of professional boxing turned away Dave Green from digging carrots in the Fens to the ring, where he has amassed a fortune. This contest with John Stracey brought him a purse in excess of £40,000.*

Dave Green, the European and British light-welterweight champion, won the most savage battle the British ring has seen for years at Wembley last night by stopping John H. Stracey, former holder of the world welterweight title, in the 10th round of a memorable contest.

The end came with Stracey, barely able to see out of a badly swollen left eye, being led to his corner by Harry Gibbs, who rightly had decided it would be unwise to allow a brave, half-blinded man to share the ring with his ferocious opponent a second longer.

From the second round onwards Stracey had fought under the handicap of a damaged eye, and obviously was not going to win this argument, even if he did stay there until the 12th and final bell.

Possibly there would have been a different story to tell if an egg-sized lump had not begun to rise over Stracey's left eye after Green had received the second of four warnings he was given for careless use of the head.

I suspect, however, that Green would have emerged triumphant even if Stracey had not been hampered by injury. This rough, tough young man from the Fen district had fought so tigerishly from the opening bell to the final moment that Stracey simply could not cope with him.

Yet, as the former champion sat, tired and dejected, on his stool when it was all over, Green looked as though he could have gone another 10 all-action rounds. He may lack class, he may not care too much at times about the Marquess of Queensberry rules, and he does not punch as hard as once did Eric Boon, that other fighting son of Chatteris. But no one can deny that Green is superbly fit, fights with savage intensity, shrugs off punishment with contempt, and hits often enough and solidly enough to wear down even the strong and the brave.

They had billed this contest as the Fight of the Year, and that it surely will prove to be. There were times when both men were locked in such angry combat that Mr Gibbs was forced to remind them that this battle was taking place at Wembley Pool, and not in a cobble-stoned backyard.

After Stracey had lost his world title to Carlos Palomino in the 12th round in this same ring last June, his appetite for the fight game was called into question. Last night he proved beyond doubt that he is no quitter.

But although Stracey from time to time put together some powerful combinations – notably in the punishing ninth round – he could not deter Green.

As the bump over Stracey's brow grew ominously larger, and his left eye narrowed to a mere slit, it was obvious that he would have the greatest difficulty in lasting the course. But not once did he ever look like giving up. Then, as Stracey twisted, trying to see another flurry of punches before they thumped on to his head, the referee decided to end his ordeal. Green now returns to Wembley on 14 June to try to take the world title from Palomino. On last night's form he must have a chance. Stracey, on the other hand, will take a long, hard look at his future.

A try to stun the mind

PETER WEST

The Times

21 March 1977 *While France were winning one Rugby title in Dublin Wales went to Murrayfield to finish top among the home countries. If the outcome was a disappointment for the Scots those who watched at least saw one of the most brilliant tries to be scored on the Scottish ground.*

Wales finally cooked the Scottish goose at Murrayfield on Saturday with a try, superbly created out of defence, which they may recall with pleasure in their dotage. So the triple crown was theirs again, with victory by 18–9 in a fierce and totally absorbing contest in which both teams won kudos. Scotland, who brought it to a spectacular climax as they threw in everything, were left to reflect that all of the last nine Welsh points sprang from their own mistakes.

Although two penalty kicks by Bennett rebounded from the posts, a brave Scottish side, playing as expansively as they have done for years, and producing their finest performance of this championship, must have felt that on the run of the game they had done enough to earn a draw. But the writing was on the wall once this resilient Welsh team had nosed in front, with the wind at their backs, and they held on firmly to win by two goals and two penalty goals to a goal and a penalty goal.

It was 9–9, midway through the second half, when Fenwick intercepted a lobbed pass by McGeechan in the Welsh 25 and kicked straight down the middle into space. Shedden had time to kick for touch but, having allowed himself to be nailed by J. P. R. Williams, he slipped a high pass that Cranston knocked on on his goal line. To make things worse, Gerald Davies was obstructed and Scotland failed to release the ball after a tackle. So instead of yielding a scrummage, Scotland presented Bennett with an easy penalty.

A few minutes later McGeechan missed what looked to be a 3–2 overlap on the right, whereupon an Irvine chip, precisely executed, touched off the fuse for Welsh genius. J. P. R. Williams made a rock-like save and, though knocked over by Carmichael, somehow fed cleanly to Fenwick, who ran flat across his posts before giving to Gerald Davies. Two dazzling sidesteps and a stern hand-off straightened up the line, leaving three would-be tacklers clutching at thin air, and there was Bennett, sprinting away up the right and giving a pass to Burcher that may or may not have been forward.

Now, as Scottish cover homed across, the Welsh centre bowled a clever, under-arm pass inside that Fenwick, under acute pressure, brilliantly flicked on to Bennett. With one conclusive side-step and swerve Bennett left the last two tacklers and shot clear to the posts. It was a lethal thrust, magnificently done, and Bennett with the simplest of goal kicks supplied the last twist.

How different the early picture, when McGeechan's left foot at once landed a 35 yards dropped goal behind a ruck set up by Biggar from the scrummage. Although Bennett soon landed a fine penalty from 10 yards farther out on the right, by the second quarter the Scottish forwards were spilling the ball out of ruck upon ruck, and the creative McGeechan on three occasions glided and jinked through inside his man. In the centre, Renwick looked sharp, Cranston powerful and uncomplicated, and the ubiquitous Irvine hungry for the slightest chance. Wales, their defence holding, could be grateful at that stage for the superlative line kicking of Bennett.

Wales, running distinctly short of good set-piece possession, but mauling the better, were frustrated by collapsed scrummages, by penalties in attacking positions, and, at the line-out, by the productive operations of McHarg, who gave Martin a difficult afternoon. The scrummaging story was curious. In the first half Wales frequently swung their opponents, but overall Madsen took three strikes off Windsor against the head – which might be bad news for the Lions tour aspirations of Clive Williams, now facing the thrusty Carmichael. At loose head, McLauchlan announced his return to Scottish ranks with a rumbustiously effective display. He may yet be summering in New Zealand and in that event could be a candidate for the Lions captaincy.

A restrained Edwards, whose kicking – by his own high standards – was inconsistent, rarely had the platform to satisfy him. Morgan, busy and sturdy, kicked shrewdly, had more opportunity to display his vision of the game and may have enhanced his claim for a Lions place. So, on the Scottish wing, did Gammell, with an all-round game of strength and good sense.

It was 3–3 at the interval, Bennett to his evident chagrin just having missed a most kickable penalty as well as having given a bad pass to Davies as Wales developed attacking rhythm. Then, when Wales switched direction, J. J. Williams spoiled things by dropping a pass directed at his navel.

Scotland regained the lead shortly afterwards when Morgan ran flat from a sound scrummage base and the scissoring Renwick, having accelerated through the middle, gave to Irvine on his right. The full back looked covered, but he stabbed inside past three defenders for a try that he himself converted from under the posts.

That was a rousing good score, as was the first Welsh try that followed it. This, too, came from a scrummage ball, Burcher making a dummy run on one side before Edwards switched to the left. The ball went swiftly and accurately via Bennett, Fenwick and J. P. R. Williams for J. J. Williams to outflank the defence, and for Bennett to convert from far out.

Then came the conclusive Welsh scoring, as already described, and the last desperate Scottish sallies, often from tapped penalties, with Irvine always in the van. Apart from one knock on of a rolling ball, Irvine had been as safe as the Bank of Scotland.

SCOTLAND: A. R. Irvine (Heriot's PP), **W. B. B. Gammell** (Edinburgh Wanderers), **J. M. Renwick** (Hawick), **A. G. Cranston** (Hawick), **D. Shedden** (West of Scotland), **I. R. McGeechan** (Headingley, capt), **D. W. Morgan** (Stewart's Melville PP), **J. McLauchlan** (Jordanhill), **D. F. Madsen** (Gosforth), **A. B. Carmichael** (West of Scotland), **I. A. Barnes** (Hawick), **A. F. McHarg** (London Scottish), **M. A. Biggar** (London Scottish), **D. S. M. MacDonald** (London Scottish), **W. S. Watson** (Boroughmuir)

WALES: J. P. R. Williams (Bridgend), **T. G. R. Davies** (Cardiff), **S. P. Fenwick** (Bridgend), **D. H. Burcher** (Newport), **J. J. Williams** (Llanelli), **P. Bennett** (Llanelli, capt), **G. O. Edwards** (Cardiff), **C. Williams** (Aberavon), **R. W. Windsor** (Pontyoool), **G. Price** (Pontypool), **A. J. Martin** (Aberavon), **G. A. D. Wheel** (Swansea), **T. J. Cobner** (Pontypool), **D. L. Quinnell** (Llanelli), **R. C. Burgess** (Ebbw Vale)

REFEREE: G. Domercq (France)

Final table	**P**	**W**	**L**	**F**	**A**	**Pts**
France	4	4	0	58	21	8
Wales	4	3	1	66	43	6
England	4	2	2	42	24	4
Scotland	4	1	3	39	85	2
Ireland	4	0	4	33	65	0

APRIL

Pride comes before cash

PETER BATT

The Evening News

1 April 1977 *The Grand National is an institution rather than a horse race, which means that the racing experts have to make room for other writers—people like Peter Batt, who put cherry trees and manure at 50p a bag into this enjoyable day-before-the-race sketch.*

Aintree racecourse is not a pretty sight. The grey, forbidding Liverpool skyline provides the kind of backcloth that, at best, can only be described as earthy. Its new caretakers, Ladbrokes the bookmakers, have attempted to inject a splash of colour by planting a few cherry trees near the barren parade ring. But at 3.15 tomorrow afternoon 43 horses, 42 men and one young lady line up for a sporting event which needs no adornment.

The Grand National paints its own pictures, grows its own plumage and decorates the senses of anyone who is privileged to witness it.

As for the thrill of competing, that was immortalised by Lord Oaksey who was up with the leaders when he jumped the last fence on Carrickbeg in 1963 and later wrote:

> It's there – the prize you dreamed of since your first child's pony – but the run in is 490 yards and an awful lot of dreams have ended between the last fence and the post.
>
> Still one horse in front and now for the first time you can hear the crowd – a murmur on the wind, faces beside the rail, your thighs burning, your whip like lead and although you are in front the winning post is still a hundred miles away . . .

On that occasion Lord Oaksey was passed by 66–1 chance

Ayala in the last 50 yards and he finished second. Ayala never won another race.

Martin Blackshaw was on holiday yesterday when he learned that he was going to be given the chance of experiencing similar bitter-sweet emotions on Churchtown Boy tomorrow.

Blackshaw, who is currently riding full-time in France, stood and cheered 9–1 winner Churchtown Boy home in the Topham Trophy Handicap and was then told by trainer Larry Salaman: 'The horse goes for the National as well, but today's jockey is already booked for Eyecatcher. Would you like the ride?'

'Would I?' echoed a delighted Blackshaw, as Churchtown Boy was having his odds slashed from 66–1 to 33–1 as a result of his triumph. He then confided:

'I had three winning rides in a week in France recently and earned as much in seven days as I used to in a season here, but money doesn't enter into it when it comes to a race like this one.'

At Blackshaw's side, nodding agreement, stood Guy Negrel, champion steeplechase jockey of France. 'I earn much more than English jockeys, but pride would be sufficient payment for tackling these fences in the National.'

'We have a stone wall to jump at Auteuil in Paris, but Aintree's fences are so high, so very high . . ."

Then, as if to emphasise the point and underline the ups and downs of these magnificent fall guys, Read promptly toppled off Mr Know All in the next race and a look of concern spread across Negrel's swarthy features as he searched his friend's eyes. Blackshaw was not responding, though. He was singing in the rain.

Pride is also propelling Miss Charlotte Brew, the 21-year-old Essex girl who will become the first woman to ride in the race when she partners Barony Fort. After braving the worst of the day's appalling weather in an early-morning canter, she said, 'I am determined to get round, even if I have to remount three times.'

Significantly, the bookmakers are beginning to respect that feminine stubbornness. They have shortened the odds on Barony Fort completing the course to 8–1.

The big race tips were as plentiful as the raindrops yesterday and not the least interesting was Johnny Buckingham's theory that victory will go to an outsider. Buckingham, who rode 100–1 winner Foinavon in 1967 and is now the weighing room valet, reckons that when the year ends with a seven luck favours the less fancied horses and he quotes Caughoo at 100–1 in 1947 and Sundew at 20–1 in 1957. His fancy tomorrow, incidentally, is Sage Merlin.

The oldest jockey in the 1977 National is 40-year-old solicitor Mr John Carden, who rides the oldest horse, 13-year-old Huperade, and the youngest is Nigel Tinkler, who partners Fort Vulgan. The luckiest owner could well be Sir Garnett's Mr Alan Kaye, who claims to have once done the next best thing to breaking the bank at Monte Carlo by cleaning out the cropiers at a Nice casino. And the most popular animal by far is Red Rum, of course. We are reliably informed that the price of his manure is 50p a bag – 15p more than the rest of his rivals. Just think what he could do for those cherry trees if he makes it three times lucky tomorrow!

Red Rum—National Hero

TOM FORREST
The Sunday Express

3 April 1977 *There are times when those from the animal kingdom reach out and come closer to the human race. A horse called Red Rum has for several years now received fan mail at his stable near Southport, held parties and even phone calls. This year he surpassed himself by winning the Grand National for the third time. Strong men wept, said one writer. Tom Forrest, in his despatch from the course, was clearly touched by the event, but he kept his feet on the ground – and his eyes dry.*

Never has heroism earned a tribute as thunderous as the wave upon crashing wave of cheering for immortal Red Rum, as he galloped gloriously to an incredible third victory – by 25 lengths over Churchtown Boy and Eyecatcher – in the News of the World Grand National.

Never in history had any horse won more than twice . . . and 'Rummy's' triple triumph, backed by two seconds on his only other attempts, add up to a record so sublime that it never will, never *can* be approached. So sublime that a tearful Tommy Stack slipped from the saddle to declare: 'Nothing can do justice to this horse, nothing I can say, and nothing you can write. He is just beyond belief!'

So emotional was the ecstatic 50,000-plus crowd's reception for its own special Aintree idol that even the irrespressible effervescence of trainer Ginger McCain dissolved from time to time into the happiest tears I have ever seen.

'Bloody marvellous,' said Ginger again and again. 'Bloody marvellous on Tommy's part and on the horse's. I thought he was a week short of peak fitness – but nothing stops him.'

And nothing could stop Red Rum's owner. Noel Le Mare – 90 in December – from being there to see his champion's historic surge to glory. Told of the tempest-force winds ripping over the Aintree track on the morning of the race, he burst out: 'I was putting up with gales on deep-sea trawlers when I was thirteen years old. Why should the winds worry me now?'

The greatest moment steeplechasing ever knew could only have happened to a phenomenon like Red Rum, who just does not know how to fail, who battles his heart out whatever the odds. But even a Red Rum could never have made it without the fast, favourable turf which strong sun and stronger winds had produced. Liverpool time records were smashed in both races before the National, and those are the conditions the great horse revels in.

And even Red Rum might never have made it but for a dramatic chain of fateful accidents which cleared the opposition right off the track. Only nine of 42 starters finished without mishap. Cheltenham Gold Cup winner Davy Lad, thrown into the handicap with only 10st 13lb, crashed at the third fence. Sebastian V was 10 lengths clear when he nose-dived at Beecher's on the first circuit. Boom Docker, even further ahead at the 17th fence, dug in his toes and refused to jump. Then it was the 15–2 favourite Andy Pandy who left the field trailing far behind, until he took his spectacular tumble at Beecher's second time round.

All the while Red Rum was making up ground relentlessly, nearer and nearer, until Andy Pandy's fall left him in command. With just three of the 30 mighty fences left to cross, jockey Stack was bothered only about two loose horses, telling himself: 'God, I'm going to get brought down at the second-last, with it all at my mercy.' What Stack did not know was that by this time Martin Blackshaw was right on his heels with Churchtown Boy . . . his mount cantering and Martin looking backwards for danger, totally confident he could take the leader.

But the loose horses switched from Red Rum, perhaps distracted Churchtown Boy, and brought a sloppy, hind-leg-dragging jump which left that horse struggling. And 'Rummy,' racing on alone and uncatchable.

After Eyecatcher – third, six lengths behind Churchtown Boy – The Pilgarlic took fourth prize ahead of Forest King, What A Buck, Happy Ranger, Carroll Street, and Collingwood. Hidden Value and Saucy Belle were remounted to finish 10th and 11th.

Winter Rain broke his neck at Becher's first time round, and Zeta's Son was put down after breaking a leg at Valentine's on the second circuit.

Charlotte Brew's dream of being the first woman to ride the big winner ended, after dogged persistence at the tail-end of the field, when Barony Fort refused at the 27th.

Top bookmaking firms reported 'the worst result possible' at starting prices of 9–1 Red Rum, 20–1 Churchtown Boy, 18–1 Eyecatcher, and 40–1 The Pilgarlic. But betting was of no importance whatever on an occasion like this. It was the wonder of Red Rum, not the winnings, which left the race crowds delirious.

The Finish:
Red Rum (Quorum-Mared) 12, 11 8 (9 – 1) T Stack **1**
Churchtown Boy 10, 10 0 (20 – 1) M Blackshaw **2**
Eyecatcher 11, 10 1 (18 – 1) C Read **3**
The Pilgarlic 9, 10 4 (40 – 1) R R Evans **4**

Gerald Ford of the track

KEITH BOTSFORD
The Sunday Times

10 April 1977 *The fast young men of the racing track are not what they seem. At the age of 37 Mario Andretti won the US Grand Prix—his first victory for six years. But as Keith Botsford points out he is just the sort of American the country needs in the art of understanding Formula One Racing.*

Mario Andretti, who won the US Grand Prix West at Long Beach, California, is no spring chicken. His first GP win was in South Africa in 1971, for Ferrari. His second, for Lotus, was last year in Japan; it was almost buried under the Fuji fireworks that accompanied Hunt's winning the 1976 championship. This season he has faced fire, explosion and failure on the way to last Sunday's victory. And he is a month past his 37th birthday.

Mario is that delicious product of the American 20th century television ethos, the old pro. It could be a gammy-legged footballer, a fighter with sprouts for ears and more scar tissue over his eyes than brain; it could be anyone in sport about whom the media can say that he has been around a long time trying, that he's always been good, and given of his best, but that he hasn't won enough to deserve to be hated. Gerald Ford was enough of an athlete to be called an old pro at politics. The words nicely combine admiration and condescension.

They also speak of timing, gags, a good delivery, a willingness to be interviewed, a freshness of language. Here is Mario, asked about the start: 'I guess Jody got me right then. Look, either it was a hell of a start he made, or we fell asleep. I saw the red go out, so the green light had to be on. Next thing he was in third gear, so sometimes you play your cards right and you don't want your wings clipped at the start, so I settled back. And I stayed so close to him I could read the labels on his collar, but he made no mistakes . . .'

Andretti's Long Beach win did, however, come in the nick of time. It made the race, threatened by unpaid bills, a worthwhile American sports event. Mario – the smiling family man, the franchised distributor of the American wise-crack – finally gave US sports writers something to do their public relations work on, being the first American ever to win a US Grand Prix. His toothy grin, his soft drawl, burly self-contained physicality, his image of being gusty without being excessive, extravagant or out of line with Middle America, is all bonanza stuff to the media.

Master James Hunt they can't understand. He seems either uninvolved or rude. Unlike the British, they're not interested in jet-set love affairs. Golden Apollos are a dime a dozen. America's mums recoil before the disasters wrought on Niki Lauda's face: 'Look what happened to him!' the matriarch will say when her big, beefy boy wants to go out on the track. And Jody is too monosyllabic, alien corn.

No, Mario's the man to put Formula One on the map Stateside. Mr Nice. An eyetie who's not a Godfather, who made his way up through the kind of motor racing Americans understand in cars that look more like their own; USAC champion in '65, '66 and '69, and Indy winner in '69. That's *comprehensible.* Not that hightly technical over-sophisticated, effete European Formula One. So Mario will maybe make it respectable, which can't hurt the sport.

The start at Long Beach is everything. After that, little passing is possible which, judging by Hunt's complaints, is something else the organisers will have to think about. Reutemann's heavy foot caused all the trouble: 'He came up like an express train, like he was heading straight for Acapulco,' said Mario. And, he should have added, never made the first corner, taking out Hunt, Peterson, Mass and, in the ensuing mess, a few other minor luminaries. Hunt got back in, but he ended up a lap behind, never really concerned in the finish.

Almost as important as Mario's winning was Jody Scheckter's losing. It was Jody's race right up to three laps from the end. And who, before the season started, ever thought Jody could win, with a new team and a new car? He was bitter about his bad luck at Long Beach: three times with a word Richard Nixon depleted from his tapes. 'I never felt so much like crying in my life,' he added. 'Mario was climbing up my backside in the first half of the race, but in the second half I thought I had him.' But with his right front tyre sucked in like an old man's cheeks, he had to let Mario and Niki by.

Niki's second place puts him level with Jody in championship points at 19, with Reutemann second at 13 and Mario third with 11, two ahead of Master James. That's a very nice line-up for this early stage of the season. All of them are basic competitors to be nth degree. Hunt is the craziest, the most erratic, but the best when his car goes well; Jody the most physical and absolute and brighter race by race; Niki the most consistent and calculating and arrogant; and Mario the wiliest, most prudent and most naturally gifted.

But after Long Beach some questions are being asked: where are the Tyrrells? What's wrong with Hunt or his McLaren? Why aren't the Brabhams, so competitive in South America, doing too well? Others are answered: Colin Chapman has his Lotus together, and Mario is a winner; Ferrari are still tops; and Jody's Wolf is anything but the joke Their Magnificences of the Contructor's Association thought it was before this year's races.

Play it again, Liverpool

PETER CORRIGAN
The Observer

Everton 2 Liverpool 2

24 April 1977 *Almost the end of April, and Liverpool are bounding along trying to spread their skills and resources to meet the demands of winning three competitions. Everton, the city's other club, held them up in the FA Cup semi-final by playing, as Peter Corrigan puts it in a vivid account, 'beyond the capabilities we had thought them to possess'. Come the replay, however, Liverpool duly triumphed 3–0.*

Those not wrung dry of the capacity to survive the tumultuous excitements of this splendid FA Cup semi-final will reassemble at Maine Road next Wednesday night eager for the resumption of a drama that refused to find a conclusion yesterday.

Liverpool's domination of this season and their promising assault on the historic 'treble' was put to the most exhaustive test by an Everton team playing beyond the capabilities we had thought them to possess and their conrtibution to the swirling splendour of a memorable game deserved no less than another chance. They might easily have won and, indeed, had a goal disallowed controversially by referee Clive Thomas. He ruled that substitute Hamilton was offside when brushing the ball into the goal five minutes from the end.

After losing an early lead to Liverpool they gathered strength and aggression to equalise and dominate the first half. Liverpool, rescuing their composure in the wind and the rain, came back in the second half to recapture the lead and then lose it once more to Everton's refusal to relinquish an ounce to their rivals.

And if one man has to be chosen it was Everton's Duncan McKenzie who managed to illuminate even this superb battle with individual artistry, scoring one goal and creating the other. It is ironic that his appearances in the team have been sporadic in the past two months.

Most of the 52,500 capacity attendance (who doubled the previous Maine Road receipts record by paying a total of £140,000) were caught in the rain, and the steam which rose from the terraces was not all passion. The teams splashed into action, realising that quick use of the brain and the foot was essential if mistakes were not to be made on the mischievous surface.

In the very first minute David Fairclough, the red-haired young forward whose unpredictability was preferred to the more experienced Johnson, launched one of his leggy, determined runs on a diagonal from the touchline to the penalty arc. The run took him fully 40 yards but just as he set himself to shoot in flight his balancing leg raised a cascade of water and he missed the ball completely as he fell flat on his back.

In the next five minutes Everton, aware that the game

suddenly offered good odds to the gambler, threw everything into attack, forced a couple of corners and, with overhead kicks from Dobson and Pearson, had goalkeeper Clemence grasping upwards for a ball which just dropped over the bar. Then McKenzie almost caught the Liverpool goalkeeper with a sly header. But there were two sudden and rare glimpses of Liverpool's class, the second of which produced their early lead. In the first Kennedy hit a clever pass out to Case on the right and although McDermott met Case's low cross first time it squirted wide and high from his right foot.

But in the second, which he received from Keegan after a Heighway break, McDermott calmed and collected himself on the rim of the box and summoned the precision to float the ball with his left foot for it to drop with telling accuracy between the desperate leap of the advancing Lawson and the crossbar.

The potency of a goal against them so early worked its way through Everton veins but all credit to them in the way they shook off its lasting effect to keep the game balanced and fluent and their equalising goal in the thirty-third minute was by no means underserved.

Pearson, an admirable deputy for the injured Latchford, sped down the right and posted the ball for the far side of the Liverpool goal where Dobson fought against the slipperiness of the pitch but only managed to knock the ball back across goal. It came into the area of McKenzie who skilfully composed himself before shooting through a crowd of players with his left foot to send the white netting billowing.

The extent to which Everton had come into the game and dominated it at this stage was certainly not in the script. Liverpool, through a combination of the pitch and Everton's aggression, were not able to build up deliberately from the back as they have been doing of late, and they looked decidedly uncomfortable as Dobson and Buckley in particular ploughed steadfast furrows deep into their half.

There was one outbreak of temper before the first half ended. Buckley was booked for a foul on Smith which left the fearsome Liverpool veteran face down in the mud. Smith was himself booked a few minutes later when he disrupted Goodlass's unity with the ground, and the outbreak seemed to have stopped, but not even the 10 minutes cooling down at the interval stopped Everton thinking positive thoughts, and one delicious and impudent piece of trickery by McKenzie as he flicked the ball around Smith showed how real the danger was to Liverpool. And when Liverpool did break through the Everton defence Keegan was speeding to the near post with the ball at his feet, only to be forcefully tackled by Lyons.

Yet the drying pitch and the inevitable fall in the pace of the game began to allow Liverpool to find their composure and rhythm and the red attacks began to infiltrate in a more telling and familiar manner. Case had a shot charged down by Lyons and Keegan brought from Lawson a flying spectacular save.

These were the signal that Liverpool were ready to occupy the game as a force once more and in the seventy-third minute Case gave them the lead again. Heighway was held up while waiting to take a free kick on the far touchline while Liverpool substituted Johnston for Fairclough. Then he floated the kick into the goalmouth where Everton failed to clear cleanly. The ball dropped to the head of Case who jerked his neck forward to send the ball looping over the chaos in front and into the top corner of the net.

Everton viewed the dwindling minutes as an enemy to be outpaced, and their second equaliser of the tie came in the eighty-fourth minute when McKenzie worked brilliantly on the right and hit a low weaving cross to the far post just out of Clement's reach and Rioch was bounding to meet it and score from a yard.

LIVERPOOL: Clemence, Neal, Jones, Smith, Kennedy, Hughes, Keegan, Case, Heighway, Fairclough, McDermott

EVERTON: Lawson, Darracott, Pejic, Lyons, McNaught, Rioch, Buckley, Dobson, Pearson, McKenzie, Goodlass

REFEREE: Clive Thomas (Glamorgan)

White Rose scattered on a Yorkshire field

GEOFFREY GREEN
The Times

25 April 1977 *Two of the outstanding football clubs of the present quarter century, Manchester United and Leeds, met to decide who would take the final step to Wembley for the final of the FA Cup. Geoffrey Green's style captures the occasion—particularly the discomfort and difficulty which the elements brought to the encounter.*

Neither strong winds, passing showers, scurrying clouds nor Leeds United could prevent Manchester United reaching Wembley for their second successive FA Cup final on Saturday with a 2–1 victory. The elements came hurtling over the Pennines; the flags of Hillsborough were stretched like fingerposts pointing the way to the future and it was Manchester who took the high road with two formidable blows by Jimmy Greenhoff and Coppell in the opening quarter of an hour to leave the White Rose scattered on a Yorkshire field.

Many had thought that the greater experience of Leeds and their midfield authority of Currie, Cherry and Frank Gray would control affairs. Events proved otherwise. They never really recovered from that crippling start. Cherry and the younger Gray were outmatched by the sharper instincts of the busy little Macari and McIlroy. Although Currie, showing many a glimpse of his refined quality, and Eddie Gray fought hard to inspire a recovery, Leeds froze as a side until a penalty by Clarke midway through the second half gave them a fighting glimpse of survival over a tingling last 20 minutes. It was then that the match suddenly hovered on a knife edge.

Victory, however, finally went to the right team. In spite of the difficult elements it was Manchester who played with a carefree air of enjoyment and the sense of balance added to the attack since last year by the arrival of the elder Greenhoff from Stoke. If the wind often blew moves off course nonetheless there were many smooth passages of triangular penetration involving Coppell, Pearson, J. Greenhoff and others which frequently had the Leeds defence on the wrong foot.

One of the keys was the freedom won by Coppell and the unpredictable Hill down the flanks, though the latter's lack of intelligence often wasted promising openings. Reaney and Hampton never truly mastered them, which brought an added responsibility and an unusual uncertainty to McQueen and Madeley in the middle. It was those two wingers who achieved the vital open sesame at the start.

After only seven minutes Coppell won a corner on the right, Hill curled a left foot inswinger which Houston back-headed, F. Gray miscued under pressure and quick as a blink Jimmy Greenhoff had hit the roof of Stewart's net. Hardly had Leeds recovered from this uppercut to the chin than J. Greenhoff, Hill and Pearson worked the left flank, Hill's shot rebounded (again from the luckless F. Gray) and there was Coppell to volley knee-high perfectly from some 15 yards to the far top corner.

There is seldom recovery from such a beginning, especially in a semi-final when fear stretches the nervous tension. Yet it was at this moment that Leeds missed a wide open chance that may have provided a key to rescue from a desperate plight. Within minutes E. Gray put Clarke clean through with a perfect pass, and only Stepney stood ahead. Nine times out of 10 Clarke would have accepted such a gift. But this was the tenth. Clark shot past the near post and when Currie and McQueen also fired wide at close range before half time Leeds clearly had wasted the help of the wind.

For Manchester it now seemed plain sailing with a full spinnaker. But with 20 minutes left an arguable penalty as Nicholl brought down Jordan offered Leeds a speck of light at the end of their tunnel. Even then Stepney almost saved Clarke's shot from the spot. But 2–1 instead of 2–0 was a different ball game. Currie, working like a beaver with persuasive footwork, and E. Gray just missed with rising 20-yard shots; Lorimer was thrown into attack in place of F. Gray from midfield and Leeds died bravely.

Manchester, however, the more articulate and creative side, rightly survived and might themselves have had a penalty near the end when Reaney floored Hill. So amid the triumphant roars of their Red Army – now well-disciplined for a change – they prepare to make amends for last year's disappointment against Southampton.

MANCHESTER UNITED: A. Stepney, J. Nicholl, S. Houston S. McIlroy, B. Greenhoff, M. Buchan, S. Coppell, J. Greenhoff, S. Pearson, L. Macari, G. Hill

LEEDS UNITED: D. Stewart, P. Reaney, P. Hampton, T. Cherry, G. McQueen, P. Madeley, F. Gray (sub. **P. Lorimer**), **A. Clarke, J. Jordan, F. Currie, E. Gray**

REFEREE: T. Reynolds (Wiltshire)

MAY

Dead-eye Dick

GARRETT COTTER
The Observer

Leeds 16 Widnes 7

8 May 1977 *The annual trek to Wembley by those northern folk who follow rugby league is less a mystery to the rest of us these days, with television serving large slices of the game from northern towns spread thick with the tones of Eddie Waring. If Widnes and Twickenham are still poles apart both live together happily; and this year only the experts were ruffled over the Rugby League Cup Final. Most of them got it wrong – but that was largely forgotten in a game of fast, exciting football.*

Leeds made fools of the tipsters by outplaying Widnes completely in a fast-flowing Rugby League Challenge Cup Final at Wembley yesterday. They trailed 5–7 at half time but shook off their inhibitions to dominate the second half. By full-time Widnes, who were making their third successive Wembley appearance, looked as groggy as a fairground fighter after 10 rounds with Muhammad Ali.

Leeds won with a mixture of flair and fortitude, holding out gamely against furious Widnes pressure in the first half. That they conceded only one try was proof of their guts and the strength of their tackling.

It was a splendid final, packed more open play than is usual under Wembley tensions. Some dubious tackling, mainly by Widnes, was the only blot on the match. Leeds played adventurously, constantly stretching Widnes with long passes from stand-off Holmes and using their barrel-chested forwards Pitchford and Cookson as human battering rams. Pitchford quickly won the crowd over with his rugged bursts, usually scattering two or three defenders before being stopped. He was awarded the Lance Todd Trophy, as the final's outstanding player, for his rumbustuous efforts.

Leeds, with things going right in the pack, were able to indulge their backs in the second half. Dick, a 19-year-old making his Wembley debut, showed not the slightest trace of nerves at scrum-half, even if Widnes's Bowden occasionally outwitted him round the scrums.

Widnes never looked like retrieving the match as the second half progressed. There were isolated flashes from Bowden, Aspey and Hughes but they never gave Leeds any serious problems. Leeds began well, with Dick kicking a penalty goal after only three minutes. Widnes, however, settled down steadily after the first shaky 10 minutes. Dutton kicked a penalty and Aspey, a well-built, fast centre, beat Hague cleverly and, with Murrell for once wrong-footed, raced to the post to score. Dutton's goal gave Widnes an ominous 7–2 lead.

Leeds somehow survived a series of fierce attacks before giving a hint of the danger they presented. Holmes kicked for the corner, the bounce beat Wright, and Atkinson, racing up from the left wing, leapt for the ball and rolled over to touch down in the corner. Dick's kick failed.

They regained the lead after 15 minutes of the second half. From a scrum Holmes's reverse passed to Dyl, coming on the burst, and the defence had no chance of stopping him as he tore away to the posts. Dick surprisingly missed the easy kick but compensated seven minutes later by nipping cheekily round a ruck of players to score after Holmes had been held on the line. This time he kicked the goal and Leeds were ahead comfortably 13–7. Dick rounded off a personally memorable match by dropping a goal and landing a 40-yard penalty. Not bad going for a teenager.

LEEDS: Murrell, A. Smith, Hague, Dyl, Atkinson, Holmes, Dick, Harrison, Ward (capt) **Pitchford, Eccles, Cookson, Fearnley,** (Subs. **D. Smith, Dickinson**)

WIDNES: Dutton, Wright, Aspey, Eckersley, O'Neill, Hughes, Bowden (capt), **Ramsey, Elwell, Mills, Dearden, Adams, Laughton,** (Sub. **Foran**)

REFEREE: V. Moss (Manchester)

The big bumper from down under

JOHN ARLOTT
The Guardian

10 May 1977 *The most significant sporting event of the year was the emergence of Kerry Packer's cricket circus. At a party in the Sussex home of Tony Greig at the beginning of May it first became known that the Australian television entrepreneur had a number of players under contract to form a 'World XI' versus an 'Australian XI' in a series of games over several seasons. In cutting across the traditional programme of the cricketing calendar Packer's scheme undermined the structure of the game. The wordage on this topic went on for miles, from the sports pages to the front page via the leader pages. Undoubtedly this was the most difficult area of choice for the editors of this book, and we have chosen this piece, by John Arlott: twenty-four hours after the announcement he was in no doubt of its importance, and his analysis puts the story in ideal perspective.*

The announcement of the formation of the freelance international cricket circus is the most historic event in the history of the modern game. The scope and the depth of the possible consequences are so immense that it is difficult to believe that those responsible, on both sides, have fully understood or considered them.

In short, 34 cricketers from five countries have signed contracts to play for a World XI in Australia during the next three Australian seasons. These contracts, it seems, have no escape clause; and the cricketers involved have already been paid advances.

Now there are two spheres of difference; the first between the star cricketers involved and their national and local authorities; the second between the top players and the rank and file professionals. There will be substantial differences in the situations in the five countries.

Fundamentally, though, the authorities will deny the right of any commercial undertaking to promote matches within their jurisdiction and of their players to take part in them. The TCCB fought this issue with the Bagenal Harvey organisation over the Rothman's Cavaliers and won, simply by undertaking to outlaw players or clubs who facilitated the appearance of the Cavaliers on television.

This is primarily an Australian commercial television operation which would presumably be extended to other countries if it proved successful here. The other four countries, however, will instantly be affected by the loss of their players in what is, for all of them except England, their domestic season.

The Australian Board of Control has always been notoriously inflexible in its handling of internal matters. It has resisted player power even to the extent, in 1912, of sending vastly weakened teams to England rather than yield to the cricketers' choice of tour manager.

The defection of the 13 who have already signed contracts would, of course, savagely reduce Australia's representative strength.

In strict practical terms, while the Board could no doubt prevent the mercenaries' matches being played on the major and normal Test grounds, the operation is intended for television and a large attendance is not at a pinch essential. If generous accommodation is wanted, some Australian Rules football grounds, if flooded and rolled would provide a hard fast surface. Alternatively, there are some mature wickets on grounds well appointed in all but their capacity for large crowds. If need be they could use synthetic pitches.

It is probably significant that Channel 9, which would show this cricket, outbid the official Australian Broadcasting Commission for this season's series in England. That has strengthened their position in some ways, especially since they have undertaken not to interrupt play with commercials; but it has not endeared them to officialdom.

In this country authority cannot tolerate a general situation in which it does not control the activities of its players; nor, particularly, one in which its reigning captain and two outstanding cricketers are not available for next winter's tour of Pakistan and New Zealand.

On the other side, the men in question probably feel that since three of the four have already had benefits (Greig is the exception), a three-year payment of £70,000 is enough to buy loyalty and compensate for a lifelong banishment from county cricket and official Test cricket which could produce £21,000 at most in the same period for three full 12-month rounds of labour.

England is for the moment the only country where the cricketers of the world can earn a professional living, albeit a meagre one by comparison with these terms.

For Pakistan the situation is doubly complicated. There the leading cricketers have recently come successfully out of a confrontation with authority. Yet they would be unlikely to find public support for playing in the same team as South Africans. In Pakistan, like India, the best cricket produces attendances of such size that they could afford to match the Australians in cash terms.

For South Africa this could prove a vast gain. They could hire the mercenaries to make good the lack of representative cricket caused by their apartheid policy to such an extent that they might find their recent relaxations unnecessary and reversible.

In the West Indies official indignation would be magnified by the fact that their representatives were playing with South Africans. By present standards that is sufficient to have the players concerned – and those from other countries who appear in the same side – banned from all play in the West Indies.

New Zealand is not yet involved, and is hardly likely to be to any important extent. They would lose few players in any case and, economically, the country is hardly within these entrepreneurs' sights.

The difference between the stars and the run-of-the-mill county professional can hardly be foreseen. Will the next echelon down feel that the defection of the upper crust will create opportunities for them to play Test cricket and, in due course, follow them on to the world television stage? Or will they, as they did on the issue of switching registrations, believe that some degree of loyalty is inherent in the game as they see it? This could prove a case similar to that in golf where the top tournament players have pulled financially clear of the club pro.

If this operation were completed the loss to county cricket

STINGER

5. *preceeding page:*
John Conteh, British world light-heavyweight champion, has U.S. challenger Len Hutchins on the ropes. Conte won by a knock-out in the third round

6. Cricket unlimited. Kerry Packer – Sportsman of the Year?

7. Centenary Test, Melbourn O'Keefe c. Brearley b. Underwood o. Knott, Chappell, umpire, Underwoc and Greig watch it happen.

8. *right* Return of the native. Geoffrey Boycott strikes Chappell for four runs in the Headingley Test. It was Boycott's hundredth hundred tailor-made for his home ground.

9. Beryl Cameron-Gibbons, gym-mistress and licensee of the Thomas à Beckett pub in the Old Kent Road. She's the only female boxing promoter in England.

10. Jack Nicklaus, the 'Golden Bear', lays a gentle hand on the shoulder of Tom Watson at Turnberry in the British Open. The two Americans left the rest of the field standing. Watson won, crushingly.

would not merely be that of the top few English players but of all the overseas players who have helped to lift the county standards. This would result in such a debasing of the county game that it might collapse altogether unless it were sustained by sponsors who could not tolerate competition from the freelances. That, however, would be improbable here. The TCCB could ensure that none of the major Test or county grounds was used. No others have remotely suitable facilities and conclusively no others could produce a pitch capable of sustaining a five-day match.

Two sets of laws apply in these matters. Those of the cricket authorities are binding only upon those who voluntarily accept them, as English county cricketers are now required to signify as a condition of the renewal of their contracts. If this dispute come to the kind of confrontation which seems certain – too many people have too much at stake to surrender – the legal systems of the countries concerned, all of which are based on the principle of equity, will be involved.

If the national authorities refused their players permission to play in these competitions at all – or in preference to official tours – would that constitute restraint of trade? If so, would all control of registration and availability be waived? In that case, would first-class cricket as it is known in England, Australia, the West Indies, India, Pakistan, New Zealand and, in normal conditions, South Africa, be destroyed? Certainly Terry Packer, the press and television magnate, who is the prime-mover in this matter, has no love of authority; he was refused television rights of Tests in Australia after making the highest bid.

This is for the moment purely an Australian operation conducted, undoubtedly, by Australian standards of behaviour, finance, and media management. The question of expansion into other countries has not yet been raised. For the moment England, probably, is the only other Test-playing country financially worth the promoters' powder and shot, though others could suffer through their activities.

It is hard to believe that commercial television here – which has not on the whole been sympathetic to cricket in the round – would allocate enough time, certainly not time comparable to that their Australian opposites want for cricket. The assumption must be that this is foreseen solely as an Australian buy.

The most bitter battle in cricket history is about to be waged. It is simply between the establishment and a form of private enterprise which if it succeeds by its own standards can only break down the traditional form of the game throughout the world.

The impact of the break of news has been such that within hours Bob Parrish, chairman of the Australian Board of Control, booked the first available flight to England. He was frustrated by an airport strike in Australia but he will be here as soon as maybe. Jack Bailey, secretary to the International Cricket Conference, has already hinted – with a speed of reaction hitherto unknown in the deliberations of that august body – that they may call an emergency meeting.

The course of the battle cannot be foreseen. Indeed, it may not be clear for a long time. Essentially it is a struggle between a deeply entrenched establishment and players who scent the kind of financial reward for their ability and crowd attraction that they and their predecessors have long been denied.

West Ham stay up

NORMAN FOX
The Times

West Ham Utd 4 Manchester Utd 2

17 May 1977 *Anyone with a friend or relative who supports West Ham had a miserable winter. From tension to despair to desperation – the West London club ranged through the gamut. Only as summer dawned did the nightmare end – and then with defeat of the club who were to win the FA Cup.*

West Ham United's long struggle with the trials of relegation were finally overcome at Upton Park last night when, in a stirring last match, they found the FA Cup finalists, Manchester United, much sterner opposition than they had expected. They are now safe for another season and, for the quality of their football, deservedly so. Now the axe hangs over Bristol City, Coventry City and Sunderland. One must join Tottenham Hotspur and Stoke City in relegation before the end of the week.

After confirmation on Saturday that Spurs were to be removed from the first division after 27 years, West Ham and, across town, Queen's Park Rangers, were playing not only for themselves but also to help save the face of London. West Ham's 19 years in the first division is a record bettered only by Everton, Arsenal and Spurs. By wide opinion they contribute too much of the attractive and precious aspects of the game to be lost from the division that sets the standards.

After threatening to rest several of his players to be sure of their fitness for Wembley on Saturday, Tommy Docherty, the Manchester United manager, changed his mind and opted for the full team except their goalkeeper, Stepney. Also, to their credit, United chose to play a committed game, heightening the excitement of the night and forcing West Ham to work for their gains and safety.

As if in reply to those who thought there would be a far-away glaze in their eyes, United stormed into the lead after only 25 seconds. They caught West Ham cold from the kick-off. When Pearson drove a pass out into the strong wind along the wing, Hill surprised Bonds by nipping inside him and shooting into the far corner with Day as dazzled as anyone.

How that goal dressed the game for the occasion! For a few minutes West Ham reeled under the surprise, their defence unsettled again when Pearson's diving header was tipped away by Day. Then Brooking, an evergreen in a threatening season, raised his team as he has so often before. He was totally involved across the whole panorama. He was less than a yard wide with a fierce shot that was the first sign that West Ham were not going to take their early setback without massive counter-action.

On the half hour, after much brilliant inspiration from Brooking, they equalized. Brooking's corner was unorthodox, merely a perfectly placed pass wide to the oncoming

Lampard who was all of 25 yards from goal when he shook the near post with a thundering shot. The ball was deflected behind Roche.

Approaching half time West Ham's first opportunity to get ahead was offered by the referee who decided that what seemed to be a slight touch on Brooking's heel by Macari was sufficient for a penalty. Perhaps it was justice when Pike raised the penalty far over the bar. Pike was not long in making his peace with his colleagues. After 52 minutes he slammed a fine shot past Roche and from then on West Ham had the measure of United.

Suddenly, the Manchester defence began to find the intensity of this revival too serious for them. On the hour, they left Robson free in their penalty area. He collected the ball from Taylor and drove in a good shot. It seemed that West Ham's problems were over but then Pearson silenced the crowd with a remarkable 25-yard volley brilliantly set up with a flicked pass by Macari.

Still more effort was needed to deflate this Manchester team who, allegedly, had little interest in the game, and it was provided, in particular, by Brooking and Robson. First Robson's splendid header was pushed over the bar by Roche and then, after 75 minutes, another corner from Brooking was met by Robson and Pearson almost together. Robson's header seemed to give the ball the greater momentum and so first division football remained at Upton Park.

WEST HAM UNITED: M. Day, W. Bonds, F. Lampard, G. Pike, T. Taylor, M. McGiven, J. Radford, B. Robson, A. Devonshire, T. Brooking, A. Taylor

MANCHESTER UNITED: P. Roche, J. Nicholl, A. Albiston, S. McIlroy, B. Greenhoff, M. Buchan, S. Coppell, J. Greenhoff (sub. **D. McCreery**), **S. Pearson, L. Macari, G. Hill**

REFEREE: G. Thomas (Treorchy)

A Richards' 100 before lunch

MICHAEL MELFORD
The Daily Telegraph

19 May 1977 *Summer for holidaymakers and cricketers seemed a long time coming (did it ever arrive?), but there were glorious days beneath skies of imperishable blue when one wondered what all the fuss had been about. On such a day Barry Richards, one of the most prolific and colourful batsmen on the English cricket stage, went to the Bournemouth wicket and smote Derbyshire's bowlers for a hundred runs before lunch. For Michael Melford it seemed the season had awoken.*

Suddenly, if belatedly, the season burst into full swing yesterday as Barry Richards scored a marvellous 100 before lunch at Bournemouth to launch a spirited day's cricket under a cloudless sky. Hampshire made 314 in exactly 100 overs, and Derbyshire, having bowled at a commendably risk rate, had 70 minutes' batting, in which they replied with 32 for no wicket.

No innings by Richards is commonplace but this, his 78th hundred, was a scintillating affair by any reckoning – 115 in 140 minutes of dazzling strokes played against good bowling on a pitch taking a little gentle spin. He was third out at 166, upon which Gilliat, in a characteristically suitable and robust innings, made 90 out of the next 129 to earn his side full batting points.

In 1976 Richards was out five times in five innings to Hendrick for a total of 28 runs, so that yesterday he was presented with something of a challenge, and he played Hendrick at first with care. Even so, when 13, he might have been caught off Hendrick as he glanced a ball to the right of backward short-leg. Cartwright had the ball in his hand, and lost it. The anguish of bowler and others at this mishap was agonising to see – not without reason.

Greenidge, a fierce, energetic contrast to the elegant Richards, made the early running before he touched a ball from Hendrick on to the stumps as he tried to force him off the back foot.

Miller started a long spell in the 10th over and was also played by Richards with much respect, during a period in which he had Turner LBW. But by now Richards had made all the reconnoissance he needed, and what followed was as near perfection as anyone present will have seen.

The bowling remained steady and accurate by most standards; the fielding was athletic and enthusiastic but to Richards's superb timing and easy destruction of anything which erred a fraction in length (and of plenty which did not err at all) there was no answer.

Having reached 50 in 90 minutes, he made his second 50, out of 67, effortlessly in the next 35 minutes. Even when he drove Swarbrook over mid-off for six he did not seem to be exerting himself. It was difficult to believe that anyone could have played better than he did in the hour before lunch. All that the bowlers could hope was that it was too good to last; and, sure enough in the second over after lunch, Richards drove over an off-break from Miller.

HAMPSHIRE: First Innings

C. G. Greenidge b Hendrick	22
B. A. Richards b Miller	115
D. R. Turner lbw b Miller	5
T. E. Jesty b Hendrick ...	28
*R. M. C. Gilliat c Tunnicliffe b Swarbrook	90
J. M. Rice c Miller b Barlow	15
N. G. Cowley c Graham-Brown b Barlow	4
M. N. S. Taylor run out ...	3
†G. R. Stephenson not out	13
A. M. E. Roberts c Tunnicliffe b Swarbrook	5
J. W. Southern run out ...	1
Extras (lb 5, nb 8).........	13
100 overs Total	**314**

Fall of wickets: 1–34, 2–65, 3–166, 4–180, 5–235, 6–248, 7–279, 8–295, 9–311

Bowling: Hendrick 21–5–49–2, Tunnicliffe 17–2–62–0, Barlow 13–1–49–2, Miller 28–7–83–2, Swarbrook 21–5–58–2

DERBYSHIRE: First Innings

A. Hill not out	11
J. G. Wright not out	10
Extras (lb 1)	2
25 overs Total 0 wkt	**32**

To bat: G. Miller, E. J. Barlow, A. J. Borrington, H. Cartwright, F. W. Swarbrook, J. G. Brown, †R. W. Taylor, C. J. Tunnicliffe, M. Hendrick

Bonus pts to date: Hants 4, Derby 4

Umpires: D. G. L. Evans & A. Jepson.

*Captain. †Wicketkeeper

Some tears for Liverpool

DAVID LACEY
The Guardian

Manchester Utd 2 Liverpool 1

23 May 1977 *Even with the growth of international competitions the FA Cup final remains one of the most important staging posts in the game—particularly for the football writers. Here David Lacey, whose football match reports, like those by most of the correspondents on the daily newspapers, are hastily written late at night, produces an excellent essay after the benefit of a day to mull the match over.*

The FA Cup went to Manchester United because for five minutes at the start of the second half the hustlers became the hustled. Having shaped the game to their satisfaction Liverpool made two mistakes and found that it had slipped irrevocably from their grasp. Liverpool's disappointment was heightened by the fact that in between United's two goals they scored with the best shot of the match from the best player of the match. Like Minnesota Fats they accepted defeat with weary good grace but without comprehending how or why they had been beaten.

The 1977 final met many of the demands made of it, not least in producing a sudden twist of plot at a time when those who had predicted a Liverpudlian victory were beginning to feel inwardly smug. Had the whole match adhered to the pattern of the first half the game would no doubt have been written off as just one more Wembley anti-climax. In fact the studious, unspectacular football of the opening 45 minutes turned out to be a perfect prologue.

The afternoon was not over-blessed with attacking skills in spite of the excellence of two of the goals. Those who had been looking forward to a broad canvas of movement were offered instead a series of contrasting sketches linked roughly to a central theme. Occasionally the play descended into the bathos which afflicts all British teams from time to time, with the ball punted aimlessly from one half to the other and back again, but there were enough strong individual performances to put the match back on course whenever it was in danger of becoming mediocre. It was not a classic Cup final along the lines of, say, 1948, but for interest and sportsmanship it compared well with most.

When the game ended the Liverpool players collapsed to their knees in the centre circle, small, white-shirted, square-shorted figures looking rather like the losers of the decisive heat in the egg-and-spoon race. They have won the prize that they were best equipped to win, the League Championship, but talk of them taking the FA Cup and European Cup as well tended to become more facile the farther one was from Anfield. Liverpool themselves never made overmuch of achieving the treble and while their captain, Emlyn Hughes, might be considered rash to have forecast that they would either win both cups or lose both he is quite likely to be proved correct.

Had Liverpool beaten Manchester United at Wembley then no doubt they would have fielded the same team against Borussia Moenchengladbach in Rome on Wednesday. Now their manager, Bob Paisley, has to look hard at Saturday's performance and decide whether he can risk replacing Johnson with Toshack and whether or not he can make better use of his substitutes given that UEFA allow him a choice of two from five on the bench. Hindsight makes every man an expert but it is true to say the first reaction on hearing that Fairclough was not in Liverpool's 12 for Wembley was one of disbelief. They were 2–1 down with 25 minutes to go when Callaghan replaced Johnson, Case moving up, but the effect of the change was merely to redistribute existing strengths rather than introduce a new and possibly crucial element into their attack.

Errors apart, one of the main reasons why Liverpool lost was that when, clearly, they were in control of the game between the penalty areas they did not have the sharpness and accuracy at the finish to disturb Buchan and Brian Greenhoff at the heart of the Manchester United defence. Case, the afternoon's outstanding player, Kennedy, who gave another thorough, phlegmatic performance, and the tidy, industrious McDermott dominated Macari, McIlroy and

Coppell for half the match only to be let down by weaknesses fore and, eventually, aft.

Liverpool's front three were disappointing for different reasons. Those who had noted, during a display of model aircraft before the game, that the victim of a mid-air collision sported Liverpool colours and fluttered to earth with a broken left wing nodded sagely when Heighway was tackled crudely amidships by Nicholl, the only bad foul of the match, and continued at reduced pace. Johnson, not a target player, languished dolefully in well-marked spaces and Keegan ended an ubiquitous week, in which his anxious features had peered out from newspapers, television, and advertisements for muscle-developers, by failing to make good use of those appearances that really matter, namely in front of his opponents' goal. To be fair, he was diligently covered throughout by Brian Greenhoff. Hamburg, new holders of the Cup Winners Cup, are the latest Continental club to show interest in signing Keegan.

Manchester United stepped out of character to win the FA Cup for the fourth time. They had been expected to go for victory on the wings and relieve the pressure on their defence by tying Liverpool up along the halfway line. Instead, though not entirely by choice, they were forced to contain their opponents deep in their own half and use the long ball in the hope that Jimmy Greenhoff and Pearson would be lucky with bounces and deflections. Buchan and Brian Greenhoff were always mindful of the way in which Southampton's winning goal had arrived in last year's final, an early through ball which caught the centre backs square, and only once did they get caught in a similar situation. That was in the first half when Case sent Keegan through, Albiston making an excellent covering tackle.

Albiston proved a sound substitute at left-back for the injured Houston, timing his interceptions well and reading the game intuitively. In attack, however, Houston's great shovelling left foot was missed and this had something to do with Hill's second indifferent final. Once again McCreery replaced him, this time to hold what United had won.

With Hill so ineffective and Macari, McIlroy and Coppell too busy in midfield to make runs for the byline Pearson and Jimmy Greenhoff had an enormous responsibility for taking the fleeting chances that might come their way. In the event they took the first and stood the game on its head. Five minutes after half-time Hughes headed firmly upfield and had the ball fallen to Case, McDermott or Kennedy no doubt Liverpool would have embarked on another controlled build-up. But Keegan met it with a vague deflection, McIlroy sent the ball back towards Greenhoff, Hughes, caught in two minds, made a half-challenge and was beaten in the air by Greenhoff, who nodded Pearson through.

Afterwards there were those who felt that, as England's goalkeeper, Clemence should not have been beaten by the near post, but this did little justice to the perfection of Pearson's shot which succeeded not only because it was low and straight but because he struck the ball as soon as it fell at his feet. Blaming Clemence was rather like asking why, from time to time, Hutton was beaten by Lindwall's yorker.

Liverpool had nearly scored at the end of the first half, Kennedy meeting a precise centre from Case by the far post only to see Stepney block the header with a foot. Two minutes after falling behind they drew level with a marvellous goal, Case bringing down Jones's cross, pivoting through 270 degrees, and walloping the ball past Stepney.

But Case had earned Liverpool a mere three minutes of hope. Macari beat a ponderous Hughes in the air, Smith was unlucky with the bounce and became entangled with Jimmy Greenhoff, allowing the ball to roll loose. Macari followed through with a shot that Clemence, mindful of the first goal, had covered but the ball struck Greenhoff and looped in over the goalkeeper's head. Poor Clemence could not bring himself to join in Liverpool's losers' lap of honour and trotted off quietly to the dressing room; his chagrin was understandable in a way although it would not be an exaggeration to say that Liverpool would never have retained the League title without his consistency in goal.

Afterwards, while the uninhibited glee of Tommy Docherty, a winner at last, was infectious, sympathy for Liverpool was widespread and they may well need more in Rome. For if Saturday's game was about differing shades of basically the same style the European Cup final should see a stark contrast in footballing concepts. Quite apart from anything else, Borussia Moenchengladbach, having just retained the West German championship by drawing 2–2 with Bayern Munich, are likely to be in a more ebullient mood than opponents who must be feeling very tired just now.

LIVERPOOL: Clemence, Neal, Jones, Smith, Kennedy, Hughes, Keegan, Case, Heighway, Johnson (Callaghan, 64 min.) McDermott

MANCHESTER UNITED: Stepney, Nicholl, Albiston, McIlroy, B. Greenhoff, Buchan, Coppell, J. Greenhoff, Pearson, Macari, Hill, (McCreery, 82 min.)

REFEREE: R. Matthewson (Bolton)

A night of triumph

DONALD SAUNDERS
The Daily Telegraph

Liverpool 3 Borussia Moenchengladbach 1

26 May 1977 *A week after Liverpool had walked, dejected and defeated, down the tunnel back to their Wembley dressing room the Olympic Stadium in Rome saw them elated as they joined Manchester United as the only English winners of the European Cup.*

Liverpool's 13 consecutive seasons of campaigning in European competitions reached a memorable climax at the Olympic Stadium in Rome last night, when they won the major trophy, the European Cup, with one of the most distinguished performances of their long history. The League champions put last Saturday's Wembley disappointment firmly behind them and swept Borussia Moenchengladbach to decisive defeat with the smoothly skilled, intelligent football we had come to believe was now a continental monopoly.

Only for 10 anxious minutes after the interval did they falter en route to a triumph that lists them alongside Manchester United as the only English winners of the trophy. And, appropriately, Tommy Smith, making his farewell appearance for the club, came to their rescue when the danger of undeserved defeat was at its height.

Smith, due to retire at the end of this season and brought back into the team only a couple of months ago, when Phil Thompson was injured, restored Liverpool's lead with a superb header in the 65th minute. He could scarcely have better timed the last and most important goal of his career. It put Liverpool back in control of their nerves, and of the match, so that Neal's penalty, seven minutes from time, was only added insurance against failure.

When it was all over Hughes led his men on the lap of honour they so richly deserved, and made sure that those faithful thousands who had made the long journey from England had every opportunity to see the gleaming trophy that has been the club's objective for so long.

When Liverpool had walked dejected off the pitch at Wembley last weekend, even some of their most ardent supporters must have wondered whether Bob Paisley could lift them back off the floor in time to cope with the German champions. We knew within a quarter of an hour that he had done so. With Case, Kennedy, Callaghan and in particular McDermott using the ball skilfully and running intelligently into space, Liverpool soon commanded midfield.

Though Vogts marked Keegan so closely that they might almost have been wearing the same pair of boots, Liverpool's front line looked much sharper than at Wembley. Indeed, the game flowed one way – towards Borussia's goal and their supporters. True, Bonhof occasionally moved forward to start a counter-attack, Simonsen attempted an occasional raid, and Steilike sometimes indicated what a gifted player he can be.

But, though Borussia replacing the experienced Wimmer with Kulik after only 25 minutes, Liverpool were so completely on top that no-one could have been really surprised when they took the lead. Callaghan instigated the move by dispossessing Bonhof before passing inside to Heighway. As the Germans hurriedly retreated McDermott spotted a gap, raced through it on to Heighway's perfectly timed pass and hit the ball hard and low into the far corner of the net.

Liverpool then began to play at a measured pace, obviously intending to conserve their energy on this warm, stamina-sapping night. Alas, they allowed their calmness to lapse into carelessness in the 51st minute – and were savagely punished. Case's misdirected pass was pounced on by the eager Simonsen, who sped into the penalty box and beat Clemence with a fierce shot.

I have little doubt that Liverpool must have feared, then, that the fate they had suffered round about the same period of the FA Cup final was about to overtake them again. For 10 minutes their composure was shattered as Borussia, sensing that they could steal victory, pushed forward with skill and eagerness in an effort to score again. But just when it seemed Liverpool might stumble to a defeat that had seemed unthinkable at half-time Smith rose nobly to the occasion. Heighway drove a corner kick firmly into the penalty box and Smith jumped no more than a foot off the ground to head forcefully into the net.

We all knew then that Liverpool would achieve the unique English double of League championship and European Cup. Though Borussia sent on Hannes for Wohlers in the 81st minute, they could scarcely have expected to catch Liverpool napping a second time. In fact, it was the Germans who were surprised – in the 83rd minute. Keegan, who had reproduced, on this occasion, the skill and eagerness that his game has recently lacked, dribbled round Vogts and was sent sprawling in the box by the veteran World Cup player. Robert Wuertz, the French referee, rightly pointed to the spot, and young Neal calmly placed his penalty in the net to make absolutely certain that justice was seen to be done.

LIVERPOOL: Clemence, Neal, Jones, Smith, Kennedy, Hughes, Keegan, Case, Heighway, Callaghan, McDermott

BORUSSIA M. G.: Kneib, Vogts, Klinkhammer, Wittkamp, Bonhof, Wohlers (sub. Hannes, 81 mins), Simonsen, Wimmer (sub. Kulik, 25 mins), Stielike, Schaffer, Heynckes

What price loyalty now?

TONY LEWIS
The Sunday Telegraph

29 May 1977 *Freedom of choice is carefully guarded in most British institutions. Within professional sport players are under contract to a club or team according to the rules of the governing body. Tony Lewis, former Glamorgan and England captain, here joins those incensed by the decision of the Cricket Council to overrule a decision preventing Imran Khan from moving from Worcestershire to Sussex.*

In the matter of Imran Khan's registration for Sussex, the Cricket Council this week overruled the decision of the Test and County Cricket Board Registration sub-committee which had resolved that Imran should wait 12 months before qualifying. The appeal to the Council's sub-committee, chaired by Oliver Popplewell, QC, brought clemency and Imran's move from Worcestershire to Sussex will now be completely with a special registration on 31 July.

Nothing has incensed the cricket fraternity more. The majority of players and administrators in the first class game believe the Council's decision is a disaster which can only impose harm on the game.

I say 'impose' because the TCCB's Committee, composed of County representatives, and including Jack Bannister, the Players' Association secretary, was unanimous in rejecting the Sussex case and Imran's testimony that life with Worcestershire was intolerable. There was not even a member of the Registration Committee invited to put their thinking to the Cricket Council's meeting. The case was simply freshly tried by new men.

So disgusted are some cricketers that three counties have already asked their committees if they can blackball Sussex by refusing to play against them. This is angry and unprecedented. Indeed, Sussex's refusal to discipline Snow last season when requested to do so by the TCCB, and the fact that Tony Greig is never far away from these disturbances, hardly leads one to think of Sussex as loyal members of the first class Board.

Or, are they the brave innovators? Could it be that cricketers selling their wares in an open market will help the game prosper? It was often maintained by Leslie Deakins, the former secretary of Warwickshire, that all registration rules should be abandoned and contracts should be negotiated by individual players. In that sort of system a form of financial compensation would then be paid to a county who had invested money over the years in developing a particular player who was about to leave them.

Down in Glamorgan, Wilfred Wooller, secretary and former captain, has no doubt about the evil committed.

Yesterday he resigned from the registration sub-committee with these words: 'It has become a toothless bulldog. This is a very bad decision for cricket made by a Cricket Council which does not and never has fully realised the requirements of the first class game.'

Worcestershire got Imran Khan started. The Royal Grammar School found him a place and after getting his A levels he went on to Oxford University, playing under a student's temporary special registration. After Oxford, many held the view that Worcestershire could not engage him because they would exceed their quota of overseas players by doing so. Worcestershire argued successfully that Imran had been virtually offered professional employment from schooldays and that the old qualifying period, five years rather than the newly introduced ten, applied in his case.

Imran has claimed to be unhappy in Worcestershire, without friends and lacking the environment in which he could happily play his cricket. He insists that money is nothing to do with it. Worcestershire offered to let him live in Oxford, Birmingham or where-ever.

The TCCB registration rules are not as restrictive as one might believe. They used to be. I myself sat on the committee when Barry Knight's was such an important test case. His move from Essex to Leicestershire incurred a two year penalty but, having proved restraint of trade, he was allowed to continue his career after one year only.

Mike Denness's case was clear-cut. Kent simply did not wish to retain his services. Bob Willis had a genuine salary grievance when he left Surry. Roy Virgin's relationship with

Somerset had totally broken down as had Bob Cottam's with Hampshire. All got their transfers within reasonable time.

The Registration Committee found Worcestershire all but blameless and Imran's reasoning not strong enough. So the reversal by the Cricket Council has left both the Players' Association and the counties upset.

It has cheapened club loyalty, diluted county identity and created a money market with all the attendant unpleasantness. Oliver Popplewell's men, which amazingly include David Brown, the Warwickshire captain, Cecil Paris and Jack Davies, have not only opened the door; they have blown it right off.

How will counties now set about developing young players? Is it worth the investment? Players can be lured away at the drop of a fiver – appealing to the Cricket Council perhaps that the local dentist does not suit them.

How will locally born and bred players see the decision? Is a steady professional career worth pursuing while the brighter lights flit club to club?

The Board has been careful not to take an entrenched position over many recent problems. Clearly they realise that the game develops all the time and always reflects our society. However, the hacking away of traditions makes no sense when the game is not improved.

Those in the game respect and live by the registration laws which they have devised. The Cricket Council has virtually told them that registration is rubbish. And that is hard to bear.

How to catch a shark

DEREK FLETCHER
The Sunday Telegraph

29 May 1977 *Angling can be quiet, leisurely—and damp. But those who go to sea to catch their fish can have more exciting adventures—as the sight of sharks reminded Derek Fletcher.*

The sharks are around early this year. Standing on a south

coast cliff-top recently I watched the surface of the water boil with mackerel, racing for their life chased by two threshers. The sharks leapt out of the water well ahead, then turned around and went straight into the shoal of mackerel, stunning them with their strong, massive tails. One wide swipe will stun or kill up to 100 mackerel, and all that remains is for the sharks to have a good meal.

Mackerel is an excellent bait for most varieties of shark. Four porbeagles recently landed in Cornish waters by anglers out from Padstow were lured by mackerel. Heaviest of the four weighed 375lb. and gave Michael Adams aching arms for almost an hour. It was quite a feat on a glass rod and wire trace.

There are many anglers who still believe threshers cannot be caught on rod and line, but this is an old wives' tale. One reads in old angling books they cannot be caught, and this is unfortunately believed. But you have to be pretty muscular to tame one. That great tail smashes all in its path, and that's why good strong tackle must be used. If it gets a chance it will slice through the strongest line.

One thresher I hooked, nearly 116lb., simply pulled my 25ft. boat along, and for a time it was in complete control. I could see the tail ripping through the water, but to try and stop it would mean disaster. In this situation one can only wait until it runs out of strength. If it feels resistance on the line it will only gain extra speed, while if it feels nothing is pulling it back it will eventually quieten.

You'll have to take my word for this, for at the time of the battle it seemed this could never happen. My boat was quite out of control, and at one stage was almost spinning round. Last year there were more threshers caught by anglers than any season I can remember, because there were more about during that long, hot summer.

Temperatures definitely make a difference to them coming within range of the angler. Some shark come very close inshore. I've seen bathers running inshore after seeing a shadowy 'jaws' come in amongst them.

Sometimes they are caught from deep water beaches. I know of one porbeagle caught from Chesil Beach by a Weymouth Angling Society member. He was after tope at the time, and his rod was nearly ripped from his hands.

JUNE

Wales find what England seek

NORMAN FOX
The Times

England 0 Wales 1

1 June 1977 *Wales's first victory over England at Wembley emphasised the problems still surrounding English football. The game was decided on a penalty goal, but that took away none of the worth of the Welsh victory.*

Wales, the emerging power among the home countries, last night beat England for the first time at Wembley. Their football contained almost everything that England still vainly seek, especially familiarity within their teamwork.

Don Revie, the manager, hoped this England side would form the basis of the team to play in the crucial World Cup match against Italy next November, against Scotland on Saturday and three South American countries on the forthcoming tour. It may still have to be because there is no time left for further experimentation, but there can now be no optimism on their behalf.

Wales, it had been suggested, would defend solidly enough to provide England with more practice in the trying art of piercing a wide, solid wall and, indeed, the Welsh did withdraw under the initial signs of pressure. Yet, after they had looked after themselves in this fashion for the first half an hour or so, they outstripped England in the alternative art of creating opportunities.

They made much the more positive contribution to a game that spent too long in a low key. Much as England's reunited forward line of Channon, Pearson and Keegan began by showing marginally more liaison than recent alignments, their penetration was always poor.

The only England player to approach what Mr Revie said he demanded, 'club form,' was Brooking, who was more comfortable in the centre of midfield, moving out towards the wings. It was surprising, therefore, that he was substituted during the second half. He was the only player to make inroads behind the Welsh defence, although nothing came of his invention deep in midfield or when he went ahead.

Wales were the first to bring a competitive feeling, albeit unfairly, when Yorath slid into Greenhoff and had his name taken. At least that showed that there was some fire in the Welsh team and, as was expected, James was the cause of England's worst embarrassment. His head down, determindedly carrying the ball along the wing, he was a constant threat. Sayer frequently moved into unmarked positions to increase England's troubles in defence.

The first time Sayer came to notice was when he whipped the ball off Hughes's feet just outside the penalty area, and although that movement came to nothing the hint was dropped.

Three times before they finally scored in the last seconds of the half, the Welsh emphasized the inadequacy of England's central defensive covering. Another fast, direct approach by James and a good centre arrived at the feet of Sayer well before he had been spotted, but Mills moved quickly to stifle the shot. Evans headed narrowly over the bar, and the Welsh kept pressing forward until Deacy was offered the ball 10 yards out and totally unmarked. Perhaps disturbed by so much freedom he fumbled his shot and Wales obtained the lead they deserved by means of a penalty.

Not that this method was an unsatisfactory means of emphasizing the uncertainties in the English defence. A forward pass from Yorath should have been intercepted by Hughes in the penalty area, but he seemed to think Shilton might come out and clear the ball. In the moment of uncertainty James rushed in, gained control but was bundled down by Shilton.

The penalty was inevitable and James put it away without difficulty. Only now, when under threat, did England enliven their game with some fresh spirit. Keegan began to win the ball and headed narrowly wide from Kennedy's centre, and Pearson broke free more frequently.

Their escape from a worrying defeat seemed certain when Brooking offered Pearson another chance on the left of the penalty area. Davies tore out to intercept and Pearson cartwheeled in the air. It was impossible to know whether the impetus was his own or Davies's contact. The referee decided there was no offence and England were left to languish in their problems.

Several of their desperate attacks over the final 15 minutes could have saved their faces, but Davies foiled Channon at the last second of a fine, swerving run and was alert to all other dangers. One was left feeling satisfied with the continuing progress of the Welsh and again dissatisfied with the entire England performance. In one week from now they play Brazil in Rio. The thought is almost frightening.

ENGLAND: P. Shilton (Stoke City), **P. Neal** (Liverpool), **M. Mills** (Ipswich Town), **B. Greenhoff** (Manchester United), **D. Watson** (Manchester City), **E. Hughes** (Liverpool), **K. Keegan** (Liverpool), **M. Channon** (Southampton), **S. Pearson** (Manchester United), **T. Brooking** (West Ham United), sub. **D. Tueart** (Manchester City), **R. Kennedy** (Liverpool)

WALES: D. Davies (Everton), **R. Thomas** (Derby County), **J. Jones** (Liverpool), **J. Mahoney** (Stoke City), **L. Phillips** (Aston Villa), sub. **D. Roberts** (Hull City), **I. Evans** (Crystal Palace), **P. Sayer** (Cardiff City), **B. Flynn** (Burnley), **T. Yorath** (Coventry City), **N. Deacy** (PSV Eindhoven), **L. James** (Derby County)

REFEREE: J. R. Gordon (Newport-on-Tay)

Epsom hails the Maestro

MICHAEL PHILLIPS

The Times

2 June 1977 *In his preview of the previous day Michael Phillips forecast the Minstrel's Derby victory in his first sentence. We could look no further than the following day's Times to read not only about the victory but to discover something more about the horse and the men behind it.*

By winning the Derby on The Minstrel at Epsom Lester Piggott demonstrated yet again why there has always been such a clamour for his services on this particular occasion. He is a law unto himself there. And it is as simple as that.

Yesterday we were witnesses to another show of pure Piggott magic. Before yesterday he had won the Derby seven times. Some of these victories were easy, some difficult, but none more difficult than this instance, when he rode like a man inspired. But, before I get completely carried away in my unstinted praise of his jockeyship, first a word about The Minstrel and his trainer, Vincent O'Brien.

I wrote yesterday that not even Piggott, who had won more Derbies than anyone else in the history of the race, is able to win without the horse. So all credit to The Minstrel and his trainer. The Minstrel had been called every name under the sun simply because he was born with a lot of white about him, and he has tended to hang under pressure in some of his previous races. But no horse could have run his heart out in a gamer fashion than he did yesterday, and no horse was better turned out looking fitter or better in the paddock beforehand. After hard races in both the 2000 Guineas at Newmarket and the Irish 2000 Guineas on the Curragh The Minstrel appeared looking just as much a credit to himself and his constitution, which can only be made of iron, as he was to his trainer, whose fifth winner of the Derby he was.

As far as the Derby is concerned, Larkspur started the ball rolling for O'Brien in 1962. Then followed Sir Ivor, Nijinsky and Roberto. Now it was the turn of The Minstrel to take the spoils back to that little town of Cashel in Co Tipperary again. Being by Northern Dancer and out of Fleur, The Minstrel is very closely related to Nijinsky, though two more different looking relations it would be hard to imagine. Whereas Nijinsky was a big, rangy bay with a look of eagles about him, The Minstrel is a short, stocky chestnut with four white stockings, and a big white blaze down his face.

Some – and there are many – will fight shy about buying a horse with so much white about him, but it did not stop Robert Sangster, his partner in this instance Simon Fraser, and O'Brien instructing Tom Cooper, the managing director of the Irish offshoot of the British Bloodstock Agency to pay $200,000 for The Minstrel when he was sold at Keenland in Kentucky at those famous sales of yearlings. By European standards, especially with the way that the pound has fallen against the dollar, that was a tall price to pay for an unproven horse, even allowing for his fine pedigree. Now they have seen their investment pay dividends, and I am particularly delighted for Mr Sangster, who has spent a small – some might say not so small – fortune on race horses in the past few years. Racing the world over would be the poorer without his ilk. Last week I wrote that Mr Sangster and his partners turned down a bid of £1m for The Minstrel in the hope that he would win the Derby, and how they have been vindicated.

Mr Sangster said yesterday that he refused that offer which was made by a group of breeders in Kentucky, primarily because he considered that The Minstrel was 'a gutsy horse,' as he put it, and precisely the sort that he and we ought to be patronizing in Europe. By beating Hot Grove by a neck yesterday The Minstrel certainly showed himself to be a supremely courageous horse. Had there been the slightest question-mark about his temperament he would never have managed to collar Hot Grove and William Carson, who were in full cry all the way up the straight.

In the heat of the moment after their unforgettable triumph neither O'Brien nor Sangster could come up with any hard and fast plan for The Minstrel, other than to say that he might well be back for the King George VI and Queen Elizabeth Diamond Stakes at Ascot in July; that he could well stay in training as a four-year old, and that there was certainly a place for him already at Coolmore, the stud they own in Ireland not many miles from where he is trained. O'Brien's own hopes of bringing off a grand slam of Derbies this year with Artaius, who will also be ridden by Piggott in the French Derby at Chantilly on Sunday, and with Alleged, who is being kept on ice for the Irish Derby later this month.

Yesterday's epic is relatively easily told. Baudelaire led early on from Milliondollarman, Mr Music Man and Valinsky, but by the time they had reached the top of the hill where there are seven furlongs left, the pace, which varied and resulted in only a moderate time of 2 min 36.34 sec, was being dictated by Milliondollarman with Baudelaire, Caporello, and Lucky Sovereign in close attendance.

Running down the hill towards Tattenham Corner, Piggott looked to his left, saw Blushing Groom in a spot of bother – the favourite returned to the unsaddling enclosure with three cuts, albeit only superficial ones on his near hind leg, having been struck into during that little bit of scrimmaging – and decided to improve his own position on the outside. At much the same time, Carson moved Hot Grove up into his challenging position nearer the rails.

Turning into the straight Milliondollarman was still in command, but by this time it was really only on sufferance. By now both Hot Grove and The Minstrel were right behind him and poised to strike. Just as soon as they were balanced and in line for home, Carson set sail on Hot Grove, and he had a fair wind behind him. For a second or so I thought that his dramatic break for glory would succeed and so I know did Piggott, who thought for a second: 'Hell, I've chosen the wrong one.'

Piggott had won the Chester Vase over the Derby distance on Hot Grove, yet still he discarded him in favour of The Minstrel, even though the latter had given no concrete proof that he would stay a mile and a half. That says something for Piggott's judgment. Yesterday Piggott never let Carson and Hot Grove out of his sights for a second and the longer that the race went on the more his eighth Derby win which began as only a dream became a reality.

Piggott's great strength towards the end finally clinched the issue, but never forget that much maligned little chestnut with four white stockings who carried him. In saying that Piggott's strength carried the day, I mean no ill towards Carson, who did all he could on a horse who certainly did likewise. On the day, they were simply beaten by a better pairing, albeit by only a neck.

Blushing Groom eventually finished five lengths behind them in third place. His jockey, Henri Samani, rode a good race, although I happen to think that he was slightly outmanoeuvred by Piggott at the top of the hill.

Samani said later that the distance was simply a shade too far for Blushing Groom. Without wishing to be wise after the event, this was always on the cards in view of the fact that he is by Red God, whose influence throughout racing has always been one of speed. Some got carried away by the reported brilliance of his gallop over a mile and a quarter at Chantilly, but there is a world of difference between a gallop over that distance and the Derby.

Samani took his defeat philosophically yesterday and the owner, the Aga Khan, took it with grace. He told me subsequently that he was thrilled simply to see his horse run well, and that he would have been disappointed only if Blushing Groom had run badly. Blushing Groom is unquestionably a very fine miler, and he may well win the best races that are run over a mile and a quarter. What his owner wants now is time in which to sit and ponder his future, knowing that he has already syndicated him for $6,400,000, which, when you come to think of it, cannot be bad business.

Monseigneur, Lordedaw, Nebbiolo, Pampapaul, and Milliondollarman were the next to follow the placed horses over the line, which does not speak volumes for the three-year-old colts currently in training in this country. English stables had to be content with second and eighth places.

The only blot on yesterday's race as far as I know was the misfortune which befell Night Before while the race was still in its infancy. After going about a furlong and a half, Night Before broke a blood vessel in his lungs or thereabouts so badly that the champion jockey Patrick Eddery had no option but to pull him up. In the circumstances it must be odds against him ever racing again.

Piggott and Mr Sangster are now in with a chance of bringing off the classic Epsom double with Durtal, who is even more firmly entrenched as favourite for the Oaks, which will be run on Saturday. But Durtal is trained by Barry Hills at Lambourn and not by Vincent O'Brien in Ireland, not that that will affect her chance.

Ladbroke's man on the spot told me yesterday that they are currently standing a number of huge doubles, The Minstrel to win the Derby, Durtal to win the Oaks. Not surprisingly, they have shortened Durtal's price for the Oaks to 9–4. Their other odds are 6–1 Triple First, 10–1 Anya Ylina, 11–1 Jalapa, Mrs McArdy and Dunfermline.

The man who knocked down Ali

DUDLEY DOUST
The Sunday Times

5 June 1977 *From a heavyweight champion Henry Cooper has moved on to become a British institution—he still gets the biggest cheer of the night when the MC introduces him from the ring at Wembley. Here Dudley Doust discovers what life is like six years after the champion had his last fight.*

In his fighting days Henry Cooper used to struggle out of bed at 3.45 in the morning and jog through the dawn, but now, aged 43 and retired from the ring, he sleeps till a reasonable hour. At his home in Hendon, North London, one morning last week, he got up at 7.30, had tea, toast and orange juice, drove his two young sons to school and returned to look at his post. It included nine fan letters – about average for the day – all of which he will answer with an autographed photograph. 'I got one of them signature stamps,' he said, 'but people like you to sign your autographs by hand.'

Cooper, six years an ex-boxer, is a modest man, and finds it hard to explain his enduring popularity as probably the most beloved British sports figure since the war. 'The public either takes to a person or they don't and, thank God, they took to me,' he said. 'I don't know why, perhaps it was because if I had a bad fight I used to admit I stunk the joint out. If you put on airs and graces you'll come unstuck. I once seen a footballer, I won't name him, who told a little kid to f—— off. Blimey, that geezer not only lost a fan but, by the time the story got around, I bet he lost a *neighbourhood* of fans.'

Over the next couple of days Henry Cooper, OBE, will visit several children's Jubilee parties. That is nicely appropriate, because this year Cooper himself celebrated his own sort of Silver Jubilee. In 1952 he won his first boxing title, the Amateur Boxing Association's light-heavyweight crown. 'I beat Joe Maclean, a big raw Scots guy, in the final,' he recalled. 'He didn't have a lot of finesse, and I knew I could beat him. I stayed clear, and knocked him silly with the old trombone left hand – boom, boom, boom.'

Cooper smiled. He drove his blue Opel towards Central London. He was dressed impeccably in a blue check suit, a regally red-white-and-blue tie, a small gold watch and black Italian shoes. The air tingled with the smell of men's cologne. At 14st. 5lb. about 11 pounds more than he weighed in 1975, when he fought his last fight (against Joe Bugner). 'I'm a burner. I can eat and drink what I like, and burn it all up. When I was in training it used to come off too quickly. The only trouble I had was building myself up.'

The second knuckle of his right hand bulges as big as a walnut. 'Cracked it as an amateur when it 'it Joe Erskine on the top of the 'ead. When I had tape round it people used to think I had something under me glove and I said, "No, it's me knuckle." '

At the traffic lights a motorist gazed over, nudged his wife. Those famous craggy eyebrows, a legacy of his raw-boned mother, also showed signs of countless amateur and 55 professional fights, despite the efforts of his peerless 'cut man' Danny Holland. 'Blimey, the advice we used to get about them scar tissues! Take a jar of pickled onions, take the onions out, and use the vinegar. Piddle in a bottle, let it cool down and use your own urine. All sorts of herbs. Crank tips – but people meant well.'

We were on our way to a cosmetic trade show at the Royal Lancaster Hotel and, providentially, a billboard appeared at Swiss Cottage. It depicted Henry Cooper and Barry Sheene, the motorcycle star, plugging a men's cologne. 'I used to use a cheap spirit-rub to tone myself up, and close up the pores after a fight,' said Cooper. 'So these cologne people, who was looking for a guy who could be stripped to the waist, legitimate, got on to me. Pretty soon they put me in a bathroom, and I'm splashing the stuff all about and telling people how good it is.' Cooper laughed. 'Gradually they got me out of the bathroom.' He now does commercials on location with Sheene, the showjumper Harvey Smith, the runner David Hemery.

Cooper spent an hour at the trade show, meeting and greeting, signing autographs, showing an amazing interest in a new line of men's lotions.

Cooper is a regular BBC fight commentator and sports-quiz panellist, a Lloyd's underwriter, a director of an insurance brokerage firm, an indefatigable fete-opener, but Fabergé takes the lion's share of his time. 'Since we've had Henry, things have been lovely,' says a company official. 'He's the man who knocked Ali on the seat of his pants.'

That fabled blow, a left hook, is the high point of post-war British boxing. It came on 18 June, 1963, in the fourth round at Wembley. In his autobiography, *The Greatest,* Ali claims he was distracted at that instant by Elizabeth Taylor screaming at the ringside. Down, Ali was saved by the bell at the count of four. 'Back in my corner, Angelo (Dundee, his trainer) discovered that the seam of my boxing glove was busted,' writes Ali. 'The cushion was coming out, and the rules and regulations in boxing are strict – the gloves must be in good condition. It took nearly a minute to make the replacement.'

That minute, in Cooper's view, was the crucial minute of the fight. 'It gave Ali another minute to recover which, to a hurt fighter, is a lifetime,' he said, flexing his fist on the steering wheel.

Cooper shrugged. 'In our second fight, at Arsenal Stadium in 1966, Ali had learned so much off the first fight that when I got him close, to go to work on him, oh boy, it was like being in a vice. The first three rounds I was falling just short with my left and, in the last rounds, when I was beginning to get the distance, my bleedin' eye slit open. The referee had to stop the fight in the sixth. So what can you do? It was a physical thing, the way I was made. If I had had negroid features, all round and smooth, maybe I'd have been the champion.'

Mild, gentle and likeable outside the ring, Cooper was known to be hard on his sparring partners, vicious in battle. He agrees. 'The real thrill in boxing is when you hit the other geezer on the whiskers and you see that look in his eyes, that blank, dead look. Some people say, "Watch the legs, the knees." That's rubbish. The eyes tell you everything and in a split second you know he's gone and he'll never get up, and it's marvellous.'

We were driving to Ealing Golf Club, Cooper's club, and the only sports moment he could compare to a knock-out blow, at least for pure exhilaration, was to hit a drive 'right out of the screws'. And 280 yards. He plays to a handicap of 12, and like most left-handers, probably *all* left-handed boxers, he plays a big, roundhouse slice. He duck-hooked one that day, snatched at it, when a passing schoolboy shouted while he was on his backswing.

'He put me off, yeah, but not for the rest of the day,' he said. 'I've always said that there was more tension in boxing than in golf because golfers bring it on themselves. After all, that golf ball is never coming up and belting you in the whiskers, is it?'

There was no arguing and, besides, we had a billboard to find for the photographers. Cooper, helpful as ever, endured the afternoon and returned home for tea. His wife, Italian-born Albina, fixed him a plate of prosciutto and a glass of red wine, and then he collected the boys, Henry Marco, aged 14 and John Pietro, nine, from school. Cooper returned for more Fabergé meeting and greeting in the evening before dining at home with his wife on grilled sole and a green salad. 'I look back at me life and I always say whatever I done I would do it again,' said Henry Cooper, a contented man. 'I don't think I made any big mistakes. I think we done it right.'

The fatal left hook

SRIKUMAR SEN

The Times

15 June 1977 *Another British boxing bubble bursts. Dave Green, who has earned more in a dozen fights than from a lifetime picking carrots in East Anglia, his other job, on his way to becoming British champion, finds that his earnest but crude approach to boxing is lost against the skills of a man like Carlos Palomino.*

Carlos Palomino, of the United States, retained the world welterweight championship at the Empire Pool, Wembley, last night, when he knocked out the British challenger, Dave 'Boy' Green, of Chatteris, Cambridgeshire, in 2min. 5sec. of the eleventh round, just when the East Anglian was beginning to find his feet. The blow was the shortest left hook I have ever seen, but it whipped in like the east wind under the door. Green was out cold, flat on his back, for a good minute, and for a while his handlers began to get worried as to why he was not coming round. To save further embarrassment he was eventually dragged glassy-eyed to his corner, where he came too quickly.

To the roar of a packed Wembley, 3000 East Anglians among them, The Fen Tiger recovered gradually from a slow start. By the ninth round he was on top, just, but Green seemed to think he had the contest in his pocket and began to come in swinging, his face sticking out before him, almost arrogantly.

This was his crucial mistake. He seemed to have forgotten that through the past eight rounds he had been up against a master of the hook. Time and time again throughout the bout Green was caught by the Mexican-American's left hook to the body, just as John Stracey, his predecessor, had been. Neither Green nor his corner saw what would happen if he continued to rush into a craftsman who had reached his optimum range with that blow.

Green took some early punishment when he tried to pace himself, and while he was concentrating on that the Mexican was scoring with body blows and moving ahead. Palomino did not allow Green to swing in. He kept close to the challenger and scored away. Green was more aggressive in the second round and did rather better when he was himself, but every now and then he started to box and that did not prove satisfactory as his left lead carried little power. Palomino still uppercut and hooked at close quarters, although Green was not particularly bothered by those punches.

The third was not a bad round for Green, and Palomino was caught several times by chopping blows which his corner preferred to call rather fancily 'bolo shots'. Towards the end of this round Green hustled Palomino. But the Mexican, a slightly-built film star of a man, remained suitably inscrutable. I gave the fourth, fifth and sixth rounds to Palomino, who began to show a variety of punches, the likes of which Green would not even have recognized.

Through all the rounds the difference in class was obvious, although neither man was showing wear and tear to encourage the other. Green wasted many punches in slaps round the Mexican's back and I began to fear for his spine. Palomino held the centre of the ring, ever weaving and moving in with uppercuts rocking Green's head back and back. The 3000 fell silent as their hero was hooked round the ring and the sages were pouting their lips and shaking their heads. Green was given a talking to and also a lot of false advice that he was coasting in. He jumped off his stool in the seventh and began to forget the boxing and be himself.

Palomino's efforts to get to close quarters were not successful, and a trickle of blood appeared over the American's left eye. Green waded in. His lunges seemed to have regained their snap. By the end of the eighth Palomino was beginning to feel the effects of those rights which seemed to start somewhere by the Wembley squash courts. By the ninth round Palomino was fighting to save his title. A curious pedigree left hook homed in on Palomino's ribs and shook him, a right sent his head dancing. The American was in trouble.

However, at the opening of the eleventh round a mouse appeared over Green's left eye. Palomino pounced on it. The mouse became a rat. Green was groping wildly, although that did not, nor could it, alter the rhythm of his swings – without shape or form, only power – that whistled past Palomino's ears. Gradually the eye became completely closed and Green would not have been able to see the fateful hook even if his head had had eyes to see it.

JULY

Three hours of summer lightning

REX BELLAMY
The Times

1 July 1977 *The task Centenary Wimbledon set us was formidable—an ocean of words spun out across a fortnight and more by correspondents and columnists both. We have kept to the nub of events by selecting a piece about the men's semi-finals, in which Bjorn Borg and Vitas Gerulaitis contributed to Wimbledon history; the men's final, a vivid piece written by Alan Hoby; and a portrait of Virginia Wade by Christopher Brasher in The Observer.*

Bjorn Borg, the holder, and Jimmy Connors, champion in 1974, yesterday qualified for the Wimbledon men's singles final. Borg's 6–4, 3–6, 6–3, 3–6, 8–6 win over Vitas Gerulaitis in three hours and four minutes was a Wimbledon classic – challenging the glittering memory of Stan Smith's win over Ilie Nastase in the 1972 final. By contrast, Connors took two hours and 37 minutes to beat John McEnroe, 6–3, 6–3, 4–6, 6–4, in a match that frankly lacked the quality expected from the semi-final round.

A year ago Gerulaitis beat Arthur Ashe, who was then the reigning champion. Yesterday he almost did the same again. In the fifth set he had a point for a 4–2 lead but stayed back on his service, and when he eventually charged to the net was off the mark with a forehand volley. Both men later agreed that this point was critical. Borg broke back for 3–3 instead of going 2–4 down.

In the 11th game Borg, serving, three times heard the umpire call 'deuce'. Again the champion was teetering on the brink of a plunge to oblivion. But three games later, somehow mustering his drained resources for a huge effort, he set about Gerulaitis's service and broke through for the match. A lob, cruel in its perfection, reduced Gerulaitis to 15–40 down. On the next point he attacked – which is in his nature in any situation and was essential now – but again misdirected a forehand volley. Different versions of the same shot, the forehand volley, thus let Gerulaitis down.

In the way of statistics, those will suffice. Beauty should be enjoyed, not measured. But how to describe this sample, save in terms of three dazzling hours of summer lightning? On the whole, grass-court tennis is not the best. But during matches such as this (if only they happened more often!) it achieves a splendour that cannot be surpassed. Borg said later that he had taken part in only one match of higher quality – against Rod Laver in the 1975 World Championship Tennis play-off series on a carpeted court in Dallas.

A reasonable man would not think it possible for two tennis players to maintain such precision at such high speed under such pressure over such a long period. The sustained quickness of footwork, reactions, and racket control was astonishing. It mattered not that – save for Borg's rocking walk, his headband, and his two-fisted backhand – he and Gerulaitis might have been brothers. They gave us plenty of variety: drops and lobs, sudden changes of pace and angle, to punctuate all the whirling, pounding agility and aggression. At times the geometry they created almost happened too fast to be properly savoured. Yet the entire match was dominated by earned points: in a context that insisted there must be a host of hasty errors.

These two know each other well. They are friends and practise together. Their personalities are complementary – Borg the introvert, Gerulaitis the extrovert. Gerulaitis, at 22, a year the senior, was born in Brooklyn of Lithuanian stock and popped over to Europe earlier this year to win the Italian championship on clay. He is wealthy enough to indulge a taste for fast, expensive cars. He owns two Rolls-Royces, a Mercedes and a Porsche. But car or no car, the man has powers of acceleration no other tennis player exceeds.

Gerulaitis put the accelerator flat down at 4.55 and kept it there until 7.59. He kept dashing to the net and relying on his quick reactions to deal with anything Borg threw his way. Gerulaitis was gambler and acrobat in one. When he opened up the court and put away a winner he often held the pose for a moment – grinning, relishing the joy of a moment in time. When serving, he made none of the fashionable fuss. He just looked at Borg: then aimed and fired.

Borg was younger, but looked older. They say he has ice in his veins. He certainly needed something like it yesterday. The storm Gerulaitis blew up was intimidating. Often Borg was on the baseline, quietly preparing a stroke when there was no warning of danger: and suddenly, there came into his peripheral vision the figure of Gerulaitis, bounding eagerly to the net with his blond hair flowing.

But Borg never flinched, never showed the slightest sign that his nerve was weakening. He said later that he was so anxious to reach the final that he was a little nervous, a little inhibited about hitting hard. But he always had more soundness and versatility in his ground strokes and, eventually, the composure to recoil from adversity to triumph. Whereupon Gerulaitis went to the interview room and chatted happily about all the funny things that had come into his mind while he was playing at Wimbledon: 'I didn't want to waste all this material. It's my winning speech . . .'

Except for the fact that neither man served exceptionally well, this was a perfect example of grass-court tennis at its best. We shall never know how Borg and Gerulaitis kept it up. But we were grateful that they did: and we shall remember them. The final can be no better. Yesterday's relative form will have to be adjusted if Connors is to confirm the evidence of last September's final at Forest Hills, where he beat Borg on clay.

For two sets, yesterday's American-Irish festival was the sort of thing that might be expected when the top seed plays a qualifier. McEnroe, aged 18, left school in May. This was his first Wimbledon – and he was the first qualifier and the youngest player to reach the last four. He had no such expectations when he turned up at Roehampton, hoping to qualify, and beat three Europeans to earn a place in the first round.

'John played really well.' Connors said after yesterday's

match. 'To get to the semi-finals on his first visit is quite something. He has a high standard to live up to. If I was him I'd be pretty proud of my performance.'

At first Connors's service returns were misfiring. But the sparks began to fly in the fifth game, and in the seventh McEnroe lost his service for the first time. Connors took five games at the cost of nine points. His shots were working now. They were working so well that he consumed McEnroe's second service – there were too many of those – and had no need of the double-faults McEnroe kept tossing his way. Three of those double-faults came on critical points. McEnroe needed to serve well but was not doing so. He looked pink and boyish and vulnerable.

In the third set, though, something went out of Connors. He did bounce back from 1–3 to 4–3. He even had a game point for 5–3. But his forehand was breaking up. First it was the volley, then the drive. We were reminded that he has yet to produce his finest tennis at this year's Wimbledon.

In the fourth set, though, Connors managed to put all the pieces together again. He hit some superb service returns – combining speed of foot, suppleness of body and controlled power of shot. Well, McEnroe never expected to make a profit out of Connors. But the young New Yorker certainly earned his ticket.

Borg is still the king

ALAN HOBY

The Sunday Express

3 July 1977 *A marathon on the Centre Court—and a dramatic turn in the final set—brought Wimbledon's centenary to a close. Connors was the player who declined to attend the Centre Court presentation on the Opening Day. That discourtesy was to have the crowd rooting for Borg.*

What do you do when your legs turn to jelly, the most important match of your life is slipping away and you have been playing more than three killing hours in the baking, airless box of Wimbledon's Centre Court?

This was the situation confronting Sweden's Bjorn Borg in a stunning fifth set as he battled to keep his crown. After leading 4–0 and with two break points for 5–0 he had dropped four successive games to Jimmy Connors – the man who nearly always beats him. Who among those 17,000 semi-hysterical spectators would have given a fig for the holder's chances? Well, it is epic history now how the slumping Borg clenched his teeth and came back from the semi-dead to snatch Connors's service in that crucial ninth game to run out the winner 3–6, 6–2, 6–1, 5–7, 6–4 after a marathon three hours 13 minutes of courage and endurance.

I do not think that Borg, who lost to the cocky American in the US Final last September, could quite believe it. Nor could anyone else – least of all the baffled and self-critical Connors. 'I played the ninth game like a real punk,' he said later. 'I had the momentum after just winning four games running and then that double fault came out of the blue.'

It certainly did. There was Connors with the pro-Borg crowd silent and still as cemetery mourners leading 15–0 with a fine serve and volley. The abrasive Jimmy was ready for the final coup; poised to bludgeon his exhausted victim out of the match when suddenly that dreadful double fault spoilt it all.

Instead of 30–0 it was 15–all. Suddenly Borg had a reprieve while Connors was an angry, rattled man. He was as disgusted with his serving as the fidgeting, anxious Borg was delighted.

Fresh adrenalin pumped through the champion's veins as left-handed Connors now proceeded to fluff his first service. A beautiful Borg drop volley took the Swede to 15–30. Amid a rustling of anticipation from Borg's army, Connors, who had been wretchedly bad on his forehand during the second and third sets, put his backhand out. 15–40.

Two break points to Borg. Then another poor service by Connors's standards had the spectators holding their breath. Could he still somehow salvage a match which had swung to and fro like a crazy metronome? No, not even Connors could perform this kind of miracle, and he delivered lawn tennis's greatest prize to the holder with another backhand error. Borg then held his service to 40–15, destroying Connors with an incredible ace.

Afterwards Borg said: 'I think winning this year has given me more satisfaction than last year. I really wanted to beat Jimmy as he has beaten me so many times before. I was very tired even at the beginning.

'Beating Jimmy must make me No. 1 at the moment. It was very important for me to win that ninth game. If he had got to 5–4 I would have been in big trouble. It was the most important game of the match.'

In the first set Connors bestrode the court as if he were Attila the Hun in tennis gear. The American took that set 6–3, breaking Borg to love in the eight game after the Swede had double-faulted. The set, clinched in 34 minutes, underlined the well-known Connors technique of trying to 'put down' his opponent right from the start. Often when the American attacked the net Borg would net. He knew that Connors was trying to psyche him and fell for it.

A new pattern began to emerge in the second set. Although Connors had four break points in the third game, eventually won by Borg, it was clear that the Swede was deepening his driving and slyly slowing the tempo at unexpected moments.

And in the sixth game he broke the abrasive 'Jimbo'. Connors was making more and more unforced errors, and with two break points to play with the cool Borg went to 4–2.

He broke Connors's serve again in the eighth game when he produced an unbelievable double-fisted cross-court backhand at advantage which had even Connors reeling.

Slicing the ball and cleverly mixing up his game, Borg shot to 4–0 in the third set taking eight games in a row. At the end of the third game Connors had won only four points.

Connors could not cope with some of the slower shots and lost many valuable points by over-hitting. Breaking Connors's service again at 5–1 after dropping the fifth game Borg finished off the set with a blinding ace.

The fourth set ground on for 51 minutes before Connors took it to square the match with a perfect lob. But in the end it was the right ending for Centenary Wimbledon. The 'nice guy' had held on to win against the man who had been cast by the crowd as the brash 'baddie'.

The changes that made a champion

CHRISTOPHER BRASHER
The Observer

3 July 1977 *Virginia Wade, at last, won the women's singles at Wimbledon. The match, the cheers, the presentation to the Queen, the tears and the interviews tumbled out on Friday night and Saturday. Meanwhile Christopher Brasher was putting together—with the help, one suspects, of his wife Shirley (formerly Shirley Bloomer and a Wimbledon doubles finalist)—a considered portrait of the champion.*

At nine o'clock on Friday morning the doorbell rang in Virgina Wade's London flat, just off Eaton Square, and there on the steps were some press photographers. Her first reaction was what one would expect from someone about to play the centenary Wimbledon final in front of the Queen: 'Oh, just leave me in peace.' And then she changed her mind: 'I thought: "This is your big moment . . . so why not just enjoy it?"' That thought would never have crossed her mind during any of the other 15 Wimbledon championships she has played in. Truly we have witnessed the transformation of a lady: a prickly, complex cocoon has opened and revealed what we least expected – a highly excited, completely professional British champion.

She has confounded us all and made life exciting not only for herself but for millions of people who could hardly believe that she, the woman named Virginia Wade who had disappointed us so often, was actually going to win the premier championship of the world in the one year when it meant so much.

Five years ago she said: 'I'm not equipped mentally to play week after week. I should never play more than three weeks on the trot because I get stale so quickly.' That is a classic English amateur attitude to sport.

This year she has played almost continuously – indeed for four weeks before she came back to Britain, at the end of the first week of June, she was 'on the road' with the New York Apples. They are just one of the teams in the American inter-city tennis league, which sprang-up four years ago, and which has survived, contrary to many expectations. The Apples played, on average, four matches a week, travelling vast distances, practising every day, moving on from city to city.

As one player says: 'You would think it was the worst possible schedule just before Wimbledon.' And certainly when Virginia came to Eastbourne three weeks ago to play for Britain in the Federation Cup she looked awful and played awfully. But she soon readapted her game to grass, and within a fortnight was playing some of the best tennis of her life against Chris Evert in the semi-final on Wednesday.

There is no doubt that her team-mates on the Apples have had a profound effect on her. First, she has seen the ultimate professional, Billie Jean King, at work – seen her train 'like a mad thing', as another English player puts it. And she has had to live with that and with the intensity of the men – Ray Ruffels, Sandy Mayer and Fred Stolle. They practise three hours a day on non-match days and two hours before every match – sometimes with two playing against one, sometimes with four players at the net banging balls at one another to speed up their reactions.

When they are 'at home' in New York – they have attracted a crowd of over 13,000 to Madison Square Garden this year – they train on two courts covered with an air balloon, on top of a garage. Virginia generally bicycles there from her flat on the East Side. She has in a sense lived with professionals and become professional. They have laughed at her bad technique until she has laughed with them and gradually changed until there are now few weaknesses.

Five years ago she said: 'I hate people who work too hard. I think laziness is the absolute end, but it is overwork that I really despise.' That, too, is a typically amateur English attitude. It has all gone now – replaced by a hard-working professionalism.

And like a good pro she has been brave. Last year her service – generally regarded as the best in women's tennis – had got into such a mess that she couldn't even toss the ball up properly. So just before Christmas she started working in New York with Ham Richardson, the American player who reached the Wimbledon semi-finals in 1956. He said that it nearly killed him to see her wasting all that energy to so little effect. They made changes, but Virginia was not entirely happy. Her confidence was in shreds, and she had what she must have considered to be two very bad losses to Sue Barker. So she went to Jerry Teeguarden, a well-known American coach, and between them they have worked on a compromise which just happens to suit her. As she herself says: 'You have to have a lot of courage to give up what you've got to get something better, and you have to try not to worry too much if you don't do quite so well in the meantime.'

It was, in fact, a very close run thing. Her new serve still wasn't working at Eastbourne. So on that rainy Sunday two weeks ago she went on to what she calls the Bambi court at her family home in Kent and served 60 or 70 balls, 'and then I felt the rhythm and I knew that I had it.'

Five years ago I wrote: 'If only someone could control her sociability, make her single-minded for a few months and tune that fine mind of hers to the one single purpose of winning.' And five years ago she said: 'It is very difficult to find someone who tells you the right thing, so that your mind can interpret it into your own style. That is what we lack in so many sports in Britain.'

She never found that one person, but maturity and a combination of circumstances in her American way of life have achieved a similar result: the sheer professionalism of Billie Jean dripping on her like a tap; the philosophy of her friend Mary-Lou Mellace (with whom she shares her New York flat) that ambition can be achieved by guts and determination. And finally there has been the presence of Jerry Teeguarden during this past fortnight, taking the worry from her practice sessions and giving self-confidence.

Five years ago she said: 'I may seem at my ease with people, but underneath there is still a terrible lack of self-confidence.' On Friday, when I repeated that to her, she said: 'I am so much more secure as a person now. When I'm at close quarters with the other players this is very obvious. When you are thrown together in dressing rooms you can see who is feeling at rest with themselves and who isn't. I just felt this week that I was far the strongest person in the dressing room. I just felt that I had more guts and felt more secure than anybody else this week.'

Part of that security stems from the New York Apples, Billie Jean, and Fred Stolle, their coach. The attitude of these Americans and Australians is that you prepare yourself as well as you can, and then, knowing that you have done everything, you go out and play your heart out – and you do not get tight if things start to go wrong. Instead you relax, confident in the knowledge that they will come right.

That is not as easy as it sounds. It requires confidence and the intelligence to read yourself. For instance when Virginia was playing Chris Evert there were signs that she was beginning to tense up. As one player puts it: 'The old Ginny would have gone on until the blood vessels were sticking out on her forehead, and she would have blown four games in the meantime. The new Virginia went and sat on the grass by the umpire's chair and relaxed her neck and back muscles. She sees the signs now. It's the same car, but it's being driven by a different person.'

That different person has also acted very differently during this past week. Instead of attempting to reject the pressure of people's expectation – something which she has accomplished easily in the past by losing to unknowns – she has put the pressure on herself by declaring that she could win. But that is just part of her perverse nature. Ten days ago, spotting my wife, who has been doing some commentating for BBC Television, she came across and said: 'Why are those BBC people writing me off? The more they do it the more I'll prove them wrong.'

And she has handled herself so well. Five years ago she said: 'Wimbledon is so difficult. The phone rings all morning with people saying "Good luck" . . . "Are you going to do well?" . . . all this sort of thing, and you can't just turn off the phone. I don't know what one does about it. Maybe one should just be mean and horrible and selfish.'

On Friday I asked her how she had avoided all those people who wanted a part of her, and she said: 'I've been much stricter. If you once look into the eyes of all those children who want autographs you've had it. You've just got to brace yourself and say I'm sorry, I can't. And I've had the pillow over the phone. This morning I had Rachmaninov's second symphony on so loud that I couldn't have heard it if it did ring!'

But all this ignores her athleticism and the talent that she has displayed over many years – she was, after all, the American champion at the age of 23. She comes from an athletic family. Her eldest brother Anthony was brilliant academically (he won a Rhodes Scholarship) and was a good tennis and squash player – a squash Blue at Oxford. He died of cancer last autumn.

Her younger brother Chris is a good athlete – a distance runner who was never able to break into the British international scene (where our best distance men are world class), but good enough to become Swedish marathon champion. He is now based permanently in Sweden. And her elder sister plays squash for her country.

Virginia herself is a natural athlete, a most beautiful mover. She is often described as tigerish, but there is a more urgent intensity about her. She is feline, but it is the movement of a feline who has her prey in sight. And she has stamina. One of the clichés trotted out this week was that Virginia, at the age of 31, would suffer most from the long baseline rallies against 22-year-old Chris Evert in the semifinal. But, of course, it is the other way round – a 31-year-old, particularly one as fit as Virginia, has far more stamina than a 22-year-old slightly above her best fighting weight.

The Wades are the children of a South African mother (with Scottish blood) and an English father, a Church of England clergyman. When Virginia was very small the whole family moved to South Africa, where her father became Archdeacon of Durban.

'I was a very energetic child, and I suppose a bit of an exhibitionist,' she says, 'always doing things that were adventurous and exciting. I had endless energy, and at school I couldn't bear ever not doing well at something I thought I could do well. I was always determined never to let myself down. Somehow we were all expected to do well, but without any pressure being put on us. Of course there was a lot of excitement when anybody did well, but absolutely no pressure.'

M

When Virginia was 15 the family came back to England, to Kent, and it was automatically assumed that after a couple of more years at school she would go to university. And so she did – to Sussex to study maths and physics (nuclear and atomic physics). But she did not really like her subjects: 'I much preferred the imagination of the artist rather than the disciplined intellectualism of the scientist. Really the English education system is ridiculous: you are forced to decide your subjects so early, committed to a course before you really know your own mind. It was only a very strong will that kept me at university.'

She had already decided that when she left she would go on to the tennis circuit for two years to see how she fared, because there is a chasm between the world class player who can earn a fortune every year and, say, the seventh-ranked British player who struggles to avoid bankruptcy. And there is an equally large chasm between those who can earn fortunes and those who can become great champions as well.

Virginia's motivation has never been money. She earns over £100,000 a year, but she doesn't need it – like all her family she can live very frugally. Instead her motivation has been to prove to all of us, the unbelievers, that 'I deserve to be out there amongst the champions. I have felt that I have been the best player who has not won Wimbledon, and that if only I had a high opinion of myself I would feel I belonged out there.'

It was, of course, merely a question of believing in her place in the world. She has believed. And she has taken her rightful place.

The Open becomes matchplay

PETER RYDE

The Times

9 July 1977 *On the Friday the Open golf championship emerged*

as a contest between two players—Jack Nicklaus and Tom Watson. Peter Ryde conveys the day to his readers superbly. Interwoven with the main contest is the way in which others falter; as well as the thunderstorm and its effect upon Trevino.

The king of golf and one who might be called his heir apparent stand at the head of the Open field as the surviving 60 or so enter the last round at Turnberry. These two, Jack Nicklaus and Tom Watson, made it an unforgettable day, in an equally unforgettable setting, by both returning 65, five under par for a three-round total of 203. Nicklaus in the past has often kept his best to the last; yesterday he decided not to delay, and although he missed two putts of four feet, the second for an eagle at the 17th, he played wonderfully well. Yet he could not draw away from Watson. The impression of them keeping stride by stride together was reinforced by their scores; both have scored 68, 70, 65 in successive rounds.

The Ailsa course was again playing short and conditions were easing in spite of a passing thunderstorm which briefly held up play, but one gets a feeling that this new course has had something to do with drawing such golf from them. Nicklaus has always said of his closest rival today that his great strength lies in his temperament and iron will. He came up against it in the Masters and had to yield to it. Now he faces him again. Because of his wonderful record in this event and his support for it I cannot help hoping that Nicklaus will prevail. I would not have him finish second for the sixth time. But if he fails it must surely be to one of two golfers of great potential. Crenshaw, finishing with two birdies, closed to within three, but it is hard to see anyone passing them.

Nicklaus had one last chance to get his nose in front for the final round, at the 17th, where his ball finished within four feet – a great stroke, although the green had been within reach of two shots all this week. But his putter skidded on the ground as he took it back and he did not stop and start again as he later said he should have done.

Horton is leading Briton after an equally brilliant round of 65, but not played under the same pressure as he will find himself today. Miller (67) is famous for making up ground but seven strokes is a great deal on two in such devastating form as these.

Trevino, safely back in the clubhouse after a round that had fallen apart round the turn, blamed his putting and not the lightning. He missed from two feet for a birdie at the seventh and that worried him almost as much as the lurking thunder. The final qualifying figure was 221 which includes Faldo.

It was a long time before those in contention took to the parched fairways. The decision to leave 80 players and ties on the third day was responsible for the last pair not going out until half past three, which assured another late home-going for those spectators who stayed to the end.

With startling rapidity, a situation which had looked likely to remain a well-kept secret for some time began to be clarified. The first of the four champions to slip was Green, the American title holder, who started by dropping three strokes at the first hole. In the highly competitive atmosphere that was enough to remove him from the leader board, and he dropped another stroke at the third.

The next to lose his grip was Trevino. He had started with four pars, but took three putts at the fifth, and did not have a champion's look about him. He could look devil-may-care and his swing could look laboured when he was winning but yesterday the same accuracy was lacking. The point is worth making because as the sky darkened, and the distant rumblings became recognizable as thunder, he dropped three shots in two holes. He more than anyone might be excused for worrying about lightning after being struck on the course two years ago and finding himself thankful to be alive.

That left Nicklaus and Watson, paired together, of the big men. Nicklaus's start was thrilling and, as the landward horizon slowly darkened, it became clear that his putting touch had returned. As in the previous round he got away to a birdie at the first hole from five feet but this time there were others to come. A huge drive along the narrow ledge of the second finished at the bottom of the bank but he was so close to the green that he can have used no more than a nine-iron and his par was never in danger. His birdies at the two short holes were from 12 feet, and 12 feet away at the sixth is as close as most have been to that distant green this week.

Further confirmation that his confidence on the greens had returned came at the long seventh when he chipped to six feet and holed an awkward downhill putt which raised him to six under par. Watson had begun equally boldly, striking a long iron to eight feet at the third for his first birdie, and tapping in his putt for a two at the fourth from no distance. But the sixth gave him a nasty jolt for he caught a left bunker, and though he came out well he had a nasty five-foot putt following Nicklaus's one of 12 feet, and he missed. With a birdie at the long seventh the only difference between them, at that point, was the two-stroke swing on the sixth. Come the brief downpour of rain with the thunderstorm and Nicklaus firmly and sensibly stopped playing.

Suspension of play lasted about half an hour, the only other casualty being the electric cable to the press tent which was soon restored. The breather ensured an even later finish but gave time for a review of most of the field who had by then completed their rounds.

Enough had finished for play not to have been wiped out for the day if the storm had continued. We were back in the same situation as at St Andrews in 1970 when Jacklin had to interrupt a brilliant round in the making and finish it the next morning. Nicklaus and Watson were luckier and two solid pars after play had resumed showed that their concentration had not been broken. The British players did not wilt badly but could hardly have kept pace with the two leaders. Butler dropped two strokes early on, recovered with birdies at the seventh and eighth, but took six at the ninth which might well have been at the height of the storm.

The best British news of that disjointed afternoon was a 65 from Horton which lifted him below par for the first time. He was not too confident in his putting but he got one in from 15 feet to save his par at the sixth and that started him off. Out in 33, he holed from six feet at the 11th and 13th for birdies and finished with two birdies, his last putt being from 20 feet. Horton finished tied fifth last year; what a prelude it would be to his captaincy of the PGA next year if he keeps his place today.

The lightning sheered off but showers continued. Nicklaus reached the turn in 31, Watson in two strokes more. One of those great chases, in which Nicklaus always seems to be one of the leading actors, was developing, with that sixth hole the only difference between them. The air, previously sultry, had cleared now, but the rain had done little more than lay the dust churned up by thousands of pairs of feet.

Leaders' scores hole by hole

J. NICKLAUS: 3, 4, 4, 2, 4, 2, 4, 4, 4 = 31; 3, 3, 4, 4, 5, 3, 4, 4, 4 = 34. **Total 65**

T. WATSON: 4, 4, 3, 2, 4, 4, 4, 4, = 33; 3, 3, 4, 4, 4, 2, 4, 4, 4 = 32. **Total 65**

B. CRENSHAW: 4, 4, 4, 3, 4, 3, 5, 4, 4 = 35; 3, 2, 4, 4, 4, 3, 4, 4, 3 = 31. **Total 65**

R. MALTBIE: 4, 4, 4, 2, 4, 4, 5, 5, 4 = 36; 5, 3, 4, 4, 4, 3, 5, 4, 4 = 36. **Total 72**

T. HORTON: 4, 4, 4, 3, 4, 3, 4, 4, 3 = 33; 4, 2, 4, 3, 4, 3, 5, 4, 3 = 32. **Total 65**

G. BURROWS: 4, 3, 4, 3, 3, 3, 4, 4, 4 = 32; 3, 4, 4, 4, 4, 3, 6, 4, 4 = 36. **Total 68**

L. TREVINO: 4, 4, 4, 3, 5, 3, 5, 6, 5 = 39; 4, 2, 4, 4, 4, 3, 4, 4, 4 = 33. **Total 72**

J. MILLER: 4, 4, 4, 2, 4, 3, 4, 5, 4 = 34; 4, 3, 4, 5, 4, 3, 3, 3, 4 = 33. **Total 67**

Card of course

Hole	Yds	Par	Hole	Yds	Par
1	355	4	10	452	4
2	428	4	11	177	3
3	462	4	12	391	4
4	167	3	13	411	4
5	411	4	14	440	4
6	222	3	15	209	3
7	528	5	16	409	4
8	427	4	17	500	5
9	455	4	18	431	4
Out	3,455	35	In	3,420	35

Watson's killer putt

RONALD HEAGER

The Sunday Express

10 July 1977 *Who, what, when and where in the first paragraph used to be drummed into the ears of young journalists by local newspaper editors. Today that style is often neglected, but not by Ronald Heager and the Sunday Express. His first 'par' is compelling for all its facts, but it's definitely not dull; and there is nothing like knowing how much someone earns to continue holding your interest.*

Tom Watson mauled 'Golden Bear' Jack Nicklaus with a devastating last round 65 to win his second British Open championship in three starts, and his second major championship of the year, at Turnberry. Watson, golf's 27-year-old Crown Prince from Kansas City, took over the throne of world's No. 1 from Nicklaus – for 1977 anyway – by repeating his US Masters triumph.

His victory added £10,000 to the £158,000 he had already won in America this year.

Watson's second successive 65 gave him a 12 under par total of 268 which smashed the Arnold Palmer–Tom Weiskopf Open scoring record by eight shots.

Yet Tom snatched victory only by a single shot. Third man Hubert Green, the US Open champion, finished 11 behind the winner and leading Briton Tommy Horton was joint ninth and 16 behind. There has never been such dominance since Palmer and Kel Nagle destroyed the opposition up the coast at Troon in 1962.

The majestic Nicklaus, runner-up for the sixth time, tried with all the strength and ferocity of a bear to keep a grip on his crown. He had a last round of 66 and said wryly: 'I felt I gave my best, but I'm tired of giving my best against Tom and not being good enough.'

Said Watson, with the grace that makes him so worthy a successor to giants like Palmer, Player and Nicklaus: 'When you beat probably the best player in the world you have to feel a great deal of satisfaction.' Jack, though, was not playing as well as he can. He did not drive well in the last two days.

The golden-haired Nicklaus and tawny-haired Watson, a sturdy 5ft. 9in. but looking boyish and dwarfed by the massive Big Jack, were locked in a duel that saw Watson come back from the discouraging deficit three shots behind after four holes of the final round.

He cut the margin to one with nine holes played, but went two behind again when Nicklaus holed from 20ft. to birdie the 12th. It was at this point that the man they call 'The Pocket Palmer,' because of his power, showed he had a core of steel. He said later: 'After the 12th I told myself "I've got to get some birdies".' He did. Titanic Tom reeled of four of them in the last six holes to burn it home in 31 against 33 by his formidable foe.

Watson nominated his 'killer shot' as the one with his putter from the left fringe of the 15th green (209 yards) which he rolled in from 20 yards for a birdie two that must have been like a sword-thrust to Nicklaus.

Just before that he had birdied the 13th from 12ft. So now they were level with three to play.

Where Nicklaus lost the championship was the 500-yard 71st – even he admitted that. A par five just was not good enough in this situation. His second was less than perfect and finished short. He chipped well to five feet, but the ball just slipped left.

Watson was home with a drive and three iron to make a comfortable birdie with two putts from 25ft.

Now they went to the 72nd tee with Watson leading for the first time all day. Nicklaus put aside his normal one-iron and staked all on a mighty drive. It found the right rough and was inches from being unplayable.

Watson hit a one-iron down the middle then he hit the stroke that clinched the title – a seven-iron to within 2ft. of the flag which brought an echoing roar from the fans packed into the massive stands on three sides of the hole.

He needed that shot for Nicklaus was not finished. He lashed an eight-iron from the edge of the bushes to within 30ft. Then he rolled in the putt.

This spectacular 'hard way' birdie was not enough. Watson completed the formality of rolling in his two-footer and spread his arms wide as he came into his kingdom.

Nicklaus had gone all day without making one bogey but was still beaten by the brilliance of Watson, who balanced two bogeys – at the second and ninth – with seven birdies.

The 15th may have been the 'killer shot' but Watson claims there had been several key strokes. He said: 'There were a lot of key shots. At the seventh I took my driver from the fairway for my second shot. There were 240 yards to the green and it went quail-high to finish 50ft. away for a two-putt birdie.

'At the sixth I made a real good par putt to keep close to Jack after hitting a three wood into a bunker. I came out to six or eight feet and made it.'

Watson birdied three holes out of four from the fifth to

11. *above* Virginia Wade at the moment of victory. She wins Wimbledon – at last – to a great ovation.

12. *over* Gentlemen in the mud. In New Zealand the Lions forwards were supreme yet the tourists lost the Test series 1–3. Fran Cotton's face tells it all.

13. Perfumes of Arabia? Don Revie leaves the field at Wembley after England have lost to Wales.

14. Phil Bull, the informed outsider who told the Royal Commission on Gambling – in 40,000 words – just how horse-racing should be run.

15. Rugby League Cup Final. One of the tries by Leeds on their way to beating Widnes.

catch Nicklaus then he fell two behind again by the 12th.

But the 15th club in wonderman Watson's bag was the king-sized heart that would not admit defeat when Nicklaus was two shots ahead of him with only six holes left.

It took a new superstar to produce four birdies in the last six holes to win the Open . . . that is Tom Watson. His victory means that he is now only £30,000 off Johnny Miller's all-time world record and there are still two tournaments to play.

Hole by hole:

WATSON: Out—4, 5, 4, 3, 3, 3, 4, 3, 5 = 34; In—4, 3, 4, 3, 4, 2, 4, 4, 3 = 31.

NICKLAUS: Out—4, 3, 4, 2, 4, 3, 5, 4, 4 = 33; In—4, 3, 3, 4, 4, 3, 4, 5, 3 = 33.

A test of character

JOHN HOPKINS
The Sunday Times

New Zealand 9 British Isles 13

10 July 1977 *New Zealand, the second Test, and the Lions win where none of their predecessors had succeeded. It was their pack, rebuilt and revitalised after their defeat in the first Test, which took control in the early stages and finally held out against the All Blacks to keep the series alive.*

Character, something definable only in moments of truth, helped the British Lions earn an exciting victory in the second Test at soulless Lancaster Park Fifty-eight thousand people packed into the Oval to see the Lions hold on to a victory that had been theirs from the opening 20 minutes and yet could have been snatched from them at any moment during a pulsating last quarter.

So what is character? It is going out on to a pitch where your countrymen have never before succeeded in a Test match and winning. It is knowing, as play starts, that you are 80 minutes away from a defeat that will kill the Test series – and then winning. It is scoring ten points in the first 20 minutes under this mental pressure and threatening to overrun your vaunted opposition. And it is, finally, what you dig into when you are so tired you can hardly run as the opposition are threatening to storm your lines in a series of unstoppable charges.

If ever their character saved these Lions it was in the last 20 minutes. Luck was on their side once when Bryan Williams horribly missed a penalty from in front of the posts, a penalty that would have made the score 9-13 with ten minutes left.

Time and again in this period the Lions had to defend desperately. Once it seemed that all was lost when full back Colin Farrell seemed to have penetrated the defensive screen, only for Phil Bennett to knock him over with a sort of tackle that makes a mockery of those oft-heard accusations that he shirks the physical. From the ruck the All Blacks switched the attack and, just as the alarm bells were sounding, Lyn Jaffray knocked on in midfield.

Again, well into injury time, the All Blacks mounted a siege and forced a line-out almost on the Lions line. A maul developed and Ian Kirkpatrick thrust his way through some red shirts before being held up. A scrum was ordered. The All Blacks heeled and the same Jaffray was set up to take the ball on the burst. He caught it two yards from the Lions line, under the posts, and as every New Zealander in the stadium rose to acclaim the impending try, he knocked it on.

These were the moments when the 1977 Lions almost went under. Yet their jubilation when the final whistle came was deserved and it stemmed from the period when they outplayed the All Blacks at the start of the game.

The Lions had made five changes among their forwards from the first Test and every one seemed to have worked for the better. They had an enormous line-out advantage at first, thanks to Gordon Brown in the middle of the line-out, Billy Beamount at the front and Derek Quinnell, valiantly protecting Willie Duggan at the back and thus neutralising Kirkpatrick and Lawrie Knight.

Gareth Evans went close to scoring a remarkable try early on after he hacked the ball 30 yards. Only the spin of the ball into touch at the last minute saved the All Blacks who had been caught out of position. Phil Bennett kicked a penalty when Going was caught offside at a scrum. Then, after a period of testing Farrell with a series of high kicks which he fielded courageously, came the Lions try, the only one of the game.

From a lone-out in midfield Bennett chipped the ball cleverly through the advancing All Blacks midfield. Quickly he darted past them as they struggled to turn on the muddy surface and kicked the ball on. It rebounded off Farrell to be picked up by a Lion. Gordon Brown charged forward with it and, when tackled, slipped it to Ian McGeechan. The centre had J. J. Williams outside him and Andy Irvine slightly behind him. A moment of confusion was all Williams needed and the way was clear for him to race 20 yards to score his ninth try of the tour. Bennett's conversion hit the right upright.

More was to come. Peter Wheeler, after taking a pass from Steve Fenwick 10 yards from the All Blacks line, was viciously high-tackled as he seemed certain to score a try on his Test debut. The penalty was a formality for Bennett, taking the score to 10-0.

With this start, and the All Blacks mounting a grandstand finish, the game was an exciting one, far too good to be held on a pitch that was a disgrace to New Zealand. It had been used for a minor game, attracting only 700 spectators, one week before the Test and heavy rain in Christchurch early last week made it a quagmire between the two ten yard lines.

The pitch and two violent outbursts of rough play were serious blots on this game. Price and Brad Johnstone detached from a line-out and while one punched, the other butted. The violence that was simmering after a number of late tackles on Bennett erupted after half-time when Kevin Eveleigh was appallingly late in tackling the Lions skipper and several Lions waded in to take retribution.

What was otherwise so striking about the game was the transformation of roles compared to the first Test three weeks ago. As usual, the Lions had the edge in the tight scrums, though the All Blacks almost neutralised this by astute wheeling. Nevertheless, the introduction of Cotton at loose head was a success because of his work in the line-outs and mauls.

Behind the scrum Phil Bennett was decisively good. Having a kick charged down late in the game hardly spoilt his overall performance. Fenwick was used on the burst more than he has been before, though, sound as he was in defence and attack, he and McGeechan still found they had their work cut out containing Bill Osborne in attack.

The All Blacks' kicking weakness was again in evidence. Williams missed five of his eight kicks at goal. The series could be South Africa 1976 all over again for the All Blacks, who then won everything bar the goal kicking. For the Lions, though, the show is back on the road. The world champions are not surrendering their status easily.

NEW ZEALAND: C. Farrell, B. Williams, B. Osborne, L. Jaffray, M. Taylor, D. Bruce, S. Going, No 8, **L. Knight,** Second row, **K. Eveleigh, F. Oliver, A. Haden, I. Kirkpatrick,** Front row, **B. Bush, T. Norton** (capt) **B. Johnstone**

BRITISH ISLES: A. Irvine, J. J. Williams, S. Fenwick, J. McGeechan, G. Evans, P. Bennett (capt) **B. Williams,** No 8, **W. Duggan,** Second Row, **D. Quinnell, G. Brown, W. Beaumont, T. Cobner,** Front Row, **G. Price, P. Wheeler, F. Cotton**

REFEREE: B. Duffy (Taranaki)

Revie: a man and his money

PETER TAYLOR and RICHARD HOLIDAY
The Sunday Telegraph

17 July 1977 *The soccer world of England, suffering badly enough on the field, was stunned when the Daily Mail, in the biggest exclusive story of the year, announced that Don Revie had resigned from the job of England manager and was to run soccer in the United Arab Emirates for £340,000. Fleet Street was bemused and, apart from the Mail, left feeling a little out in the cold. One week later The Sunday Telegraph pulled together the strands of the story in a piece which, while written by correspondents outside the immediate soccer world, put Revie's career in useful perspective.*

The strange story of Don Revie reflects the sort of pressures that the modern football manager must endure. With the growth of sponsorship in the last decade the game has become incomparably richer and more competitive than in the days when great players like Matthews and Finney took to the field in flapping shorts and short, unflapping hair. In abandoning his £25,000-a-year contract as England's manager (it still had two years to go) for a £340,000 contract in the twilight world of Arab soccer, Revie has raised a lot of questions about his motivation, and his decision to leak the story to a newspaper before telling the Football Association, his employers, has lost him a great deal of face.

On the field of football management reputations are forged slowly and lost quickly. At his peak the successful manager is as much a star as any of his highly publicised players, and those fortunate enough to retire on a crest soon pass into legend. But results are all, and in the quest for trophies one manager's theories about the game are as good as last season's results.

In addition to being a formidable (and controversial) strategist Revie has always had a reputation for enjoying the financial rewards of success ('Don Readies' is the nickname that persists in the soccer world), but in this he only treads the same path as a host of back-street youngsters before him who saw soccer as an escape to fame and fortune.

Don Revie was born on 10 July, 1927 at the family home in Bell Street, Middlesborough, a two bedroomed terraced house only yards from Middlesborough Football Club's Ayresome Park ground. Times were hard. Revie's father, a joiner, was frequently unemployed in work-starved Teesside. Football, cheap and wholesome entertainment, provided the jobless population with a weekly release. Revie was first taken by his father to the Middlesborough terraces at the age of six, and acquired a pair of football boots when he was nine.

There are some in the terraced street who remember the boy and his ways. A neighbour: 'Little Don was football mad. I'm glad he's done well because the family never had a lot of money to throw around. He always did have a way of looking after the pennies.'

At 12 his mother died, an event that affected Revie deeply, and he became a 'latch-key kid,' spending his waiting hours kicking a rag ball against a wall. He had already shown considerable football skills and was playing for Newpark Boys Club when he suddenly figured for the first time in a soccer transfer – still at the tender age of 12. He was signed on by a club known as 'Middlesborough Swifts' for five shillings. The Swifts could afford to throw money around.

The Swift's manager, engine driver Bill Sanderson, was to have a surprising influence over Revie. Sanderson held regular pre-match meetings at his council house home, attended by his players. There he would produce detailed dossiers on the opposition teams Swifts were to play. In later years with both Leeds United and England, Revie became renowned for his obsession with dossiers packed with facts and figures, even flying thousands of miles to spy in advance on the opposition.

Revie left elementary school at 14 to begin an apprenticeship as a bricklayer, and at 16 he joined Leicester City. Five years later, in 1949, he married Elsie Duncan, daughter of the then Leicester City manager Johnny Duncan. His moves as a player took him to Hull City and then Manchester City, where his tactics as a deep-lying centre forward became known as the 'Revie Plan'.

Revie later played for Sunderland, but it was at Leeds, where he arrived in 1961 as player-manager, that he laid the foundations of his fortune. One of the first people he went to see for advice was Matt Busby of Manchester United (who is on the FA committee that will now have to choose his successor as England manager). Matt, later to be knighted for his distinguished services to soccer, noted: 'Don was a shrewd, firm character as well as a straight one, and I liked something else I saw. He was an intense character, bursting to start building and to justify himself, bursting to succeed.'

As manager of Leeds Revie built a remarkably successful side which many believe should have won far more honours than it did. Players have since suggested that his superstition – his preoccupation with talismen and lucky suits – and his basic uncertainty communicated themselves to them.

As a group they were isolationist to a degree, intolerant of outsiders, closely-knit, a family with Revie cast as Godfather. They were far from popular, employing gamesmanship, physical intimidation and thinly-disguised attempts to unhinge the confidence of referees. Alfred Delcourt, a leading Belgian official, once stopped a match and called to Billy Bremner, the captain: 'Before we go further would you tell me whether you are going to referee this match or am I?'

When they started one season with a string of victories one leading coach alleged that clubs were afraid of Leeds. 'They are lying down because they are afraid of their reputation,' he said.

There were hints of an even darker side. In 1972, Leeds, who had beaten Arsenal two days earlier in one of the most boring FA Cup finals ever seen, had to play Wolves in a match which would decide whether, like Arsenal the previous year, Leeds would win the League and Cup double.

In the event Leeds lost and Derby took the title. Subsequently, a Sunday paper published a story that, some days before the match, three Wolves' players had been approached to 'throw' the match. An inquiry was ordered but the findings were inconclusive, although at least one Wolves player confirmed that he had received a sinister phone call.

Towards the end of Revie's reign at Leeds a 'reformed' side emerged. Gone were the old time-wasting tactics (once, when Leeds were playing West Ham, even the Leeds crowd began to jeer when Revie's team persisted in running the ball to the corner flag and keeping it there). This late repentance was greeted cynically by other managers. Said one: 'What do you do when a man who has been burgling your house for five years comes to tell you he's reformed?'

Last week Revie hit back at critics who accused him of being money-mad by claiming that for three years Leeds kept him on '£38 a week'. However, there were fringe benefits provided by the club. Not least of these was Three Chimneys. This was a large detached house in Sandmoor Drive, Alwoodley, a leafy suburb of the city, which the club purchased for Revie for £18,000 from its chairman, the millionaire Manny Cussins. The house, together with an annexe, stood in an acre of ground and contained five bedrooms and a four-car garage.

Some time after moving in Revie and his wife – both golf fanatics – had a nine-hole putting course laid out in the grounds. Revie remained at Three Chimneys until March 1974, three months before the confirmation of his England appointment. It was then that a wealthy Leeds businessman bid £40,000 for the property, which was by then in Revie's ownership. The sale was completed, but Revie and family did not move far – to a bungalow in the same grounds. This was sold separately in April 1977.

Apart from property there were other perks. Leeds United had one of the most successful players' pools in football, the envy of many a club. Its squad, which included many international stars, enjoyed the benefits reaped from advertising, and Revie is recognised by many as the originator of much business off the football pitch.

Mr Richard Langridge, marketing director of Stylo Matchmakers International, the sports footwear firm, said that since becoming England manager Revie had signed a contract with the company to boost its boys' soccer boots. This follows a previous contract with the Leeds players' pool which also undertook to wear Stylo boots. Mr Langridge refused to say how much money had changed hands on either deal, but he said: 'Don impressed me as an astute businessman. He's got his head screwed on properly.' However, Revie's current contract, which started last September, may now come to an abrupt end. His decision to depart for the Middle East had 'put a different complexion' on the arrangement with the firm, Mr Langridge said.

But suggestions that Revie had a direct hand in the much-publicised contract between Cook and Hurst, the Leicester-based manufacturers of Admiral sports wear, and the Football Association, brought a denial from company chairman Mr Bert Patrick. The company is sponsoring the FA to the tune of £250,000 in return for the England squad wearing the Admiral strip.

Mr Patrick said: 'Our contract is with the FA – not with Don Revie. We had no relationship with him and he played no part in the negotiations.'

He also denied that advertisements for Admiral bearing Revie's name and photograph in European sports magazines were part of a private deal between the firm and the ex-

England manager: 'There has been no personal deal with Revie.' Even so, the relationship between Revie and the sportswear firm was close enough for *Sunday Telegraph* soccer correspondent Colin Malam to remark during a lamentable England performance at Wembley: 'I wonder if Admiral make a towel for Revie to throw in.'

Revie's decision to allow the *Daily Mail* to announce his resignation before he had told either his employers, the FA, or his loyal friend and assistant, Les Cocker, has brought much speculation about how much he was paid. A figure of £15,000 has been rumoured.

Last year many people in the game were astounded to receive circulars announcing that Mr Revie was available for soccer seminars at £200 a time. One of the recipients was Danny Blanchflower, who, in a newspaper column, questioned the wisdom and propriety of certain business relationships of Revie's. The plan was hastily shelved, but Revie was recently reported to have 'appeared' at a World Cup promotion at a London hotel for £250.

Revie has, at least, completed the success story of the rag-ball kid who became the world's richest football manager. Indeed his new wealth is exceeded only by the ironic richness of his parting: the man who abandoned the most worthy and honourable job that English football can offer, to build a new reputation on sand.

Kent are left whimpering

JOHN ARLOTT
The Guardian

18 July 1977 *It was a strange world at Lord's for the Benson and Hedges final, with 'new-fangled' devices such as rosettes and rattles on view. The cricket did not match up to expectations, either.*

Gloucestershire beat Kent by 64 runs in the final of the Benson and Hedges Cup at Lord's on Saturday to the delight of those with West Country sympathy or who like to see favourites beaten. The match stirred loyalties now generally expressed at these new-fangled rosette-flaunting, rattle and chant-sounding Lord's finals which keep cricket's coffers so healthily full. As a contest, though, it was an anti-climax, an almost cruel demonstration of the fact that one-day cricket, in its artificiality, can end anywhere between an excruciatingly close finish and a pure Eliot whimper.

Prediction was reduced to nonsense. Not only were the favourites roundly beaten, but even those expected to play major parts for the unfancied Gloucestershire were outshone by a less fancied performer. That was the most surprising aspect. Defeat of a fancied side is always possible in a sudden-death match; but it is generally achieved by a few predictable players on the other side.

The pattern of both innings was established from the start. Of course there have been remarkable instances of collapse and recovery; though never to such an extent as is common in the three-day, two-innings game. Now, though, Gloucestershire started their innings well and, if the initial quality was not fully maintained, their eventual score was – by one run – the highest ever recorded in these finals. Kent made a dismal start, and their attempts at recovery were never strong enough to give them a genuine prospect of winning. It might, too, be argued that in spite of – or perhaps because of – their great wealth of talent they made errors of selection; while Gloucestershire, reduced by injuries and ineligibility to their only possible XI, made the best of it.

Procter can hardly have been completely happy to win the toss which gave him the choice to bat or indicate doubt about his batting fully justified by several earlier performances this season.

All too often it has been a case of Sadiq and Zaheer or nothing except a rescue act by Shepherd. Now, although Sadiq glanced the first ball of the day for four, he was soon out-paced by Stovold, a sturdy, homespun, Bristol-born player of unvarnished strokes. Stovold worked his passage by batting better than the first-choice wicketkeeper, Brassington. Jarvis and Julien were not always tidy, and he thumped their vagaries for nine fours in an opening partnership of 79. Then Sadiq, never so fluent as his partner, drove at Woolmer, and Hills took a good one-handed catch at mid-on.

Zaheer soon slipped into his characteristically pleasant, easy style, and he and Stovold put on another 65. When Stovold clipped Underwood to mid-on the score was 144 for two and the innings was as securely founded as is possible in the over-limit game. Zaheer and Procter scored another 55. Underwood, regarded as the infallible scoring break in this cricket, bowled his first 10 overs – mainly directed at or outside the leg stump – for 22 runs; his last one cost 10. When Zaheer drove Jarvis's half-volley to Shepherd Gloucestershire were 204 for four. In spite of the rapid departures of Shepherd and Graveney an unexpectedly dogged Foat and Vernon took the total to a record 237.

Kent had left out their opening batsman, Johnson – Gold Award winner in last year's final – for Clinton, who was presumably intended to anchor the innings. In the event Brain hit the top of his off stump before he had scored. Procter had Rowe caught by Stovold and Kent were five for two. Soon, in a shrewd psychological move, Procter called up his second-line bowlers. Asif was the man likeliest to revive the innings; but Stovold caught him off Vernon. Ealham, Kent's last hope for a long, fast score, slashed at Vernon, and Stovold, hurling himself far to his right, caught him, one-handed, where a second slip would have been. The Gloucestershire players' congratulations for Stovold recognized that as the decisive stroke.

Now the second puzzle of the Kent selection emerged. To prefer Hills to the young Cowdrey – who, in the quarter-finals, made the highest score ever recorded for Kent in this competition – was logical only for Hills's bowling; but he did not bowl at all. So Kent had simply deprived themselves of a man capable of a major innings. Woolmer, the core of the batting, was caught forcing the pace; so was Knott; and, although Shepherd went down with all his favourite guns firing, Kent never looked like closing the gap. The individual Gold Award went, of course, to Stovold, in a surge of broadly accented euphoria.

For scoreboard see following page

GLOUCESTERSHIRE:

Sadiq Mohammad c Hills b Woolmer	24
A. W. Stovold c Underwood b Shepherd	71
Zaheer Abbas c Shepherd b Jarvis	70
M. J. Proctor c Knott b Julien	25
J. C. Foat not out	21
D. R. Shepherd b Jarvis	9
D. A. Graveney c Underwood b Julien	1
M. J. Vernon not out	3
Extras (lb 7, w 2, nb 4)	13
Total (for 6, 55 overs)	**237**

Fall of wickets: 79, 144, 191, 204, 220, 223.

M. D. Partridge, J. H. Shackleton, B. M. Brain did not bat.

Bowling: Jarvis 11–2–52–2, Julien 11–0–51–2, Shepherd 11–0–47–1, Woolmer 11–0–42–1, Underwood 11–1–32–0.

KENT:

R. A. Woolmer c Shackleton b Graveney	64
G. S. Clinton b Brain	0
C. J. Rowe c Stovoid b Procter	0
Asif Ibqal c Stovoid b Vernon	11
B. D. Julien b Graveney	1
J. N. Shepherd c Procter b Brain	55
A. P. E. Knott c Zaheer b Partridge	14
R. W. Hills c Procter b Shackleton	6
D. L. Underwood b Brain	8
K. B. S. Jarvis not out	0
Extras (lb 7, nb 2)	9
Total (47.3 overs)	**173**

Fall of wickets: 4, 5, 24, 64, 65, 100, 122, 150, 166.

Bowling: Procter 7–1–15–1, Brain 7.3–5–9–3, Vernon 11–1–52–2, Shackleton 10–0–40–1, Graveney 9–2–26–2, Partridge 3–0–22–1.

Umpires: H. D. Bird and W. L. Budd.

The Minstrel gives his best

BROUGH SCOTT
The Sunday Times

24 July 1977 *The Minstrel gave his backers a fright but another marvellous victory in the main event at the Ascot July meeting. Brough Scott emphasises the courage of the horse and once again the skill of Piggott, who avoided panic when the odds seemed heavy against him.*

The Minstrel ran a race of superb courage at Ascot yesterday to edge out last year's third Orange Bay in the £100,000 KingGeorge VI and Queen Elizabeth Diamond Stakes but still left us wondering at how much difference a few inches can make.

For it was by that margin that The Minstrel got home against his elders yesterday, and it was also only by inches that he won our Derby, and that victory was the central part of his fame that led to a ten-million-dollar bid from the Canadian E. P. Taylor last week. If both verdicts had gone against him his present value would be scarcely $2m. But since The Minstrel's connections refused the Canadian offer one's mind boggles at today's price on the chunky chestnut who had seemed a failure just two months ago, but whose total earnings of £317,316 have now passed Grundy's previous record.

The Minstrel, with his ears stuffed with cotton wool to calm him during the pre-race parade, was returned a 7–4 favourite. But those odds hardly looked generous when the stalls opened and he stood in his place for a full second after his 10 rivals jumped out. This manoeuvre cost him some five lengths, but Piggott has not won his immortality nor taken five previous runnings of this race without developing an immunity to panic, and he now calmly settled The Minstrel down at the back of the field while the Irish challenger Mart Lane cut out the running from the Spanish horse Rheffissimo, Lucky Wednesday and the French Derby winner Crystal Palace.

The pace was not a great one, and the final time of 2–30.48sec. was exactly 2½ seconds outside Grundy's astonishing run two years ago. One's confidence in Piggott's judgment was fully tested as he stayed at the tail of the field, and in fact still only had the moody Norfolk Air behind him with four furlongs to run. By then Eddery had already put Orange Bay close up behind Mart Lane and Lucky Wednesday, and with a brilliant tactical ploy swept ahead on to the rails as they straightened up for home.

Anyone less alert than Piggott or on a horse less handy and determined than The Minstrel would certainly have been beaten by Eddery's enterprise and Orange Bay's tremendous spurt. But Piggott is a master round Ascot, and just as some of his rivals, notably the French horse Exceller, seemed to lose ground, he swept through to face the straight four lengths adrift of Orange Bay and still with plenty of horse beneath him. Mart Lane, Lucky Wednesday, Bruni and Crystal Palace were also close up, but only Exceller had the legs to come through and join in the chase.

The pursuit was deadly but Orange Bay fought every stride to the line. A furlong out The Minstrel was almost level, his neck stretched out and ears laid back in effort, but with Piggott still not resolving to his final blitz. Exceller was two lengths off and the rest well beaten. Two hundred yards from the line Piggott went for everything, and The Minstrel struggled a neck ahead. But Orange Bay came back so bravely that only The Minstrel's bottomless courage kept him the race by the minimum distance.

Immoral tails

MICHAEL LEAPMAN
The Times

25 July 1977 *The sports pages are not the only ones to contain extraordinary sporting revelations. Michael Leapman, retired Times diarist, returned briefly to London to report the damage that promiscuity among our race horses and the doings of Tony Greig are having on the image of British sport abroad.*

I fear I am pulling out of Britain at a time of collapse. I am not referring to the total economic collapse which has been imminent ever since my return from my last spell in New York in 1972, and which will no doubt be more imminent still when I come back again. I mean a collapse in standards in sport.

This might strike you as odd. British teams have not done well at sport for years, and have we not, after all, just won a Test match at cricket and reached the final of the European Cup at athletics? Standards of performance in sport seem, therefore, to be improving, if anything: what is in sad decline is the moral climate in which these standards are achieved.

To have England's cricket captain and football manager

selling out to foreigners is bad enough. I am sure, though, that fans are more horrified by Tommy Docherty's relationship with the wife of his football team's physiotherapist; and most horrified of all by the outbreak of venereal disease in our racehorses.

The report on our front page a couple of weeks ago was the first that I had seen which fearlessly named the equine scourge. The equine epidemic has been the subject of speculation on the sports pages for some time, but since sports writers are people of sensibility they have not been able to bring themselves to define it.

I cannot say I am surprised at the revelation, for it has long seemed to me that our bloodstock is forced to maintain a way of life stained by grave moral turpitude. A reasonably successful and well-bred male horse will, when put to stud, have fleeting affairs with dozens of mares, many of whom he will be meeting for the first time and some who might be quite close relatives. Any racecard showing the names of the parents of runners at a meeting is a sordid chronicle of promiscuity.

The most successful make a lucrative career of it, complete with perks like extensive foreign travel. The Minstrel, this year's Derby winner, will next season commute between Ireland and Australia for the purpose of fathering issue.

An American racecourse stages a race every year which brings the whole business down to a disgraceful level of commercialism. The race, called by some coy romantic name which escapes me, is for female horses. Included in the winner's prize is the opportunity to be closeted with a desirable stallion. The second and third placed horses win the services of marginally less attractive stallions, while the winning jockeys simply get their usual commission.

Given that this immorality is officially condoned, not to say encouraged, by those who run the sport, it is hardly surprising that there should be an outbreak of that disease which is commonly recognized as retribution for such behaviour. Loose living has brought the downfall of many past civilizations, and will no doubt bring about the collapse of the bloodstock industry unless it switches quickly to the path of virtue.

It is curious how standards differ from one sport to

another. The powers that organize cricket, far from being prepared to countenance lax moral behaviour, are unwilling to sanction any deviation from a strict conformist position. I can think of no other institution which would fine a club £500 because its captain was so bold as to criticize the wicket on a Test match ground.

Tony Greig's 'offence', for which Sussex have to foot the bill, was to make 'a derogatory public pronouncement detrimental to cricket'. Worse, he did so 'without having obtained the proper consent'.

It happened that Greig's view on the wicket was wrong. It played well enough for the duration of the match. But if I had to cough up £500 for every wrong prediction I had made in public, or for any derogatory pronouncement detrimental to the press in general or *The Times* in particular, I should be heavily in debt.

It is an important infringement of Greig's liberty to prevent his expressing his views concerning the game at which he makes his living. Only in countries with dictatorial regimes of the left or the right are such practices commonplace.

Greig is out of favour with the cricketing establishment because of his involvement with Kerry Packer's enterprise: and, as I pointed out in the long article on cricket I wrote a couple of weeks ago, so are his county, Sussex. Last season the county refused a recommendation from the Test and County Cricket Board that they suspend John Snow, their fast bowler, for wearing advertising about his person during a televised Sunday match.

There was more trouble over Sussex's request for the special registration of Imran Khan, the Pakistan all-rounder. The county appealed to the Cricket Council, who reversed the TCCB's decision that he could not play for them this season.

If, as some predict, the very structure of cricket as we know it is at risk as a result of Packer's initiative, Sussex would be in a splendid position to lead a breakaway group of counties and set up a rival organization, free from the TCCB's iron clasp. Say they were to recruit about half the 17 county sides, they could mount an alternative county championship, attracting its own sponsorship.

The existence of two cricket leagues would introduce an element of competition in the promotion of the game which could result in better pay and conditions for all players. When the initial bitterness had passed, they could play representative matches against each other and stage a grand final between the champion teams of the two leagues.

Such a system works well in the United States, where baseball teams belong to either the American or the National League, with the World Series between the two champions to round off the season. The result is a high degree of professionalism in the playing and the promotion of the sport. Nobody is prevented from making derogatory or detrimental remarks – indeed it seems at times as though they do little else. It may be unseemly, but it is fun.

By the time you read this I ought to be halfway across the Atlantic in the QE2.

This, then, is the final answer to the hundreds of kind well-wishers who, during the two months since I gave up the editorship of the Diary, have asked me unceasingly and with growing incredulity: 'And when exactly *are* you going to New York?'

When I visited New York in May and wrote a few columns from there, many assumed that I had already gone for good, although I explained quite meticulously that it was only an advanced sighting visit. Many a pair of diplomatic eyebrows were therefore raised in puzzlement when I made my positively final appearance last weekend in the annual cricket match between the Foreign Office News Management Department and the Diplomatic and Commonwealth Writers. (Though I am neither a Foreign Office spokesman nor a diplomatic correspondent, I qualify for the latter team by virtue of once having been one.)

I have written about this match in previous years; but the Foreign Office news people, who are trained to notice such things, point out that it is my habit only to give the result on the rare occasions when our side wins. Though this practice seems to me to be in the best tradition of diplomatic reporting, I shall break with it and confess that for the second successive year we lost quite convincingly.

Unsportingly, though, I shall add sourly that we might have won if their umpires had not been prone to signal boundaries for their side as soon as the ball penetrated the close field, and if I had snapped a catch at the wicket offered by their most successful batsman. (The chances are, though, that the umpire would not anyway have given him out: I understand why our colleagues in Europe find British diplomats such tricky people to deal with.)

The wicket, dare I say it, was not too good, sloping alarming at one end. But at least nobody, as far as I could detect, made off with anyone else's wife.

Botham makes his debut

JOHN WOODCOCK
The Times

29 July 1977 *The first Test against Australia was drawn, the second won by 9 wickets. In a cricketing year that had its Greig, Randall, Packer and Boycott, it might easily be overlooked that Ian Botham from Somerset in his first match for England played a crucial part in the series. On the first day of the third Test he cut through the Australian middle order, taking five wickets for 74 runs. John Woodcock's piece is also as good a report as any written during the series on how the Australians let their batting collapse.*

Except for the first two in their order and the last three, Australia batted no better when the third Test match began at Trent Bridge yesterday than they did at Old Trafford in the second. After an opening partnership of 79 they were bowled out for 243, Ian Botham, in his first Test match, having most to do with this by taking four wickets in the hour before tea for 17 runs in seven overs.

While McCosker and Davis were together during the first 90 minutes of the day there were thoughts of an Australian total of 500. Everything seemed in favour of it, except for the uncertainty which the Australians must feel about their future. At lunch the sun went in and the batting declined.

England's fielding had a lot to do with it. They were offered five slip catches and held them all, one by Hendrick being positively brilliant and three of the others very good. Before his home crowd Randall saved numerous runs by his anticipation and agility. Yet to lose six wickets for 54 runs, as Australia did in the afternoon, was a spectacularly inept piece of batting.

Of the England bowlers, Hendrick was better than Willis, who was not at his best; Underwood was, as ever, reliable. Greig took a wicket and Miller was never used. The honours went to Botham who must have been uncertain when he arrived at the ground soon after breakfast whether he would even play. After a loose first spell Brearley probably brought him on for his second, in the middle of the afternoon, with some misgivings.

What Brearley did know, though, was that with 75 wickets already to his name Botham has been the most successful bowler of the current season. He is 21 years young and conspicuously strong. He is fit, too, having bowled more first-class overs in the past three months than anyone else. It was a happy time to choose to make the impact he did, having, as he does, no Packer strings attached to him. Thompson, who has just severed his, was cheered all the way to the wicket yesterday afternoon, as spontaneous an indication of what the public think about the 'circus' as there could have been.

While it was disappointing for England that Australia's last two wickets should add 88, it brought home to them just how well they had done to account for the main batting so cheaply. O'Keeffe always sells his wicket dearly, playing straight and attempting few of the strokes that get others out. If he is not quite the batsman one would have chosen to entertain the Queen on her annual visit to Test cricket, she would have recognized his resolution and realized how badly it must have been needed.

The gates were closed an hour after the start of play, for the first time at Trent Bridge since 1948. It was a lovely morning, full of warmth and light. Of enthusiasm, too. England left out Roope, which opened the way for Botham, the first young Somerset player to win a cap since Maurice Tremlett 30 years ago.

The first ball of the match was enough to show that the pitch was not as fast and resilient as Willis, who bowled it, must have been hoping. When, later in the over, he let a bouncer go, it barely carried to Knott. Reassured by the sight of this McCosker played his best innings of the series, Australians say his best of the tour. Although beaten once by Willis and once by Hendrick, and fortunate to edge Botham's second ball in Test cricket just wide of second slip, he was 51 not out at lunch, his runs neatly, competently and comfortably made.

From the way McCosker and Davis made their runs there was no way of telling how fortunate they were to be getting another chance of opening Australia's innings. Davis played some good on-side strokes, once hooking Hendrick for six. In his first six overs Botham conceded six boundaries, all to McCosker and five of them to leg. At 67 he was replaced by Underwood, who in his third over had Davis caught at mid-on, driving too soon at Underwood's slower ball.

At lunch the clouds appeared. Not only this. England bowled afterwards as though they had resolved to do away with those long hops of which there had been too many in the morning. McCosker stayed for another 35 minutes without adding to his score before being nicely caught low down at first slip off Hendrick. It was while Chappell and Hookes were together that Australia last looked like making a total. Chappell seemed ominously determined, Hookes casually confident. When drinks were taken in the afternoon they had added 30 together; Hookes had twice creamed Willis effortlessly through the covers.

But as we say when unable to think of a better cliché 'the drinks proved fatal'. The first ball afterwards was a long hop from Botham which Chappell dragged into his stumps, attempting a forcing stroke. Off the first ball of the next over Hookes was marvellously caught at third slip by Hendrick off Willis. The ball went low and far to Hendrick's left. How he got a hand to it was remarkable, how he got two to it was more so, how he held it was miraculous.

For the next three-quarters of an hour Australia's innings was processional. Walters and Robinson each flashed a boundary or two, which is more than most of the others did. Walters was out as he often is, caught in the gully playing his sparring stroke. Robinson was well caught high up at first slip, throwing his bat at a wide half volley without letting go of the handle; Marsh was leg-before to Botham, shuffling across his stumps; Walker was caught at third slip by the reliable Hendrick off the revelationary Botham. The threat which Marsh represents to any side batting at No. 7 (he scored 110 not out in the second innings of the centenary Test) is hardly shown by his recent form. In his last six innings he has made 18 runs.

To help stop the rot after tea O'Keeffe had first Thomson with him, then Pascoe. The ninth wicket partnership was worth 41, the last wicket partnership 47. All three batted with a lack of difficulty which must have caused some blushes on the Australian balcony and given England fair reason for looking forward to batting today, so long, at any rate, as the sun shines. Last night Boycott and Brearley, cheered as enthusiastically as Thomson had been, survived the three overs that were bowled at them with more inward than outward concern. Boycott had three balls to face, all from Pascoe. Those who wish to be sure of seeing his confrontation with Thomson must catch the early bus this morning.

AUSTRALIA: First Innings

R. B. McCosker c Brearley b Hendrick	51
I. C. Davis c Botham b Underwood	33
*G. S. Chappell b Botham	19
D. W. Hookes c Hendrick b Willis	17
K. D. Walters c Hendrick b Botham	11
R. D. Robinson c Brearley b Greig	11
†R. W. Marsh lbw b Botham	0
K. J. O'Keeffe not out	48
M. H. N. Walker c Hendrick b Botham	0
J. R. Thomson c Knott b Botham	21
L. S. Pascoe c Greig b Hendrick	20
Extras (b 4, l-b 2, n-b 6)	12
Total	**243**

Fall of wickets: 1–79, 2–101, 3–131, 4–133, 5–153, 6–153, 7–153, 8–155, 9–196, 10–243.

Bowling: Willis 15–0–58–1; Hendrick 21.2–6–46–2, Botham 20–5–74–5, Greig 15–4–35–1, Underwood 11–5–18–1.

ENGLAND: First Innings

*J. M. Brearley not out	5
G. Boycott not out	1
Extras (nb 3)	3
Total: (no wkt)	**9**

R. A. Woolmer, D. W. Randall, A. W. Greig, A. P. E. Knott, G. Miller, J. T. Botham, D. L. Underwood, M. Hendrick and R. G. D. Willis to bat.

Bowling (to date): Thomson 2–1–2–0, Pascoe 1–0–4–0.

Umpires: H. D. Bird and Constant

A man at odds

MICHAEL PARKINSON
The Sunday Times

31 July 1977 *The return of Geoff Boycott to the England cricket side was one of the most important events of the year—and not just for the part he played in Australia's defeat. Michael Parkinson, a fellow Yorkshireman—and, with Brian Clough, one of Boycott's few close friends in public life—brought a closer understanding of the cricketer than most writers.*

He carries with him the air of a man perpetually at odds with the world. No one suffers the slings and arrows of outrageous fortune – real or imagined – more publicly than Geoffrey Boycott. When his recall to Test cricket was announced – surely a matter of personal joy – he was heard on television predicting that there would be many people hoping he would fail at Trent Bridge. This comment surprised no one who has closely observed The World versus Geoffrey Boycott.

Of all the athletes I know none has worked more assiduously to become the greatest player of his generation, and, similarly, no one of my acquaintance has paid so little attention to the inevitable consequences of succeeding in that ambition; namely the business of being a public figure.

Geoffrey Boycott, who neither knows nor cares overmuch about anything else outside of cricket, would claim that his job was to play like the great cricketer he is and not bother about winning any charm contests. Yet there is little doubt – and he knows it, too – that his career in the game would have been a whole lot less turbulent and troublesome had he been able to apply to his life off the field the intelligence and tactical awareness he reveals on it.

Geoffrey Boycott's ruthless drive to succeed has cost him dear in what might be termed his 'social development'. At 36 and with 15 or more years behind him of playing sport at the topmost level, meeting people from all sections of society, travelling the world, he can still be a gauche uncertain figure. No more, you might say, than many other athletes with the same kind of experience. Which is true, except Geoffrey Boycott is much more intelligent than the average athlete.

The paradox of Geoffrey Boycott is that the man who is absolutely self-sufficient in making such difficult decisions, who has mastered in his own way the intricacies of the most complex of games, is the same person who presents himself as a slightly bitter, embattled figure only at ease in the company of his own beloved Yorkshire team or the handful of people he trusts with his friendship.

The answer as to why he chose this course of action, and the answer to a lot of other questions about Geoffrey Boycott, was probably given much later in his career when, as England's opening batsman, he was en route to Australia with Mike Smith's team. Stopping over in Sri Lanka every player in the party had to fill in a form stating, among other things, the purpose of their visit. Everyone completed the form by stating 'cricket'; everyone, that is, except Geoffrey Boycott, who wrote, simply: 'Business.'

It is difficult for anyone, including fellow players, to calculate completely Boycott's total absorption in the game he loves. His idea of relaxation is a three-hour net practice, his sole topic of conversation cricket. He is single, teetotal, non-smoking and still living at home with his mother. In his obsessive dedication to physical fitness, his careful diet, his abhorrence of late nights, he further isolates himself from the majority of his fellow cricketers who as much enjoy the social side of the game as the playing of it. Indeed, when playing on overseas tours, on free days when the rest of the team were to be found relaxing on the beach or round the pool, Boycott used to retire to his room and stay there all day with curtains drawn in the belief that exposure to the sun would sap his strength and therefore reduce his ability as a player.

Boycott at first swallowed his pride under Denness because he calculated, and correctly, that his days were numbered. It was when Greig was given the vice-captaincy that Boycott foresaw a future whereby he was kept from his ambition to captain England himself, not only by one less experienced but, moreover, a foreign player. He was deeply hurt by what he considered to be an insulting rejection of his claims. Not for the first time in his life he went his own lonely way.

What changed his mind was Greig's departure and pressure from people around him to display his great talents in the settings they deserve. Anyone who loves the game and delights in watching a great batsman at work can only rejoice at his return.

He is a loner; more, I suspect, by the circumstances that shaped him rather than by any natural inclination. From the very first moment he played cricket in the Yorkshire mining village where he was born he was determined not simply to play for Yorkshire and England but to be the pre-eminent batsman of his generation. In other words, his ambition was not simply a Yorkshire cap but the laurel wreaths worn by Sutcliffe and Hutton.

I met him first when he came to play for Barnsley at the age of 15. In those days, not fully fleshed out and wearing National Health Service spectacles, he looked an unlikely and puny recruit to a notoriously tough league which took no prisoners. But from the beginning he showed himself to be an exceptional talent with an insatiable appetite for learning the game. There was also the first indication of the ruthless streak in his character that later led him into conflict with some fellow players and the executive.

The story goes that he was playing a friendly Sunday fixture and batting well when play was interrupted to hand him a message asking him to report the next day to Headingley to join the Yorkshire first team squad. Geoffrey Boycott read the message and walked to the pavilion even though his innings was not finished. He was pursued to the pavilion gate by the opposing skipper who, not unnaturally, pointed out that it was courtesy to ask his permission before departing the field of play. Moreover, where was he going? Geoffrey Boycott looked at him and said: 'I've finished with this kind of cricket.' And he had.

If Geoff Boycott can now loosen just a little the tight rein of his self discipline and vaunting ambition we might be lucky enough to see the re-emergence of a great international batsman in the Test arena, and, more importantly, the emergence of a remarkable man with a lot to offer cricket both on and off the field.

There are propitious signs. Recently Yorkshire were playing Nottinghamshire at Trent Bridge and bowling badly. In his endeavour to stem the flow of runs Boycott was handicapped by injuries to two of his key bowlers. After retrieving the ball from the mid-wicket boundary Boycott was addressed by a spectator who, in a loud voice, demanded to know why Robinson wasn't given a bowl. Boycott explained that Robinson was injured. Next over, retrieving yet another ball from the same spot, the spectator inquired why Cope wasn't bowling. Again Boycott took time out to explain, patiently and politely, that the bowler was injured. When the same thing happened again a few overs later Boycott told the man that he would speak to him at close of play.

Thus, at stumps, Geoffrey Boycott walked across to the spectator and patiently explained his tactics during the last session. After 10 minutes of detailed insight into his captaincy and problems he said to the man: 'Now, does that satisfy you?' 'All I can say is God help us if they mek thee t'captain of England,' said the spectator, and went home.

The point is Geoffrey Boycott told this joke against himself last week. And laughed at the humour of it all.

Up and under

CLEM THOMAS
The Observer

New Zealand 19 British Isles 7

31 July 1977 *The British Lions managed to lose their way in the third Test against New Zealand at Carisbrooke, where the All Black backs produced a harder—and cleaner—brand of rugby.*

Virtue certainly found its reward when a cleaned-up All Black side reverted to playing some fine rugby behind the scrum, nullifying a superb performance by the Lions' forwards, and breaking the dominance of British rugby since 1974. The All Blacks won a thoroughly deserved victory –

against which there can be no complaint of any kind – by a goal, two penalty goals, a dropped goal and a try to a penalty goal and a try.

It was strange to see how the wheel seems to have gone full circle, for here was a British pack dominating in possession but the game being won by the skilful, inventive and attractive approach of their opponents. For this New Zealand must thank the boldness of the selectors who went for their lives for the attacking approach.

Bevan Wilson, the new cap at full back, had a dream debut and his stability brought a new confidence into his team. Brian Ford, another new cap, also showed that he too might become a fixture in the side.

The Lions' forwards were magnificent, and they have every cause to resent the appalling play of their own midfield which was bereft of almost any attribute. For the first time in the series they totally outplayed their opponents for the whole 80 minutes – apart from some familiar driving loose play by Kirkpatrick, Haden and Mourie. The Lions took the line-out by 22 to 14, took the only two tight-heads and generally played with a vigour that any competent back division could have translated into a decisive win.

A few chickens came home to roost and it was evident early in the game that Brynmor Williams had not recovered from his hamstring injury. He finally left the field 10 minutes into the second half to be replaced by Doug Morgan. It was also apparent that Gareth Evans is not a Test wing, and on this evidence neither is Dave Burcher a Test centre. Phil Bennett must take the major blame, however, for seldom has he played so badly. He constantly crabbed across field, gave his centres an extraordinary range of bad passes, and appeared to have no notion of any strategy.

Throughout the tour the Lions' backs have never in my view aligned properly and it was interesting to hear Carwyn James confirming this. He also said about the Lions' forwards: 'This is the best pack I have ever seen. I never thought that I would see the day when a Lions' team would win so much possession against an All Black pack.'

There was a capacity crowd at Carisbrook when the All Blacks kicked off on yet another excruciatingly heavy pitch and within the minute went into the lead. From the first line-out they set up a ruck for Lyn Davis to throw a huge pass which found the All Blacks' threequarters clear. Bev Wilson came into the line but Bill Osborne wisely missed him out and put the ball to Bruce Robertson. He swung out and chipped back for the line where the predatory figure of Ian Kirkpatrick picked up a yard out and went over; Wilson converted.

The ease with which they scored was ominous, but within seven minutes the Lions recovered with a try by Willie Duggan after a blind-side break from Brynmor Williams.

The more positive play of the All Blacks, however, quickly brought them another score. Doug Bruce carried to the blind side from a scrum. Bruce Robertson and Ford took the ball on to the line, and there Haden prised it from a ruck to dive over. The Lions lost J. J. Williams with a pulled muscle – McGechan replacing him – 10 minutes from half-time when the score was 10-4.

After Brynmor Williams went off, the Lions forwards were going really well and when Andy Irvine kicked a 32-yard penalty (Kirkpatrick and Norton were offside in the loose) the game was really on again for the Lions.

The turning-point came in the fifteenth minute of the second half when, after winning two successive scrums in the All Blacks' 25, Bennett had a kick charged down. At once the All Blacks took the game to the other end of the field where Cotton got offside and Wilson kicked an easy penalty. He then kicked another, and Bruce Robertson finished matters with a dropped goal from the last kick of the match.

So the Lions lost heavily to an All Blacks team which not only played and behaved impeccably but broke the supremacy of the British Isles. The tourists now have the Herculean task of saving the series in a fortnight's time at Auckland.

NEW ZEALAND: B. Wilson, B. Williams, B. Robertson, B. Osborne, B. Ford, D. Bruce, L. Davies, B. Bush, I. Norton (capt) **J. McEldowney, I. Kirkpatrick, F. Oliver, A. Haden, G. Mourie, L. Knight**

BRITISH ISLES: A. Irvine, J. Williams (I. McGeechan, 38 m.), D. Burcher, S. Fenwick, G. Vans, P. Bennett (capt), **B. Williams (D. Morgan, 58 m.), G. Price, P. Wheeler, F. Cotton, D. Quinnell, G. Brown, B. Beaumont, T. Cobner, W. Duggan**

AUGUST

Small fry, big chips

IAN BAIN
The Observer

7 August 1977 *The commercialisation of tennis, golf and now cricket has been inevitable, if not always acceptable; the thought of angling for cash from a river bank seems the very end of the line.*

The competitive element in most sports is something to be encouraged. Golf, football, tennis and athletics were all designed to match one man against the next, and there would be little pleasure for participant or spectator if that were not the case.

The competition in that supposedly tranquil pursuit of angling is becoming more keen and less easy to defend. Fishing, throughout its history, has always been either for food or fun and the comparatively recent innovation of big money in match angling has done much to change the entire outlook of its followers.

On any Saturday or Sunday afternoon of the nine-month coarse season there are something like 100 to 150 contests involving 100 or more anglers taking place up and down the country. The aim is basically to haul in more fish than any other competitor, and the simple pleasure of catching is greatly overshadowed by guessing the possible value of each specimen as it is slipped into the net.

The matchman, then, is an entirely different creature from the ordinary angler. He is nurtured by greed and glory and becomes expert at his task, for it is a vital ability to read a water and judge immediately how it should be fished and what it could contain. There is also the decision to be made whether to concentrate on small fry by the side or wait hopefully for big ones in the middle. The fish doesn't matter, it's the weight that counts.

Cash is a driving force, for an average match winner can pick up £250 in prize money, pools and bets he has had on himself with the ubiquitous bookie who shouts the odds along the towpath and riverbanks of rural England. Ladbrokes have even involved themselves in this new and lucrative market. In really big matches, like the Embassy Challenge final, the victor will walk away with nearly £4,000.

It cannot be denied that the matchman is far better at his sport than the pleasure angler, but he fishes more frequently and even practices on waters where a match is impending. The difference between a professional and an amateur footballer is the nearest comparison.

But the professional's trouble is that he involves himself deeply in the politics of his sport, and in angling that is particularly so.

A glance at the stories in the current *Angler's Mail* underlines this. 'Cup Tie Row' blazes one headline, and it goes on to relate how Bradford City and Birmingham angling associations are fighting over when to fish their round in the East Anglian Cup contest and how both teams could be eliminated by default.

Birmingham, a giant of a club, with 60,000 members, said they were not prepared to abandon any weekend matches to fish the tie. They offered a midweek date instead and £2 towards each Bradford man's travelling costs.

'We regard this as contemptuous,' the paper quotes one Bradford official as saying.

Another story is headed: '4,000 Showdown. England team gets cash challenge from "Outcast".' It begins: 'Southern match ace Ray Mumford, shunned by England yet again, has thrown down a staggering £4,000 cash challenge to the team to fish in the World Championships in Luxembourg this year.'

Apparently Mr Mumford is so upset that he has not been included in England's eight-man squad that he has bet each of the eight £500 that he would catch more fish than them in duels which have yet to be arranged – if there were any takers. 'I want to show the selectors that I should at least have been given a chance,' he said.

A third story in the *Mail* goes further. Angry match-men in the North East have flooded the organisers of a big invitation event with complaints that their local hero hadn't been invited.

It would be easy to accuse the angling professionals of pettiness if they didn't take these matters so seriously. They regard them as vitally important, for they seem quite removed from the concept of what angling really is about. And that's a terrible shame.

Boycott's century of centuries

MICHAEL MELFORD
The Daily Telegraph

12 August 1977 *Boycott's great day seems almost a story from a pre-war Wizard (Wilson surely achieved this feat), but in recording the historic event of his hundredth century Michael Melford does not let his readers go short of the rest of the day's play.*

Only the most macabre imagination could have pictured Geoff Boycott failing to make his 100th hundred on his return to Test cricket at Headingly, and at 10 minutes to six yesterday evening the feat for which one and all were waiting was duly accomplished. The day's play thus ended amid tremendous scenes of jubilation, and the fact that England's score stood promisingly at 252 for four did nothing to detract from them.

The churlish might say that 67 runs after tea was a poor haul against tiring bowling lacking variety on a splendid batting pitch. For once, however, England have time on their side and do not need to take risks; moreover, only 87 overs were bowled. In this context, of course, they had the ideal batsman in charge in Boycott, with his massive concentration and unflagging technique. He was all but caught at the wicket when 22, but otherwise played with a look of permanence which made the occasional mishap at the other end seem of minor concern.

The gates were closed before the start of play on a superb cloudless morning with none of Wednesday's haziness. England, as expected, left out Miller and Australia preferred the brisk left-arm spin of Bright to the wrist spin of O'Keeffe.

Whatever effect this Australian change may have had on England's batsmen it relieved their bowlers of having to probe the near impregnable defence of O'Keefe which can be irksome late in the innings, especially if somone is batting well at the other end.

It seemed a wonderful toss for England to win, not least in their strange and felicitous position of being two up; but in three balls Brearley was out, caught at the wicket off a good one from Thomson which he had to play.

Until lunch Boycott and Woolmer put things in perspective, batting with care, restrained confidence and just a little luck. Boycott gave a hard low chance off Walker in front of first slip which Marsh reached and would have held in more prosperous times; but not here.

When Boycott was 26 Pascoe bowled him one of the morning's few bumpers which lobbed up into the slips, apparently off Boycott's forearm, but otherwise they played some tidy bowling strictly on its merits – Boycott producing one fine square cut.

The bowling still gave little away after lunch and nothing was attempted unless the length erred a lot. Only six runs had been added in 15 minutes after lunch when Woolmer pushed out to Thomson and was picked up, low down at first slip, by Chappell.

Randall breezed in and out again, making 20 runs in 25 minutes, with some quick, wristy cutting before he played round a ball from Pascoe and was lbw.

Boycott made three runs in nearly 50 minutes after lunch, but, at about the same time as at Trent Bridge, he had completed the reconnaissance and was prepared to advance on all fronts. His 50 received a rapturous ovation, which was a merciful restoration to normality after the hostility which had greeted Greig a few minutes before.

However, there are problems in differentiating between

the goodies and the baddies when the alleged baddies are on your side and Greig, on his luckier days, is undeniably a useful batsman to have in when the tempo needs raising. When the ball was pitched up or nearly so he unfolded his long reach and played some good strokes through the covers. Though the ball was not always in the middle of the bat he hooked Chappell for six and England had only one bad moment before tea.

The Australians appealed at full throttle for a catch at the wicket on the leg side when Boycott was 75. When it was refused they expressed such disappointment, some of it presumably verbal, that umpire Alley spoke severely to the bowler, Bright. After tea, when the fourth wicket had added 96 in 105 minutes, Greig was out in a not unfamiliar way, bowled driving outside a ball from Thomson which came back to hit his off stump.

Roope in his early stages would not be recommended watching for those of a nervous disposition, but nothing seemed likely to dislodge Boycott as he made five in 45 minutes after tea and moved on towards the inevitable moment of glory.

A hook off Pascoe produced another four, but Walker, in a fine spell of 10 overs for 14 runs, made him work hard and it was a straight drive to the football stand off Chappell which eventually brought about the historic event. The ball was not half way to the boundary when the hero's bat was raised on high and amid a rare hubbub small boys were converging on him from all over Yorkshire.

When he reappeared from the melee five minutes later he was without his cap, but it was returned by a repentant souvenir-hunter before he resumed operations, looking understandably weary.

There was another, almost equally unusual interruption when Thomson had to be stopped from taking the new ball because only 81 overs had been bowled and not 85, as shown on the scoreboard. It was eventually taken for the last two overs, wherein Thomson was driven by Boycott and Walker cut by Roope, who by now was looking safe without finding the gaps.

And so they came in, followed to the pavilion by a large proportion of the 22,000 who sang and waved and cheered until the genial hero made his last balcony appearance and was escorted off in royal state by the police.

ENGLAND: First Innings

*J. M. Brearley c Marsh b Thomson	0
G. Boycott not out............	110
R. A. Woolmer c Chappell b Thomson	37
D. W. Randall lbw b Pascoe	20
A. W. Greig b Thomson ...	43
G. R. J. Roope not out......	19
Extras (b 1 lb 3 nb 17 w 2)	23
Total (4 wkts)	**252**

To bat: I. T. Botham, *A. P. E. Knott, D. L. Underwood, M. Hendrick, R. G. D. Willis

Fall of wickets: 1–0, 2–82, 3–105, 4–201.

Bowling: Thomson 21–4–78–3, Walker 27–12–59–0, Pascoe 20–7–48–1, Walters 3–0–5–0, Bright 6–3–14–0, Chappell 10–2–25–0.

AUSTRALIA:

R. B. McCosker, J. C. Davis, *G. S. Chappell, D. W. Hookes, K. D. Walters, R. D. Robinson, †R. W. Marsh, R. J. Bright, M. H. N. Walker, J. R. Thomson, L. S. Pascoe.

Umpires: W. L. Budd and W. E. Alley

*Captain †Wicketkeeper

Yorkshire to the marrow

JACK FINGLETON
The Sunday Times

14 August 1977 *Watching and observing are very different exercises. Most sports writers perform the latter well, though some would wish they could do it as well as Jack Fingleton does, in this typical piece on Geoff Boycott.*

Geoff Boycott is so much a victim that he's predictable. I don't wish to add a syllable to what I wrote about him when he made that century many moons ago against the Australians for Yorkshire at Scarborough nor what I anticipated would happen when he returned, as he had to, to the English team.

He made 191 against us at Headingly but what the scorebook doesn't tell us is that he touched the ankle of his right foot at the rate of 40 an hour for every hour that he batted, that he took off his cap and wiped his perspiring brow 364 times and that he conducted spirited mid-wicket conversations with his various partners at the end of every over. And he played 466 balls.

Boycott has other mannerisms. He diligently marks his guard twice every time he gets down the business end, one at the usual mark, the other inside his crease. I anticipated that we would watch him for many hours in the middle and that he would monopolise this series as soon as he returned. He did just that at Trent Bridge and again at Headingley and he will set himself to do it again at the Oval.

I sat here and talked with Tim Rice, the playwright, one day and he told me that Boycott rang him after he, Rice, made mention of him in an article. I believe Boycott to be so thorough that he reads everything that is written of him. Tim is a wary fellow and having friends who can imitate accents and pull his leg he had doubts that it was Boycott. He didn't believe it until Boycott told him how many centuries he made in 1972 and what his average was.

That is Boycott. He can bore with his grim methods, his unrelenting love of piling run upon run and the relish he gets from being just in the middle. But Headingly accepted he was there on Thursday to prove a point and the whole country was behind him and cheered him.

He resolutely defends and defends until the ball of poor merit comes along which he then puts where it belongs with infinite certainty. It is then that he removes his cap, wipes his brow with his sweat bands on both wrists, gives a thought possibly to what that last four makes his average, marks out his crease again and bends, now squarer to the bowler than a few years ago, to his unremitting task.

Boycott is Yorkshire to his marrow and he never believes in giving anything away. He it was who put England in its unassailable position. He has no fears of pace bowlers. Indeed, he now gives himself a little ground to meet them head on, as I noticed him standing out of his crease to them.

Hutton and Sutcliffe are other Yorkshiremen who batted by the day rather than the hour against Australia. At short leg to those two, I frequently thought I knew why Yorkshire was called the county of Broad Acres. Hutton at the end of the over would take off his cap, throw his hair back and smooth it and replace the cap from the front.

Herbert had one mannerism when taking guard: he would mark it with the reverse side of the bat and then meticulously wipe the bat. Sutcliffe knew his moments of luck against us, as has Boycott here and at Trent Bridge, but that is our fault, not Boycott's. He accepts that as his right as Sutcliffe did.

Boycott has other mannerisms, such as taking his gloves off frequently, and I arrived at my totals above by noting them over the hour and multiplying them by the 10½ hours he batted. If anybody missed them they will be on show at the Oval, mark my words. Geoff sought me out during that Centenary Test in Melbourne to contest something I had written about his running between the wickets. As I said, he does not miss anything critical or analytical. I add quickly that his running here was flawless, turning many twos into threes, and stealing many short singles with extreme safety. He ran as well as Sutcliffe ever did.

England turned the Australian batsmen inside out. It is no excuse that our men have spent several tiring days in the field. The Australian batting crumpled in abysmal manner, with no application or heart. We capitulated – and how much we would have give for a Boycott with his intensity of purpose.

One other thing about him. Despite his success of 107 and 80 not out at Trent Bridge I got the impression by his demeanour in the field that he felt himself on the fringe of the team. Here he seemed to be there as by divine right, in his rightful place. If it were put to him, I would not be surprised if he admitted he had done a few foolish things in recent years and wants to forget all about them.

New peaks at Helsinki

CLIFF TEMPLE
The Times

15 August 1977 *Besides the achievements of the East Germans in the European Cup the British efforts do not appear to add up to much.*

But team competitions in athletics, however clever the points scoring system, tends to bury individual performances—and, as Temple's report shows, Britain had several outstanding ones.

With points from some unexpected sources, Britain's athletes reached a new level in team competition when our women's team finished third in the European Cup final at Helsinki yesterday, their highest position in the competition, while the British men equalled their best-ever placing, fourth. Yet between them they produced only two winners, with Nicholas Rose's gritty victory in the 5,000 metres yesterday adding to Steven Ovett's 1,500 metres win on Saturday. But the solid points scoring came from other British athletes who also refused to be overawed by the occasion or the tough opposition.

If it is traditional that our runners do well then it is no surprise that the two victories came on the track. But the fourth places of Keith Connor in the triple jump and of Brian Hooper in the pole vault, plus the third place on Saturday of Roy Mitchell in the long jump, were all examples of the British field eventers rising to the occasion where the ranking list predictions had been more gloomy.

For the girls, two fourth places yesterday were my pick as the team heroines, because on the day that mattered they produced their lifetime best performances. Ann Ford, from Feltham, knocked seven seconds from her best time in the 3,000 metres with 8 min. 55·9 sec. and, if she had not run wide for a considerable distance, would surely have broken the United Kingdom record, which stands just two-fifths of a second faster. But she was still mixing it with the first three right up to the final 250 metres in a race won by the Russian world record-holder, Lyudmila Bragina.

Then, in the high jump, the shy Brenda Gibbs, from Leicester, cleared a personal best of 6ft. 0½in., an improvement of an inch. If the gap between that performance and the new world record of 6ft. 5½in. set by the winner, Rosemarie Ackermann, of East Germany, seems considerable, it misses the point that this type of competition is exclusively about team struggles and Miss Gibbs had been forecast to finish a fairly distant last.

Nicholas Rose must also rate as a great competitor after

the 5,000 metres in which he destroyed the field as effectively as, and in a similar manner to, Brenda Foster, winner of the past two European Cup final 5,000 metres in 1973 and 1975. The lanky Rose, whose mane of hair makes him look like a lead guitarist in search if a pop group, was content to sit back early on, as a sudden heavy rainstorm drenched the field.

After 2,000 metres he went ahead, and began a series of bursts which strung his rivals out, and left only Karl Fleschen, of West Germany, the fastest man in the race, on his heels. After the first burst the rest gradually caught up, but no sooner had they regained contact than Rose pushed the accelerator again, and they drifted back to contest the minor placings.

'I didn't expect to get rid of them that early,' Rose admitted afterwards. Even Fleschen, with his upright style and low arm carriage contrasting with Rose's loping run, had eventually to allow daylight between himself and the leader and the gap stretched from ten metres to 20, and 40 by the bell. Fleschen himself was caught for second place by the last lap sprint of Enn Sellik, of the Soviet Union, but Rose was safe, winning in 13min. 27.84sec.

'I was really glad to see that finishing line,' he said. 'I didn't dare look round to see where Fleschen was in the closing stages. But now maybe people will credit me with having beaten some good guys. I'm always being accused of never running against the best. Well, Fleschen and the others are no mugs, are they?'

It took a foreign journalist to needle the normally placid Rose, who has lost none of his native Bristol accent despite his recent college years spent in Western Kentucky, where he returns in the autumn. He asked: 'Are you Brendan Foster's reserve?' Rose's reply was suitably brusque.

Rose will now surely be asked to run the 5,000 metres for the European Select team in next month's World Cup, but he is only 'fifty-fifty' certain that he will accept such an invitation. 'I've run a lot of races since March, and I think I need a rest. I'll talk it over with my coach when I get back to Bristol.'

The European Select team, which is announced today, should also include Steven Ovett in the 1,500 metres, Alan

Pascoe in the 400 metres hurdles, Sonia Lannaman in the 100 metres, Tessa Sanderson in the javelin, and perhaps one or two more British athletes, as a result of their performances here. It may also include Brendan Foster himself at 10,000 metres, as he has given tantalising glimpses of good form this summer, and his failure to earn selection for the European Cup has not, I understand, ruled him out of World Cup contention altogether. Sadly, Tony Simmons, who finished last in the 10,000 metres here on Saturday, must have greatly diminished his chances for the World Cup as a result of an uncharacteristic poor performance, which he was at a loss to explain. A very heavy racing programme recently may have contributed, however.

The rough tactics which one has almost come to expect in these European Cup races reared up both in the men's 1500 metres on Saturday and in the 800 metres yesterday. In the shorter race, Sebastian Coe, who is making a comeback to the sort of form which won him the European indoor gold medal last March, was suddenly projected sideways about 70 metres from home when making his run for the tape.

It was a crowded, niggling race, but Coe had just passed the eventual winner, Willi Wulbeck, of West Germany, when 'I felt Wulbeck grab my arm and push me out into the third lane. I was going well, and I knew exactly what I had to do up to that point, but all of a sudden I was desperately trying just to keep on my feet'. A protest over the incident was lodged by British officials, but almost inevitably it came to nothing.

So Coe had to settle for fourth place, and nurse a couple of spike wounds which he had incurred early in the race.

The British men finished two points ahead of their old rivals, Poland, for fourth place, and if we introduce the 'ifs and buts' element I suppose the Soviet Union, who were just six points ahead of Britain in third place, were within range. But the British performance, which matches the 1975 placing in Nice, was satisfying.

East Germany and West Germany are the two men's teams to qualify direct for the World Cup in Düsseldorf, while East Germany and the Soviet Union go through in the women's contest. The British girls never really had a chance of a place in the first two, but beating West Germany was a great achievement. Both countries scored the same number of points, 67, and the normal way of deciding a tie, the greater number of winners, did not apply, as neither nation had an individual victor. Even looking at the second places did not break the tie, so the decision finally went Britain's way as a result of more third places.

The Lions throw away their chance

JOHN REASON
The Daily Telegraph

New Zealand 10 British Isles 9

15 August 1977 *After a tour which had many problems, particularly off the field, the Lions came to their final match needing victory to square the Tests against New Zealand. With their pack again playing a dominant part they lead 9–3 midway through the second half, but then came a curious change of tactics and defeat. Altogether the Lions won 21 of their 25 matches.*

The British Isles threw away a wonderful chance of winning the final Test at Eden Park and saving the 1977 series against New Zealand. The Lions forwards had played so well, and scrum-half Doug Morgan so sensibly to keep them in command that midway through the second half the game was there for the taking.

At that point, though, the Lions suddenly loosened their grip and abandoned the game that had given them a 9–3 lead. Instead of sticking to their policy of keeping the ball in front of their forwards and kicking for touch they began some almost suicidal speculations in midfield.

This was quite unnecessary, because the Lions forwards had control of the line-out. However, Phil Bennett, the Lions captain, threw out a couple of passes that caused his centres considerable embarrassment and gave renewed life to the All Blacks.

Their forwards had been given the most humiliating pounding, but they hauled themselves off the floor and chased after the Lions in the hope of exploiting a mistake which might give them a chance to save the match.

That mistake was duly made. The All Blacks duly exploited it and in the first of five minutes of injury time Lawrie Knight, the All Black No. 8, scored a try which won both the match and the series for New Zealand.

At that point the British Isles were leading by a goal and a penalty goal to two penalty goals kicked by Bevan Wilson. Knight's final try gave New Zealand victory by one point and the series by three matches to one.

Even then the Lions nearly won the match, because in the last four minutes they forced an attacking five-yard scrum and then another a yard from the New Zealand line.

On the first occasion the All Blacks saved themselves only by collapsing the scrum, which is never penalised, as it should be, in New Zealand; and on the second occasion Andy Irvine, the Lions full-back, dropped a poor pass in midfield.

By then, though, the Lions were conscious that a Test match and a series had been thrown away. Bennett has not had a successful tour, either as a captain or as a player, but I doubt whether even he will ever be able to explain to himself why he turned away from the game which had put the Lions in command of the match.

Sadly, it was Bennett's missed touch-kick which gave the All Blacks their try. He went back to tidy up the ball in defence in a situation where he needed to kick with his left foot to be absolutely sure of finding touch. Bennett does not kick with his left foot, of course, and he had to put in an ambitious hook kick over his left shoulder while running backwards. Distance was not a consideration; the ball had only to go into touch.

It did not do so, and when Bill Osborne caught it in the New Zealand centre he returned an up-and-under which Steve Fenwick caught under pressure and passed to Peter Wheeler, who lost the ball in a tackle. Even then the gods were frowning on the Lions, because the ball bounced straight to Knight and he ran through to score.

In that one moment the Lions squandered another matchful of tremendous work by their forwards. As ever, the Lions scrummaging was overwhelming, but their greatest triumph at Eden Park was the domination that Gordon Brown, Jeff Squire and Willie Duggan achieved in the line-out.

Most of the ball that New Zealand tried to throw to numbers five and seven in the line-out was either taken by the Lions or spoiled, though it must be said that the All Blacks' throwing into the line-out on the left wing was so poor, particularly when Taylor replaced the injured Ford, that their jumpers stood little chance.

The All Blacks also lost their loose-head prop, John McEldowney, with a ricked neck, and while they were waiting for Billy Bush to replace him they twice put only their front row into a scrum against the Lions. Nothing could have been a more conclusive demonstration of the Lions' domination of the scrummage in this series, and of New Zealand's acceptance of it.

However, the object of winning possession is to score points, and the Lions did not do so. Their loose-forward moves were a failure and their backs have long since lost their confidence in attack.

The Lions' only try was scored by Morgan after an excellent line-out peel initiated by Duggan was carried to a successful conclusion by Cotton, Beaumont, Price and Fenwick. Morgan converted the try, and also kicked a penalty goal.

NEW ZEALAND: B. Wilson, B. G. Williams, W. M. Osborne, B. J. Robertson. B. Ford, O. D. Bruce, L. Davis, J. T. McEldowney, R. W. Norton (capt), **K. K. Lambert, F. J. Oliver, A. M. Haden, I. A. Kirkpatrick, G. Mourie, L. G. Knight**

Replacements: M. Taylor for Ford (45 mins), W. K. Bush for McEldowney (60 mins).

BRITISH ISLES: A. R. Irvine, H. E. Rees, S. P. Fenwick, I. R. McGeechan, G. L. Evans, P. Bennett (capt), **D. W. Morgan, F. E. Cotton, P. J. Wheeler, G. Price, W. B. Beaumont, G. L. Brown, A. Neary, J. Squire, W. P. Duggan**

REFEREE: D. Millar

Close bows out

HENRY BLOFELD
The Guardian

27 August 1977 *A fifteen-over game to decide who should go to Lord's for the final of the oldest one-day knock-out competition is a nonsense; when it marks the departure of a man who has served the game as long and as diligently as Brian Close then commercialism is as close to strangling the sport as it has ever been. Henry Blofeld never lost sight of the match itself but he captured its sadness too.*

Brian Close's dream of winning the Gillette Cup and taking Somerset to their first major title in his last year in county cricket ended sadly in 80 minutes yesterday morning at Lord's. In this time Somerset battled disastrously in their fifteen-over semi-final against Middlesex and were bowled out for 59 in 14.4 overs. Middlesex themselves were given a good start by Radley, and some firm strokes by Gatting enabled them to win with comfort by six wickets with 3.3 overs to spare. They reached 61 for four in 11.3 overs.

Any side which after five blank days loses a match which should have been played over 60 overs and is then truncated to fifteen overs is bound to feel that they have been treated badly. It was decided to play a fifteen-over match starting at 11 o'clock because the weather forecast was bad and it was desperately important with the final only eight days away that a result should be achieved.

If this situation should happen again one wonders if the authorities will not decide to postpone the final. In this case it might have been put off for a week to allow a proper semi-final to be played at Lord's next Saturday. It was decided that this was not possible, however, and so in front of a gate of two or three thousand, instead of 20,000, Somerset lost and Middlesex won. Who can blame Somerset if they feel they would have had a fairer chance over sixty overs?

As it was they batted badly, but the toss was extremely important. Close guessed wrong and Mike Smith put Somerset in to bat. For the side fielding first a 15-over match is solely a question of preventing runs and hoping that their opponents will get themselves out; for the side batting first it becomes a matter of slogging and hoping. It is almost impossible to decide what will constitute a satisfactory score.

Somerset slogged and got out for 59. How much better it would have been for them if they had tried to build an innings of around 80, but that is, of course, a thought in retrospect. Richards, on whom most of their hopes lay, drove Selvey off the back foot over long off for six in the second over and then failed to pick up a full toss from Daniel in the third and was LBW. Close off-drove Selvey for four and the third boundary of the Somerset innings was a cover drive by Burgess – the only player to reach double figures – off Daniel.

Wickets fell all the time. Denning, Close – who retired to the pavilion at Lord's for the last time, head down – and Rose all drove across the line and were bowled. Kitchen hit a full toss to square leg, there were three hopeless run outs and Burgess was bowled having a heave right at the end. Daniel is too quick to slog and, like Selvey, bowled a full length and profited. Daniel finished with four for 24 and was made man of the match and Selvey took three for 32.

Radley was soon square cutting Garner when Middlesex went in and although Garner was always hostile and took four wickets Dredge was not such a solid support to him as Selvey had been for Daniel. By the time Close came charging in from square leg to catch Radley it was virtually all over. It was a sad and anti-climactic end to a remarkable cricketer's last game at Lord's.

SOMERSET:

I. V. A. Richards lbw b Daniel	8
P. W. Denning b Selvey	4
D. B. Close b Selvey	9
M. J. Kitchen c Barlow b Selvey	3
B. C. Rose b Daniel	3
J. Garner run out	2
G. Burgess b Daniel	12
D. Breakwell run out	6
V. J. Marks run out	3
D. J. S. Taylor c Butcher b Daniel	5
C. H. Dredge not out	1
Extras (lb 2 nb 1)	3
Total (14.4 overs)	**59**

Fall of wickets: 13, 21, 27, 29, 34, 43, 52, 58.

Bowling: Daniel 7.4–0–24–4, Selvey 7–0–32–3.

MIDDLESEX:

Total (for 4 wkts 11.3 overs) **61**

Umpires: H. D. Bird, B. J. Meyer

SEPTEMBER

Middlesex take the cup

ROBIN MARLAR
The Sunday Times

4 September 1977 *The Gillette Cup has since its inception been a sure way of filling the seats at Lord's—which on most summer days are empty. This year there was song for the occasion, too.*

The Gillette was 15 years old before it bred a Welsh finalist. Not before time. The sospan fach singers sounded better in the sunshine than they do at Twickenham. Now so well established, the prize of the cup cannot easily be snatched at the first tilt, and though Glamorgan twice looked as though they might follow Northamptonshire's victory over Lancashire last year with another equally surprising success, they failed to make enough runs.

Middlesex hit the 178 runs they needed for their own first cup with five wickets and more than four overs remaining. There was one outstanding hit: the biggest six most of the ground had ever seen, by Llewellyn, on to the top of the pavilion, and one outstanding innings, Radley's 85, which won the match for Middlesex and earned him the Man of the Match award. And what must Brearley have felt near the end of his summer on a green carpet of magic, for all that his batting companion this time was a duck?

A short story. A reminder of what we now take for granted. In 1963 Frank Woolley, the great Frank Woolley, as tall and dignified in his seventies as he was batsman of grace and style in his thirties, a cricketer who by his very skill as a bowler managed to convey the notion that putting the ball into play was no lesser an activity than its magisterial dispatch with the bat, was invited to judge the Man of the Match at the very first-ever significant 60-over match – a preliminary tie to the first round at Old Trafford between

Lancashire who won by 101 runs, and Leicestershire. Woolley, ever the perfectionist, insisted even on this bitter May day that the only place on the ground from which he could conscientiously discharge his arduous responsibility in this new brand of cricket was alongside the sight screen. A special chair was placed for him there and he sat on it until the very end of the game.

Those were brave experimental days: Basil d'Oliveira, judging this final, looked much more relaxed in the pavilion. But then it was, after all, a lovely sunny day. Amazingly the match began on time. Brearley won the toss, and expecting that the rain must have done something to the square which has been more of a playground for ducks than cricketers these last three weeks, decided to show what they could do on a slow wicket in their first final. It was a shrewd decision.

Although Daniel conceded five runs in his first over and eight in his second to Alan Jones, Glamorgan's captain, Selvey bowled a most accurate spell, taking two wickets for 22 as Brearley let him bowl through his overs in the hope of settling the match there and then. With more luck Selvey could have done that. In fact, only Jones and King succumbed.

Hopkins, short, right-handed, dark side-boarded, and thick of girth, proceeded to play an important innings on the ground where he learned his trade, hitting the ball hard and often with short arm strokes, cricket's equivalent of uppercuts – and just as dangerous to the opponent. He found an ally in Llewellyn, left-handed, slightly taller, a player who had his share of illness as a child but now reveals himself as an attacking hitter. Off 30 overs Glamorgan made 99 for three but it was after that that they became stuck.

The Middlesex spinners, Edmonds and Emburey, bowled at the right pace for the wicket, and after lunch when Glamorgan desperately needed half-an-hour without the loss of a wicket Edmonds succeeded in bowling both Hopkins and Richards, whom he might have had stumped earlier. Llewellyn, however, was far from finished. He reached 50 to the great joy of the daffodillies and then hit Emburey's last ball so high up against the pavilion that Daniel on the boundary underneath it was reduced to looking upwards like an observer of unidentified flying objects.

At the other end Featherstone bowled and Llewellyn hit him even higher. This hit passed over Brearley who, in an interesting show of emotion in the crisis of the match, whirled round with finger pointed to young Gatting, placed on the long-on boundary at the Nursery end. Catch that, my son, was the message, or else. Gatting caught it with real cool and later pocketed Nash, taking that catch baseball style. Nash, meanwhile, had featured in a silly run-out. Facing Daniel with some apprehension he set off when the first ball hit him and Jones, the wicket-keeper, running to take the bowling, was thrown out by Barlow.

It seemed that Glamorgan could only get back into the game by taking two Middlesex wickets cheaply. They got one – Brearley's. Jones the Keeper caught him off Nash's first ball. Unfortunately for the Welshmen catches were put down thereafter and Smith's wicket did not fall until Middlesex had made 45.

Gatting also fell before Middlesex reached the home straight. Their driver was Clive Radley, the Middlesex beneficiary, so consistent a player over the years, who was able to unleash the best running between the wickets of the match with Barlow, and also managed to find one ball an over worth hitting for four – even off Cartwright.

The Welsh singing grew lower and lower and not even the loss of Barlow and Featherstone in quick succession could revive either the singers or the match, as Radley and Edmonds knocked off the final 25 runs to end what has to be recorded as one of the plainer cup finals.

At Lord's. Middlesex won toss

GLAMORGAN:

*A. Jones lbw b Selvey	18
J. A. Hopkins b Edmonds	47
C. L. King c Barlow b Selvey	8
R. C. Ontong c Gould b Gatting	0
M. J. Llewellyn c Gatting b Featherstone	62
G. Richards b Edmonds ...	3
†E. W. Jones run out	11
M. A. Nash c Gatting b Featherstone	3
A. E. Cordle not out	8
T. W. Cartwright st Gould b Featherstone	3
Extras (b 7 lb 5 w 2) ...	14
Overs 60 Total (9 wkts)	**177**

Fall of wickets: 1–21, 2–47, 3–50, 4–115, 5–129, 6–163, 7–163, 8–171, 9–177.

Bowling: Daniel 11–0–41–0, Selvey 12–4–22–2, Gatting 7–1–28–1, Edmonds 12–3–23–2, Emburey 12–2–32–0, Featherstone 6–0–17–3.

MIDDLESEX:

*J. M. Brearley c E. W. Jones b Nash	0
M. J. Smith lbw b Cartwright	22
C. T. Radley not out	85
M. W. Gatting c Hopkins b King........................	15
G. B. Barlow lbw b Richards	27
N. G. Featherstone b Nash	3
P. H. Edmonds not out ...	9
Extras (b 6 lb 11)	17
Overs 55.4 **Total** (5 wkts)	178

Fall of wickets: 1–0, 2–45, 3–72, 4–146, 5–153.

Bowling: Nash 12–3–31–2, Cordle 8.4–1–29–0, Cartwright 12–2–32–1, King 5–1–19–1, Richards 12–2–23–1, Wilkins 6–0–27–0

Umpires: D. J. Constant and T. W. Spencer

Middlesex won by 5 wickets

Half-marathon man

CLIFF TEMPLE
The Times

7 September 1977 *Steve Ovett was Britain's most successful runner of the summer, with British records for the Mile and 1500 metres and a host of other important victories as well. On track he is often flamboyant, a style which is sometimes mistaken for arrogance; off it he prefers to avoid the limelight. After Ovett's victory in the World Cup Cliff Temple traced the runner's rise to the top.*

Steven Ovett, the winner of the 1,500 metres in the World Cup in Düsseldorf on Saturday night in the United Kingdom record of 3min. 34.5sec., is the most exciting, and still untapped talent in international middle-distance running. In a sport where the stop watch is supposed to tell all, it says nothing about Ovett's ability to put together speed, endurance and competitive flair.

Yet, in what has been a highly successful season, he has not come under pressure. If it had happened it should have been in the World Cup where his rivals included the Olympic champion, John Walker, of New Zealand. But the race turned out to be a relative doddle for Ovett.

He was so clearly in command in the last 200 metres that

he waved to the stand, a habit which is now almost his trademark, 50 metres from the line. The gesture was not arrogance. It was merely to reassure his parents, who travelled to Düsseldorf by overnight coach and ferry, that everything was all right. The year has been outstanding for Ovett.

As the fifth man in the 1976 Olympic 800 metres final, speed had always been his forte. But he not only moved up successfully to 1,500 metres: he also dabbled, with similar results at 5,000 metres and cross-country. His most remarkable run came not in a packed stadium but around the roads of Dartford last month where, on an impulse, he entered a half marathon over 13½ miles.

'I had just driven my training partner, Matt, up to the race from Brighton and my legs were a little stiff when I got out of the car. So I asked the referee if I could run in the race too. I had meant to drop out after a few miles, but I felt good, so I carried on.'

He won the event comfortably, and still looks back on it, in a session which has included victories in the European and World Cup 1,500 metres and a United Kingdom mile record, as probably his most satisfying, and his most surprising, performance. ('Mind you, I could hardly walk for a couple of days afterwards.') That is part of Ovett's strength.

He is unpredictable in attitude, but consistent in racing – an unconventional but uncompromising athlete. No other athlete possesses his extraordinary range, from 200 metres in 22.5sec. to beating the AAA marathon champion in a 13½ miles road race.

Optimism about Ovett's future is not misplaced. Athletics is a sport littered with memories of those who had tremendous talent as youngsters but who either could not cope with increasing pressure of training or who lacked sufficient motivation. Their places are taken by those with limited talent but a burning desire to overcome those limitations. Ovett is a young man who has always been an outstanding runer ('at school I was always stuck on the wing or the boundary because of my speed') who has adjusted to higher planes, both physically and mentally.

He was born in Brighton on 9 October 1955, and the Sussex town is still the place in which he is happiest. In

Stanmer Park and Preston Park he pounds out the hundreds of training miles necessary each winter month to lay the foundations of summer success.

He resisted the approaches of more than 40 United States colleges, keen to recruit him on an athletics scholarship, when he left Varndean Grammar School after his A levels in 1974. By then he was already the European junior 800 metres champion, but that was no solid guarantee for future success. Others had reached that stage only to fall by the wayside. Ovett, however, did not. The following summer, still only 18, he won the silver medal in the European senior 800 metres in Rome. But he was furious with himself afterwards, not so much for losing but because he thought he had run a tactically poor race and cheated himself out of any chance of challenging Luciano Susanj, of Yugoslavia, for the gold medal.

In 1975, after winning the 800 metres in the European Cup semi-final round at Crystal Palace, he also felt that he was dealt with harshly by certain sections of the press for saying that he would not run in the Cup final at Nice because he wanted to hitch-hike to Athens instead. In fact, he did run in the final and won decisively for Britain. But he later refused and still refuses to return to the interview room at the Crystal Palace press box. 'We run our guts out on the track, and if we've pleased them enough for them to want to talk to us we get this demand to attend the press box interview, like some sort of Royal command.'

In turn, Ovett's description upset some journalists, but it is probably the most accurate yet from the other side of the fence. In isolation, it sounds like an angry young man speaking. But he is a straight talker, a self-confessed loner, who enjoys running, winning races, being at home with his family at Brighton and not being involved with the circus on the fringe of any big meeting.

He is artistically, as well as psysically, talented and has been studying business administration and photographic art at a local college this year. Again, he is reluctant to move away from Brighton. His family is close. His parents are still in their late thirties and he has a younger brother and sister.

'We discuss everything fully and I never make a decision without talking it over with the others,' he said. 'Of course, we are always disagreeing. That's because we all speak our minds. The blazing rows we have are marvellous things. They get rid of the old pressures and really clear the air.'

His coach, Harry Wilson, has guided him through a sparing, if varied pattern of competition this summer which has left Ovett neither weary nor stale. 'Steve has one big advantage in that he has been quietly preparing for his races at home, and we've been racing and travelling all summer,' John Walker said before Saturday's World Cup event.

That was merely a matter of preference. Ovett had the opportunity, but not the inclination to race all over Europe this year. He will have even more opportunities now, but will probably take few of them.

'I simply prefer being in Brighton' he says. 'I wouldn't mind running in this "Dream Mile" in Vancouver on 17 September, but it would mean having to leave home a week early to get used to the time change, and I'm not sure I fancy that part of it so much.'

Riding to victory

CAROLINE SILVER
The Sunday Times

11 September 1977 *Lucinda Prior-Palmer showed she was one of the outstanding three-day event riders of all time when she became the only person ever to win the European title twice in succession. She also helped Britain to win the team event. Here, with one day to go, Caroline Silver made compelling Sunday-morning reading: the depth of her knowledge, her eye for minute detail and her economy in writing left very little about the day unsaid.*

After yesterday's speed and endurance phase of the European Three Day Event Championships, held at Burghley Park, Lincolnshire, Great Britain is in a near-unassailable position for the team gold medal and has also as good a chance of retaining the individual prize as a Grand National winner has of outjumping a camel.

Germany's Karl Schultz and Madrigal, the best dressage performers in eventing in the world and also, since last summer, one of the boldest cross-country, remained in the individual lead last night, with a total score for the first two days of only 29 penalty points. But their Achilles heel, as those who watched them drop from a certain Olympic gold to a dull bronze at Bromont last year because of the miserable failure of two small rails to stay in their cups will recall, is their show jumping.

This afternoon only one show jumping error stands between them and the defending European medallist and three-times Badminton winner, Lucinda Prior-Palmer.

For sheer luminosity, Lucinda's ascendant star dazzles the mind. Riding for a safe round to ensure that we finished ahead of Germany, she also retained the precise judgment of pace needed to keep herself less than one fence behind Karl Schultz today. Hers was the fifth fastest cross-country time of the day. Earlier, during the steeplechase phase, she and wise 12-year-old George fell on the flat, got up and got back together, unshaken, and went on at such a speed that they incurred no time penalties.

Lucinda's was not the only British performance to make the Burghley crowd fly a mental flag. Chris Collins and Smokey VI, the first to go of our four-strong team, galloped round with such authority that, alone of all the 41 competitors, they incurred no time penalities. Forty dressage penalties from the first of the three phases leaves them temporarily in fourth place, but again just one show jump stands between them and Lucinda and the third-placed individual, Horst Karsten and Sioux. And there are two between Collins and Karl Schultz.

Another great British performance came from Jane Holderness-Roddam and Warrior, who rode in the responsible No. 3 spot. This experienced pair went boldly and faultlessly to complete a clear round.

The four-and-three-quarter mile cross-country course, on thick turf all the way, rode extremely well. It was a galloper's course, a test of stamina as well as cleverness, and it found out the unfit as surely as an overcrowded bus rejects the weak in rush-hour. Poland, with a valiant young team, were consistently outpaced and outjumped and Italy's chances shimmered into memory when the first of their three-strong team retired after the steeplechase and their next to go was eliminated in the cross-country.

As so often happens on a cross-country, it was a few of the less formidable fences that caught the riders napping. Most, having paid anxious attention, did well at the famous Trout Hatchery water and creditably over the formidable Double Coffin. But fence 27 of the 33, a post and rails on a downhill slope that was straighforward enough if the horse took off from the top of the bank, proved bad news if approached too closely.

With eight British riders finishing in the first 15 it might seem a British benefit event. It was not. It was a test of fitness. Performances this afternoon should confirm it.

TEAM: **1** GB 131.25 penalties, **2** Germany 171.9, **3** Ireland 237.9, **4** France 265.55, **5** Poland 370.70, **6** Russia 397.48

INDIVIDUAL: **1** **Karl Schultz** riding Madrigal (Germany) 29.00 penalties, **2** **Lucinda Prior-Palmer** riding George (GB) 37.35, **3** **Horst Karsten** riding Sioux (Germany) 38.2, **4** **Chris Collins** riding Smokey VI (GB) 40, **5** **Diana Thorne** riding The Kingmaker (GB) 52.3, **6** **Jane Holderness-Roddam** on Warrior (GB) 53.9

THE YEAR'S RESULTS

From 18 September 1976 to 11 September 1977

Below are a selection of results of the major sporting events of the year, or events involving British sportsmen. We have necessarily had to be selective but trust that an overall picture of Britain's main sporting achievements over the year is presented, while at the same time the results may be a useful adjunct to the rest of the book.

ASSOCIATION FOOTBALL

League Champions
Liverpool
F.A. Cup
Semi-finals
Hillsborough—Manchester United 2 Leeds United 1
West Bromwich—Liverpool 2 Everton 2
Replay: Loftus Road—Liverpool 3 Everton 0
Final
Manchester United 2 Liverpool 1
F.A. League Cup
Semi-finals
Aston Villa 0 Queens Park Rangers 0
Queens Park Rangers 2 Aston Villa 2
Replay; Aston Villa 3 Queens Park Rangers 0
Aston Villa won 5–2 on aggregate
Everton 1 Bolton Wanderers 1
Bolton Wanderers 0 Everton 1
Everton won 2–1 on aggregate
Final
Everton 0 Aston Villa 0
1st Replay; Old Trafford—Everton 1 Aston Villa 1
2nd Replay; White Hart Lane—Everton 2 Aston Villa 3
F.A. Charity Shield
Wembley—Manchester United 0 Liverpool 0
European Cup
Final
Liverpool 3 Moenchengladbach 1
Home International Tournament
Wembley—England 2 Northern Ireland 1
Glasgow—Scotland 3 Wales 2
Birmingham—Northern Ireland 1 Scotland 2
Walsall—Wales 1 England 0

Walsall—Wales 3 Northern Ireland 1
Wembley—England 0 Scotland 2

English South American Tour

7 June—Montevideo—Uraguay 1 England 1
10 June—Buenos Aires—Argentina 1 England 2
13 June—Sao Paulo—Brazil 1 England 1

Other International Matches

5 Nov—Wembley—England 0 Holland 2
3 April—Wembley—England 5 Luxembourg 0
27 April Scotland 3 Sweden 0
West Germany 5 Northern Ireland 0
4 May—Rome—Italy 2 England 0
—Walsall—Wales 3 Czechoslovakia 1
3 June—Northern Ireland 1 Wales 1
4 June—Wembley—England 1 Scotland 2
9 June—Rio de Janeiro—Brazil 0 England 0
11 June—Buenos Aires—Argentina 1 England 1
16 June—Santiago—Chile 2 Scotland 4
—Montevideo—Uraguay 0 England 0
24 June—Rio de Janeiro—Brazil 2 Scotland 0
6 Sept—Wrexham—Wales 0 Kuwait 0
7 Sept—E. Berlin—East Germany 1 Scotland 0
England 0 Switzerland 0

ATHLETICS

UK Championships at Cwmbran, 12 & 13 June

Men

100 Metres A. Bennett (Birchfield) 10.63 sec
200 Metres A. Bennett 21.2 sec
400 Metres W. Taylor (Army) 47.5 sec
800 Metres D. Warren (Epsom & Ewell) 1 min 50.4 sec
1500 Metres S. Ovett (Brighton) 3 min 37.5 sec
5,000 Metres N. Rose (Bristol) 13 min 20.6 sec
10,000 Metres I. Stewart (Tipton) 27 min 51.3 sec
110 Metres Hurdle B. Price (Cardiff) 14.9 sec
400 Metres Hurdle P. Kelly (Wolverhampton) 51.74 sec
3,000 Metres Steeplechase T. Staynings (Bristol) 8 min 31 sec
High Jump M. Butterfield (RAF) 2.10 metres
Long Jump T. Henry (Shaftesbury) 7.6 metres
Triple Jump A. Moore (Birchfield) 15.80 metres
Pole Vault J. Gutteridge (Windsor, Slough & Eton) 5.00 metres
Shot G. Capes (Enfield) 20.04 metres
Discus P. Tancred (Wolverhampton & Bilston) 55.44 metres
Javelin P. de Kremer (Bournemouth) 75.82 metres
Hammer P. Dickenson (unattached) 64.88 metres

Women

100 Metres S. Lannaman (Wolverhampton) 11.3 sec
200 Metres S. Lannaman 23.16 sec

400 Metres D. Hartley (Stretford) 51.88 sec
800 Metres L. Kiernan (Havering) 2 min 1.5 sec
1500 Metres H. Hollick (Sale) 4 min 13 sec
3,000 Metres G. Penny (Cambridge) 9 min 20 sec
100 Metres Hurdle S. Colyear (Stretford) 13.5 sec
400 Metres Hurdle C. Warden (Wolverhampton) 57.6 sec (UK rec.)
High Jump B. Gibbs (Leicester) 1.78 metres
Long Jump S. Colyear (Stretford) 6.42 metres
Shot V. Head (Bristol) 15.72 metres
Discus M. Ritchie (Edinburgh) 53.9 metres
Javelin T. Sanderson (Wolverhampton) 60.24 metres (UK rec.)

European Cup, Helsinki, 13-14 Aug

Men East Germany 123
West Germany 110
Russia 99
Great Britain 93

Women East Germany 114
Russia 93
Great Britain 67

Emsley Carr Mile
1 S. Coe (GB) 3 min 57.7 sec
2 F. Baryi (Tanzania) 3 min 57.91 sec
3 M. Ledere (W Germany) 3 min 58.3 sec

BADMINTON

All England Championships, Wembley, 23-26 Mar

Men's Singles
Flemmig Delf (Denmark) bt Liern Swie King (Indonesia)
15–17; 15–11; 15–8
Women's Singles
H. Yuki (Japan) bt L. Kopper (Denmark)
7–11; 11–3; 11–7
Men's Doubles
Tjun Tjun & Johan Wahjudi (Indonesia) bt
Ade Chandra & Christian (*sic*) (Indonesia) 15–7; 18–15
Women's Doubles
E. Toganoo & E. Ueno (Japan) bt
M. Lockwood & N. Perry (England) 15–3; 15–10
Mixed Doubles
G. Gilks & D. Talbot (England) bt
M. Perry & M. Tredgett (England) 15–9; 15–9

BOXING

1976

14 Sept British Middleweight Title: Alan Minter, holder, outpointed Chris Finnegan—Royal Albert Hall
9 Oct World Light Heavyweight Title: John Conteh, holder, outpointed Alvaro Lopez (US)—Copenhagen
12 Oct European, British & Commonwealth Title: Joe Bugner beat

Richard Dunn; K.O. 1st—Wembley

7 Dec European Light Welterweight Title: Dave Green beat Jean Baptiste Piedvache (France); ret. 9th—Royal Albert Hall

1977

1 Feb British Light Middleweight Championship: Jimmy Batten beat Albert Hallman; ret. 7th—Royal Albert Hall

4 Feb European Middleweight Title: Alan Minter beat Germano Valsecchi (Italy); K.O. 5th—Rome

5 Mar World Light Heavyweight Title: John Conteh beat Len Hutchins (US); K.O. 3rd—Liverpool

8 Mar British Light Heavyweight Title: Bunny Johnson beat Tim Wood; K.O. 1st—Wolverhampton

15 Mar World Light Middleweight Title: Eckhard Dagge (W Germany) and Maurice Hope, drew on points over 15 rounds; Dagge retained title—Berlin

7 May European Light Middleweight Title: Maurice Hope outpointed Frank Wissenbach (W Germany)—Hamburg

1 June British Middleweight Title: Kevin Finnegan beat Frankie Lucas; referee stopped fight, 11th—Royal Albert Hall

14 June World Welterweight Title: Carlos Palomino (US) beat David Green; K.O. 11th—Wembley

6 Aug European Lightweight Title: Jim Watt beat Andre Holyk (France); referee stopped fight, 1st—Glasgow

Amateur Boxing Association Finals, Empire Pool, Wembley, 6 May

Light Flyweight Winner: P. Fletcher; Runner-up: R. Jones
Flyweight Winner: C. Magri; Runner-up: M. Younns
Bantam Weight Winner: J. Turner; Runner-up: V. Praise
Featherweight Winner: P. Cowdell; Runner-up: I. McLeod
Lightweight Winner: G. Gilbody; Runner-up: A. Mann
Light Welterweight Winner: J. Douglas; Runner-up: C. Sanigar
Welterweight Winner: C. Jones; Runner-up: A. Salmon
Light Middleweight Winner: C. Malarky; Runner-up: L/Cpl T. Williams
Middleweight Winner: R. Davis; Runner-up: M. Shone
Light Heavyweight Winner: C. Lawson; Runner-up: P. Gonzalez
Heavyweight Winner: G. Adair; Runner-up: G. Scott

CRICKET

Benson & Hedges Cup, Lord's, 16 July

Final

Gloucestershire 237 for 6, 55 overs
(Stovold 71; Zaheer Abbas 70)
Kent 173, 47.3 overs (Woolmer 64)

First Test, Lord's, 16-21 June

England 216 (Woolmer 79; Randall 53; Thomson 4 for 41)
& 305 (Woolmer 120; Greig 91; Thomson 4 for 86)
Australia 296 (Sergeant 81; Chappell 66; Walters 53)
& 114 for 6

Second Test, Old Trafford
Australia 297 (Walters 88)
& 218 (Chappell 112; Underwood 6 for 66)
England 437 (Woolmer 137; Randall 79; Greig 76)
& 82 for 1

Third Test, Trent Bridge
Australia 243 (O'Keefe 48 n.o.; Botham 5 for 74)
& 309 (McCosker 107; Willis 5 for 88)
England 364 (Boycott 107; Knott 135; Pascoe 4 for 80)
& 189 for 3 (Brearley 81; Boycott 80)

Fourth Test, Headingley
England 436 (Boycott 191; Knott 57; Pascoe 4 for 91)
Australia 103 (Botham 5 for 21)
& 248 (Marsh 63; Hendrick 4 for 54)

Fifth Test, Oval, 31 August
England 214 (Malone 5 for 63) & 57 for 2
Australia 385 (Hookes 85; Walker 78 n.o.; Malone 46; Willis 5 for 102)

Test Series, England v. Australia
AVERAGES

England—Batting

	M	I	N.o.	R.	H'st	Ave.
G. Boycott	3	5	2	442	191	147.33
R. Woolmer	5	8	1	394	137	56.28
A. Knott	5	7	0	255	135	36.42
D. Randall	5	8	2	207	79	34.50
A. Greig	5	7	0	226	91	32.28
M. Brearley	5	0	0	247	81	27.44
R. Willis	5	6	4	49	24*	24.50
D. Underwood	5	6	2	66	20	16.50
C. Old	2	3	0	46	37	15.33
D. Amiss	2	4	1	43	28*	14.33
M. Hendrick	3	3	0	20	15	6.66
J. Lever	3	4	0	24	10	6.00

Also batted: G. Barlow 1*, 5; I. Botham 25*; G. Miller 6*, 13; G. Roope 34, 8, 38. *Not out

England—Bowling

	O.	M.	R.	W.	Ave.
Miller	24	7	47	3	15.66
Willis	166.4	36	534	27	19.77
Botham	73	16	202	10	20.20
Hendrick	128.4	33	290	14	20.71
Underwood	169.1	61	362	13	27.83
Greig	77	25	196	7	28.00
Woolmer	16	5	31	1	31.00
Lever	75	22	197	5	39.40
Old	77	14	199	5	39.80

Australia—Batting

	M	I	No	R.	H'st	Ave.
K. O'Keefe	3	6	4	125	48*	62.30
G. Chappell	5	9	0	371	112	41.22

	M	I	N.o.	R.	H'st	Ave.
D. Hookes	5	9	0	283	85	31.44
R. McCosker	5	9	0	255	107	28.33
D. Walters	5	9	0	223	88	24.77
M. Walker	5	8	1	151	78*	21.57
C. Serjeant	3	5	0	106	81	21.20
R. Marsh	5	9	1	166	63	20.75
I. Davis	3	6	0	107	34	17.83
R. Robinson	3	6	0	100	34	16.66
R. Bright	3	5	1	42	16	10.50
J. Thomson	5	8	1	59	21	8.42
L. Pascoe	3	5	2	23	20	7.66

Also batted: K. Hughes 1; M. Malone 46.

Australia—Bowling

	O.	M.	R.	W.	Ave.
Malone	57	24	77	6	12.83
Thomson	200.5	44	583	23	25.34
Pascoe	137.4	35	363	13	27.92
Bright	72.1	27	147	5	29.40
Walker	273.2	88	551	14	39.35
O'Keeffe	100.3	31	305	3	101.6

Also bowled: Walters 6–1–10–0; Chappell 39–5–105–0.

Centuries:

England—5: 2. G. Boycott. 191—4th Test Leeds
107—3rd Test Nottingham
2. R. A. Woolmer. 137—2nd Test Old Trafford
120—1st Test Lords
A. P. E. Knott. 135—3rd Test Nottingham

Australia—2: G. S. Chappell. 112—2nd Test Old Trafford
R. B. McCosker. 107—3rd Test Nottingham

Averages for the Test series against India appear on pp. 85–86.

Prudential Trophy—Oval

England 242, 54.2 overs (Amiss 108; Brearley 78)
Australia 246, 53.2 overs
(Chappell 125 n.o.; Robinson 70)

Edgbaston

England 171, 53.5 overs
(Chappell 5 for 20; Cosier 5 for 18)
Australia 70 (25.2 overs) (Lever 4 for 29)

Old Trafford

Australia 169 for 9, 55 overs
England 173 for 8, 45.2 overs

Final Averages for 1977

Batting: Qualifications—8 innings

	I	N.o.	R.	H'st	Ave.
R. Baker	12	9	215	77*	71.66
G. Boycott	30	5	1701	191	68.04
V. Richards	35	2	2161	241*	65.48
G. Greenidge	32	3	1771	208	61.06

	I	N.o.	R	H'st	Ave
G. Roope	31	5	1431	115	55.03
Zaheer Abbas	36	6	1584	205*	52.80
D. Amiss	34	5	1513	162*	52.17
K. McEwan	37	4	1702	218	51.57
B. Woods	34	6	1439	155*	51.39
F. Hayes	26	3	1152	157*	50.08
R. Woolmer	30	4	1238	137	47.61
J. Edrich	26	4	1044	140	47.45
K. Wessels	17	3	663	138*	47.35
M. Brearley	31	4	1251	152	46.33
Mustaq	37	5	1469	147	45.90
B. d'Oliveira	36	7	1257	156*	43.34
J. Hampshire	23	5	779	100*	43.27
C. Balderstone	38	8	1297	178*	43.23
K. Fletcher	37	6	1331	106*	42.93
J. Whitehouse	41	5	1543	158*	42.86
A. Knott	20	2	771	135	42.83
B. Richards	25	3	927	115	42.13
A. Kallicharran	36	4	1340	149*	41.87
G. Turner	38	5	1380	153	41.81
J. Miandad	39	6	1326	111	40.18

*Not out

Bowling: Qualification—10 wickets

	O	M	R	W	Ave.
R. Woolmer	134.1	50	289	19	15.21
M. Hendrick	565.4	188	1068	67	15.94
W. Daniel	516.1	142	1233	75	16.44
Sarfraz	486.4	130	1246	73	17.06
R. Hills	215.3	60	566	33	17.15
G. Miller	655.4	223	1551	87	17.82
M. Procter	777.3	226	1967	109	18.04
J. Emburey	691.1	205	1488	81	18.37
D. Underwood	436.2	172	896	46	19.47
M. Selvey	629.1	158	1540	78	19.74
P. Booth	179	37	494	25	19.76
A. Roberts	349.2	112	793	40	19.82
J. Shepherd	738.4	216	1734	87	19.93
J. Garner	215.1	63	539	27	19.96
A. A. Jones (Middx)	139.4	32	421	21	20.04
R. East	658.4	196	1477	73	20.23
R. Willis	399	91	1183	58	20.39
B. Wood	120.3	40	306	15	20.40
K. Shuttleworth	293.4	57	825	40	20.62
J. Inchmore	244.2	55	685	33	20.75
R. Illingworth	388.4	143	777	37	21.00
K. Stevenson	190.5	38	550	26	21.15
D. Brown	405.1	76	1209	57	21.21
B. Brain	569.1	134	1637	77	21.25
J. Simmons	592.2	199	1313	61	21.52

Final County Table

	P.	W.	L.	D.	Bonus Pts. Bt.	Bw.	Pts.
1. Kent (14)	22	9	2	11	54	65	227
Middlesex (1)	22	9	5	8	43	76	227
3. Gloucestershire (3)	22	9	5	8	44	70	222
4. Somerset (7)	22	6	4	12	58	64	194
5. Leicestershire (4)	22	6	4	12	44	73	189
6. Essex (6)	22	7	5	10	38	65	187
7. Derbyshire (15)	22	7	3	12	38	64	186
8. Sussex (10)	22	6	5	11	52	60	184
9. Northamptonshire (2)	22	6	6	10	43	68	183
10. Warwickshire (5)	22	4	8	10	61	72	181
11. Hampshire (12)	22	6	5	11	53	54	179
12. Yorkshire (8)	22	6	5	11	36	63	171
13. Worcestershire (11)	22	5	10	7	29	55	144
14. Glamorgan (17)	22	3	7	12	36	60	132
Surrey (9)	22	3	6	13	42	54	132
16. Lancashire (16)	22	2	4	16	36	57	117
17. Nottinghamshire (13)	22	1	11	10	34	52	98

1976 positions in brackets

CYCLING

Tour of Britain, 29 May-11 June

1 S. Gusseinov (USSR) 48 hrs 22 mins 13 sec
2 A. Segersall (Sweden) 48 hrs 22 min 21 sec
3 P. Carbutt (GB) 48 hrs 22 min 32 sec
Team event: U.S.S.R.

EQUESTRIANISM

Badminton Trials, 23-25 April

1 George (Lucinda Prior-Palmer) 37.65 pts
2 The Kingmaker (D. Thorne) 59.0 pts
3 Killaire (Lucinda Prior-Palmer) 65.6 pts

European Three-Day Event Championship, Burghley, 10-12 Sept

1 George (Lucinda Prior-Palmer; GB) 37.35 pts
2 Madrigal (K. Schuitz; W Germany) 39.0 pts
3 Sioux (H. Karsten; W Germany) 48.20 pts
4 The Kingmaker (D. Thorne; GB) 52.3 pts
5 The Warrior (J. Holderness-Roddam; GB) 53.9 pts
6 Cambridge Blue (J. Watson; Ireland) 58.05 pts

Team event

1 Great Britain 151.25 pts
2 West Germany 221.9 pts
3 Ireland 237.9 pts

GOLF

English Championships, 23 July—Walton Heath

Final

Shingler bt Mayell; 4 and 3

Semi-final

T. R. Shingler (Blackwell) bt
M. J. Kelley (Scarborough North Cliff) 3 and 2
J. M. Mayell (Copt Heath) bt
M. C. Hughesden (Sunningdale) 20th

Walker Cup, 28 August—Shinnecock Hills

United States—16
Great Britain—8

British Ladies Open Championships, Lindrick, 31 Aug-2 Sept

1 V. Saunders (England)—306 (won with lower last round total)
2 M. Everard (Hallomshire)—306
3 D. Henson (W Byfleet)—307

European L. P. G. A. Championships, Sunningdale, 3-6 Aug

1 J. Rankin (US)—281
2 N. Lopez (US)—287
3 S. Little (S Africa)—289

Open Scots Championships

P. McAvoy (Copt Heath) bt
Hugh Campbell (Falkirk Tryst) 5 and 4

HOCKEY

Men's Hockey: International Results 1977

12 Mar	England 3 W. Germany 4 (London) T
13 Mar	Spain 2 France 1 (London) T
	W. Germany 3 Spain 2 (London) T
	England 1 France 0 (London) T
25 Mar	Ireland 6 Poland 1 (Glasgow) T
26 Mar	Scotland 2 Ireland 0 (Glasgow) T
	Wales 1 Poland 1 (Glasgow) T
27 Mar	Scotland 0 Poland 1 (Glasgow) T
	Wales 1 Ireland 0 (Glasgow) T
22 Apr	Ireland 1 Netherlands 1 (Dublin) T
23 Apr	England 2 Netherlands 2 (Dublin) T
	Ireland 1 Scotland 0 (Dublin) T
24 Apr	Ireland 0 England 1 (Dublin) T
	Scotland 0 Netherlands 6 (Dublin) T
19 June	Austria 1 Scotland 2 (Vienna) Euro Q
21 June	Netherlands 3 England 1 (Amsterdam) T
22 June	England 1 Japan 1 (Amsterdam) T
24 June	England 2 Netherlands Jnrs. 2 (Amsterdam) T uno
25 June	W. Germany 1 England 2 (Amsterdam) T
26 June	Spain 1 England 1 (Amsterdam) T

Women's Hockey: International Results 1977

5 Mar	England 0 New Zealand 1 (London)
	Wales 0 Ireland 1 (Bangor)
12 Mar	Scotland 2 England 4 (Ayr)
19 Mar	England 1 Wales 0 (Leeds)
26 Mar	England 1 Ireland 2 (Cambridge)
	Wales 0 Scotland 2 (Llanelli)
2 Apr	Wales 0 Netherlands 2 (Cardiff)
2 Apr	Ireland 1 Scotland 0 (Dublin)
16 Apr	Scotland 0 West Germany 2 (Edinburgh)
23 Apr	Netherlands 2 Scotland 2 (Amsterdam)
6 May	Spain 1 England 4 (Santander) T
7 May	France 0 England 2 (Santander) T
	West Germany 2 England 1 (Santander) T

T = tournament Q = qualifier uno = unofficial

LAWN TENNIS

Italian Open, Rome, 15-22 May

Men's Singles
V. Gerulaitis bt A. Zugarelli 6–2, 7–6, 3–6, 7–6
Women's Singles
J. Newberry bt R. Tomanova 6–3, 7–6
Men's Doubles
B. Gottfried & R. Ramierez bt
S. Stuart & F. McNair 6–7, 7–6, 7–5
Women's Doubles
B. Cuyters & M. Kruger bt
B. Bruning & S. Walsh 3–6, 7–5, 6–2
No mixed doubles

French Open, Paris, 23 May-5 June

Men's Singles
G. Vilas bt R. Ramierez 6–0, 6–3, 6–0
Women's Singles
M. Jausovec bt F. Mihai 6–2, 6–7, 6–1
Men's Doubles
B. Gottfried & R. Ramierez bt
W. Fibak & J. Kodes 7–6, 4–6, 6–3, 6-4
Women's Doubles
R. Marsikova & T. Teeguardian bt
R. Fox & H. Gourlay 5–7, 6–4, 6–2
Mixed Doubles
J. McEnroe & M. Carillo bt
I. Molina & F. Mihai 7–6, 6–3

Wimbledon Championships, 20 June-2 July

Men's Singles
B. Borg (Sweden, 2) bt J. S. Connors (US, 1)
3–6, 6–2, 6–1, 5–7, 6–4

Women's Singles
S. V. Wade (GB, 3) bt B. F. Stove (Netherlands, 7)
4–6, 6–3, 6–1
Men's Doubles
R. L. Case & G. Masters (Australia, 7) bt
J. G. Alexander & P. C. Dent (Australia) 6–3, 6–4, 3–6, 8–9, 6–4
Women's Doubles
R. L. Cawley (Australia) & J. C. Russell (USA) bt
M. Navratilova (USA) & B. F. Stove (Netherlands) (1) 6–3, 6–3
Mixed Doubles
R. A. J. Hewitt & Miss G. R. Stephens (S Africa) bt
F. D. McMillan (S Africa) & Miss B. F. Stove (Netherlands) (1)
3–6, 7–5, 6–4

Forest Hills Open, 31 Aug-11 Sept
Men's Singles
G. Vilas bt J. Connors 2–6, 6–3, 7–6, 6–0
Women's Singles
C. Evert bt W. Turnbull 7–6, 6–2
Men's Doubles
B. Hewett & F. McMillan bt
B. Gottfried & R. Ramierez 6–4, 6–0
Women's Doubles
M. Navratilova & B. Stove bt
R. Richards & B. Stuart 6–1, 7–6
Mixed Doubles
F. McMillan & B. Stove bt
V. Gerulaitis & B-J. King 6–2, 3–6, 6–3

Australian Open—yet to be played

MODERN PENTATHLON

British Championships, Walton, 14 Aug
1 D. Nightingale 5601 (British Record)
2 P. Whiteside 5546
3 N. Clark 5516

MOTOR CYCLING

World Championships
Final Positions—500 cc
1 B. Sheene (GB) 107 pts
2 S. Baker (USA) 80 pts
3 P. Hennen (USA) 67 pts

Sidecar Championships
1 G. O'Dell (GB) 64 pts
2 R. Biland (Switzerland) 56 pts
3 W. Schwarzel (Germany) 46 pts

RACING

Champion Hurdle, 16 Mar

1 Night Nurse—P. Broderick (15–2) Trained: M. H. Easterby
2 Monksfield (15–1)
3 Dramatist (6–1)

Cheltenham Gold Cup, 17 Mar

1 Davy Lad—D. Hughes (14–1) Trained: M. A. O'Toole (Ireland)
2 Tied Cottage (20–1)
3 Summerville (15–1)

Grand National, 2 April

1 Red Rum—T. Stack (9–1) Trained: D. McCain
2 Churchtown Boy (20–1)
3 Eyecatcher (18–1)

2,000 Guineas, Newmarket, 27 April

1 Nebbiolo—G. Curran (20–1) Trained: K. Prendergast (Ireland)
2 Tachypous (12–1)
3 The Minstrel (6–5 fav.)

1,000 Guineas, Newmarket, 28 April

1 Mrs. McArdy—E. Hide (16–1) Trained: M. W. Easterby
2 Freeze the Secret (11–2)
3 Sanedtki (12–1)

Derby, Epsom, 1 June

1 The Minstrel—L. Piggott (5–1) Trained: M. V. O'Brien (Ireland)
2 Hot Grove (15–1)
3 Blushing Groom (9–4) fav.)

Oaks, Epsom, 4 June

1 Dunfermline—W. Carson (6–1) Trained: W. Hern
2 Freeze the Secret (7–1)
3 Vaguely Deb (14–1)

King George VI & Queen Elizabeth Stakes, 23 July

1 The Minstrel—L. Piggott (7–4 fav.) Trained: M. V. O'Brien (Ireland)
2 Orange Bay (20–1)
3 Exceller (11–2)

St. Leger, Doncaster, 10 Sept

1 Dunfermline—W. Carson (10–1) Trained: W. Hern
2 Alleged
3 Classic Example

REAL TENNIS

World Championships, Hampton Court, 13 June

Howard Angus (GB) bt Eugene Scott (USA)
6–2; 5–6; 3–6; 6–1; 6–5; 6–4; 6–2; 6–1; 6–4; (7–2)

ROWING

Henley Regatta, 30 June-3 July

Grand Challenge Cup: Final
University of Washington bt Leander Club & Thames Tradesmen
1 Length; 6 min 27 sec
Ladies' Plate: Final
Trinity College, Dublin bt Pembrooke College, Cambridge
2⅓ Lengths; 6 min 53 sec
Thames Cup
Semi-finals
Leander Club bt Kingston
1¼ Lengths; 6 min 50 sec
London RC bt University of London
1½ Lengths; 6 min 47 sec
Finals
London RC bt Leander Club
2¾ Lengths; 6 min 37 sec
Princess Elizabeth Cup: Final
Ridley College, Canada bt Hampton School
1 Length; 6 min 53 sec
Stewards' Cup Final
London RC row over; no other entries; 7 min 24 sec
Prince Phillip Cup: Final
Garda Siochana, Rep of Ireland bt Thames Tradesmen
2¾ Lengths; 7 min 35 sec
Visitor's Cup: Final
University of Washington bt Lady Margaret BC, Cambridge easily;
no time taken
Wyfold Cup
City Orient bt University of London
2 Lengths; 7 min 15 sec
Britannia Cup: Final
Tideway Scullers' School bt Henley RC
2⅓ Lengths; 7 min 28 sec
Silver Goblets & Nickalls' Cup: Final
J. Clark & J. Roberts (Thames Tradesmen) bt
J. MacLeod & A. N. Christie (St. Thomas's Hospital & London RC)
3 Lengths; 7 min 54 sec
Double Sculls: Final
M. J. Hars & C. L. Baillieu (Leander) bt
G. Stone & C. R. Wood (Harvard University)
easily; 7 min 20 sec
Diamond Sculls: Final
T. J. Crooks (Leander) bt J. W. Dietz (New York AC)
3⅔ Lengths; 8 min 11 sec
Special Race for Schools
St. Edward's School bt Radley College
2 Lengths; 4 min 38 sec

World Championships, Amsterdam, 20-28 Aug
Germany: 6 min 39.16 sec
Double Sculls
Great Britain (C. Baillieu & M. Hart): 6 min 42.83 sec
Coxless Pairs
USSR: 7 min 6.19 sec
Sculls
East Germany (J. Dreifke): 7 min 12.22 sec
Coxed Pairs
Bulgaria: 7 min 21.72 sec
Coxless fours
East Germany: 6 min 16.73 sec
Quadruple Sculls
East Germany: 5 min 57.44 sec
Eights
East Germany: 5 min 45.36 sec
Lightweights
Sculls—Switzerland; 7 min 18.58 sec
Coxless fours—France: 6 min 30 sec
Eights—Great Britain: 5 min 57.37 sec
Women (1000 *metres*)
Coxed fours—East Germany: 3 min 20.59 sec
Double Sculls—East Germany: 3 min 16.83 sec
Coxless Pairs—East Germany: 3 min 27.89 sec
Sculls—East Germany: 3 min 34.31 sec
Quadruple Sculls—East Germany: 3 min 10.11 sec
Eights—East Germany: 3 min 00.23 sec

RUGBY LEAGUE

Northern Rugby League Cup Final, Wembley, 7 May
Leeds 16 Widnes 7
World Championships Final, 29 June—Sydney
Australia 13 Great Britain 12

RUGBY UNION

Rugby Union Tour
13 *August—Auckland*
New Zealand 10 Great Britain 9
30 *July—Dunedin*
New Zealand 19 Lions 7
9 *July—Christchurch*
New Zealand 9 Lions 13
20 *June—Wellington*
New Zealand 16 Lions 12
Home International Tournament
Twickenham 15 Jan England 26 Scotland 6

Cardiff, 15 Jan Wales 25 Ireland 9
Dublin, 5 Feb Ireland 0 England 4
Paris, 5 Feb France 16 Wales 9
Twickenham 19 Feb England 3 France 4
Murrayfield 19 Feb Scotland 21 Ireland 18
Cardiff 5 Mar Wales 14 England 9
Paris 5 Mar France 23 Scotland 3
Murrayfield 19 Mar Scotland 9 Wales 18
Dublin 19 Mar Ireland 6 France 15

SAILING

Admiral's Cup, Cowes, 28 July
1 Britain
2 United States
3 Hong Kong

SPEEDWAY

World Pairs Championship, Belle Vue, 2 July
England 28 (P. Collins 15; M. Simmons 13)
Sweden 18
West Germany 18

SQUASH

Women's Open Championships, Wembley, 3 Mar
H. McKay (Australia) bt B. Wall (Australia)
9–3; 9–1; 9–2
Men's Open Championship, 4 April
Geoff Hunt (Australia) bt Cam Nancarrow
9–4; 9–4; 8–10; 9–4

SWIMMING

National Swimming Championships, Leeds, 20-23 July
Men
100 Metres Freestyle M. Smith (Radcliffe) 53.25 sec
200 Metres Freestyle G. Downie (Warrender) 1 min 55.69 sec
400 Metres Freestyle G. Downie 4 min 3.49 sec
1500 Metres Freestyle P. Sparkes (Merton & Swordfish) 15 min 50.91 sec
100 Metres Backstroke G. Abraham (Southampton) 59.8 sec
200 Metres Backstroke J. Carter (Paisley) 2 min 8.65 sec
100 Metres Breaststroke P. Naisby (S. Shields) 1 min 5.72 sec
200 Metres Breaststroke P. Naisby 2 2 min 4.31 sec

100 Metres Butterfly J. Mills (Sutton & Cheam) 57.80 sec
200 Metres Butterfly P. Sparkes (Merton) 2 min 5.19 sec
200 Metres Ind. Medley D. Cleworth (Manchester) 2 min 11.57 sec
400 Metres Ind. Medley A. McClatchey (Warrender) 4 min 37.18 sec

Women

100 Metres Freestyle V. Bullock (Cardiff) 59.14 sec
200 Metres Freestyle S. Davies (Plymouth) 2 min 8.15 sec
400 Metres Freestyle S. Davies 4 min 26.72 sec
800 Metres Freestyle L. Heggie (Warrington) 9 min 9.62 sec
100 Metres Backstroke J. Beasley (Junction 10) 1 min 6.82 sec
200 Metres Backstroke S. Davies (Plymouth) 2 min 21.18 sec (British rec.)
100 Metres Breaststroke M. Kelly (Cumbernauld) 1 min 15.32 sec
200 Metres Breaststroke M. Kelly 2 min 39.45 sec
100 Metres Butterfly J. Hull (Basildon) 1 min 5.45 sec
200 Metres Butterfly S. Jenner (Mermaid) 2 min 5.45 sec
200 Metres Ind. Medley S. Davies (Plymouth) 2 min 22.95 sec (British & English rec.)
400 Metres Ind. Medley S. Davies 4 min 56.28 sec (British rec.)

TABLE TENNIS

World Championships, Birmingham, 26 Mar-5 April

Swaythling Cup (Men)
China bt Japan 5–0

Corbillon Cup (Women)
China bt South Korea 3–0

Men's Singles Final
M. Kohno (Japan) bt Kuo Yao Hiia (China)
17–21; 21–9; 21–13

Women's Singles Final
Pak Yung Sum (N. Korea) bt Chang Lei (China)
21–15; 24–22; 22–20

Men's Doubles Final
Li Chen Shih & Liang Lu Yuan Sheng (China) bt
Wuang Liang & Lu Yuan Sheng (China)
22–20; 21–18; 21–11

Women's Doubles Final
Pak Yung Ok (N. Korea) & Yang Ying (China) bt
Ywei Li-Cheh & Chu Hscang Yun (China)
21–18; 26–24; 16–21; 21–13

Index